civilization: a developed culture and mode of life;

man's "improvements" on nature; man's advance from

pushing a plow to pushing a button.

corrupt: to make rotten; to defile; to contaminate; to make evil; to bribe;

putrid, depraved, tainted with vice or sin; influenced by

bribery; spoiled, by mistake, or altered for the worse.

DARK CITY

The Lost World of Film Noir

Cover
    Photo montage featuring
    Humphrey Bogart and Liz Scott in
    Dead Reckoning (Columbia, 1948)

Frontispiece
    711 Ocean Drive (Columbia, 1950)

Title Page
    Woman on the Run (Fidelity/Universal-International, 1950)

DARK CITY
The Lost World of Film Noir

EDDIE MULLER

St. Martin's Griffin   New York

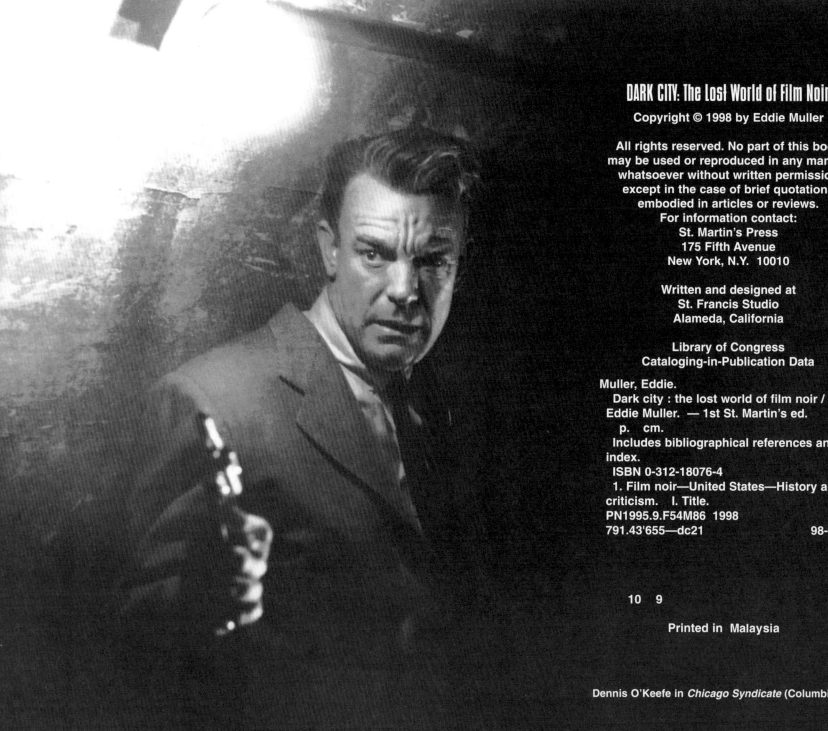

DARK CITY: The Lost World of Film Noir

Copyright © 1998 by Eddie Muller

For information contact:
St. Martin's Press
175 Fifth Avenue
New York, N.Y. 10010

Written and designed at
St. Francis Studio
Alameda, California

Library of Congress
Cataloging-in-Publication Data

Muller, Eddie.
  Dark city : the lost world of film noir /
Eddie Muller. — 1st St. Martin's ed.
    p.   cm.
  Includes bibliographical references and
index.
  ISBN 0-312-18076-4
  1. Film noir—United States—History and
criticism.   I. Title.
PN1995.9.F54M86 1998
791.43'655—dc21   98-5677
                                       CIP

        10   9

            Printed in Malaysia

Dennis O'Keefe in *Chicago Syndicate* (Columbia, 1955)

CONTENTS

Acknowledgments

Crafting a book is a caper. It requires a dedicated and resourceful crew.

Erik McMahon was a mastermind, boxman, and hooligan all in one; he had my back through the whole run. I couldn't have asked for a tougher, sharper, more literate lieutenant.

Lester Glassner went deep into his photo archive to find spectacular visual material. He also found a friend; my debt to him will never be repaid.

Lawrence Chadbourne supplied an arsenal of films, feeding me hard-to-find titles with unsurpassed generosity and kindness. His henchmen, Dave Martin, Bob Yamada, and Arthur McMillan, all came through in a pinch.

Eric Sagen and Michael Wong generously contributed posters from their terrific collections, as did Michael Abbott and Allen Michaan. I also thank Michael for a major post-production assist.

Movie Image in Berkeley, California deserves recognition as the most discriminating video store in existence. My gratitude to owner Roland De La Rosa, and staffers Randy Beucus, Jeremy Gross and Will "Vic Valentine" Viharo.

Every takedown needs an underwriter, and I was lucky enough to have the dynamic duo of St. Martin's Press, Cal Morgan and Gordon Van Gelder. They're smart enough to leave no finger-prints, but they can be held entirely responsible. A tip of the lid to others in the Flatiron trenches: Nelson Taylor, John Karle, Dana Albarella, Jennifer Starrels, and Corin See.

Along the way, many others weaved their way through the plot. Whether they knew it or not, they all had an impact on the outcome. Ted Bonnitt came through with an invaluable ass-kick at an auspicious moment. Paul Toner orchestrated a vital connection. Abraham Polonsky helped scratch out an early spark. Geoffrey O'Brien offered the inspiration of his superb book, *The Phantom Empire*. What did Jerry Ohlinger do? He was *there*. (He rates a cameo in any New York noir.)

Lisa Ryan was wonderfully open about her father, Robert. Ron and Maria Blum at Kayo Books in San Francisco were Johnnies-on-the-spot. Andrew Taylor contributed vivid reproductions of the posters. Pierce Rafferty at Fossil Photos in New York excavated the chapter-opening sidebars, and spectacular cityscapes. Mary Corliss and Terry Geesken at the Museum of Modern Art, and staffers at the Margaret Herrick Library at the Academy of Motion Picture Arts and Sciences were also helpful. Dennis Parlato furnished invaluable camaraderie, and a hideout, when I was on the lam.

The spirit, and humor, of the late Tracey Janzen (O.C.M.) cracks wise in many of these pages.

As for the dozens of other authors to whom I'm indebted — pick up your cut in the bibliography.

Lastly, I thank my wife, Kathleen, who gives me no good reason to travel to Dark City.

Introduction

FILM NOIRS WERE DISTRESS FLARES launched onto America's movie screens by artists working the night shift at the Dream Factory. Some of the more shell-shocked craftsmen discharged mortars, blasting their message with an urgency aimed at shaking up the status quo. Others went off like firecrackers – startling but playful diversions. After the explosions, the foul whiff of cordite carried the same warning: we're corrupt.

The collective sigh of relief heaved on V-J Day ought to have inspired Hollywood to release a flood of "happily ever after" films. But some victors didn't feel too good about their spoils. They'd seen too much by then. Too much warfare, too much poverty, too much greed, all in the service of rapacious progress. A bundle of unfinished business lingered from the Depression – nagging questions about ingrained venality, mean human nature, and the way unchecked urban growth threw society dangerously out of whack. Writers and directors responded by delivering gritty, bitter dramas that slapped our romantic illusions in the face and put the boot to the throat of the smug bourgeoisie. Still, plenty of us took it – and liked it.

I took it somewhat later, because I grew up in the Sixties. By then Hollywood's hold on adolescent dreams had been watered down, siphoned from opulent motion picture palaces to discount television sets. I'm grateful for the family Philco, though, and the TV tower on Twin Peaks, because they tapped into *Dialing for Dollars*. Every afternoon at one o'clock, KTVU in Oakland, California would broadcast old movies and entice viewers to wait by their phones, in case host Pat McCormack happened to dial them up at random and ask "What's the count and the amount?"

Before I could tell Richard Widmark from Richard Conte I knew the kind of film I'd play hooky to watch. *Thieves' Highway. Night and the City. Crime Wave. The Big Heat.* In fact, if any movie with *City*, *Night* or *Street* in its title was listed in that week's TV Guide — you could mark me absent from sixth period on. Not long after, I learned the delirious pleasure of watching old "B" movies in the dead of night, thanks to Jay Brown, "The Price Slasher," a Bay Area used car salesman who hosted movies from midnight 'til dawn.

I went AWOL plenty from catechism, as well. Realistically, how could Sister Gretchen compete with Lizabeth Scott or Joan Bennett? The lessons that Father McTaggert tried to impart didn't seem nearly as crucial as the ones instilled by Robert Mitchum and Humphrey Bogart. If they really wanted us to understand the Ten Commandments, they couldn't have done any better than screening *Out of the Past, Force of Evil, They Won't Believe Me, Side Street* — come to think of it, the Good Book would make one hell of a film noir.

Watching these movies transported the viewer to another place. It was still recognizable as our world, but it had been stripped down, juked up, and slapped around. Landmarks were cloaked in shadowy mist. But that fog was far more arresting than the flower-power incense cloud that swirled around my generation. I related to the jaded, hard-ass attitudes, the billowy suits and sleek gowns, the meticulous manners and nail-spitting dialogue. One's first impression of film noir fixes on all this window dressing. When you've gotten a ration of these films, the patterns and point of view emerge. Pretty soon you're recognizing familiar faces on the grainier edges of the frame. You greet Marie Windsor, William Talman, and Charles McGraw as if they lived at the dark end of your own street.

Once I started to research the films, and the filmmakers, the line blurred between the pictures and the lives of the people who made them. Tom Neal, that grungy guy in the seedy noir classic *Detour:* shot his wife in the head — "accidentally" — and drew a stretch for manslaughter. Alan Ladd, the icy, unflappable straight-shooter who wore a fedora better than anyone: tried to blow a hole in his heart, but botched it. Gloria Grahame, sexy siren of so many dark dramas: initiation rites with her thirteen-year-old stepson nearly destroyed her career. Her husband, the brilliant director Nicholas Ray: spent his wedding night, and forty grand, in a Vegas casino. He wound up a virtually destitute alcoholic, playing Fascination dusk till dawn in Times Square.

The world of film noir was an alternative environment, in which real and reel life were entwined. In the self-absorbed Seventies, an ever-expanding catalogue of criticism emerged that diligently tried to capture and deconstruct every frame of noir. Essayists argued about what it was, and which films qualified. Was noir a genre? Was it a style? The academics tried to pin it down and dissect it. In the process they managed to drain most of the life's blood out of the films.

This book is an attempt to resurrect these movies for another generation, to make them as vivid as they were when I first saw them, or when our parents did.

Of all the varieties of films Hollywood produced during the glory days of the studio system, film noirs hold up best. They've got vivid characters and thematic weight, and an inspired vision that preserves their vitality. When they fail to meet that tall order, they've got style and sass to die for. While other studio fare of the Forties and Fifties has slid into campiness, or decayed into a nostalgic toothlessness, film noir has kept its bite. Enjoy it for the surface allure, or venture further into the scorched existentialist terrain.

Conventional wisdom has branded these films bleak, depressing and nihilistic — in fact, they're just the opposite. To me, film noirs were the only movies that offered bracing respite from sugarcoated dogma, Hollywood-style. They weren't trying to lull you or sell you or reassure you — they insisted that you wake up to the reality of a corrupt world. Quit kidding yourself. Stand up, open your eyes, and be ready for anything. Prayers go unheard in these parts.

Film noir pointed toward the black core of corruption in our "civilized" society and our primitive essence. The struggle of the individual to transcend or escape provided the emotional tension. That's the theme that makes noir so compelling for the contemporary crowd. The films still connect, even without dissertations on the men and women who made them, or classes on the social pressures that informed their creation. Of all the postures proffered by Hollywood in this century, noir has proven the most prescient. Sadly, we're nowhere near as stylish anymore — but the corruption is thicker than ever.

The High Wall (MGM, 1947)

SO LOCK YOUR DOOR, WOULD YOU? And hold on. We're taking a little ride. Seat belts wouldn't do much good, even if we had them. Remember, once we cross the Dark City limits, the meter's double and there's no going back.

This trip is going to take us through all the finer neighborhoods. We'll hit Sinister Heights, Shamus Flats, Blind Alley, Vixenville, and maybe Loser's Lane, if we make it that far. We'll be hustling in and out of cheap hotels, seedy nightspots, and lonesome roadside diners. You'll get reacquainted with some folks in these dank corners, ready to spill a bitter life story before retreating to the shadows. Be ready to crack wise even if a trickle of cold sweat's running down your spine.

While we're rolling, stay calm, act natural, and keep the windows rolled up. Dark City was built on fateful coincidence, double-dealing, and last chances. Anything can happen, and it will.

Jean Hagen and Sterling Hayden flee *The Asphalt Jungle* (MGM, 1950).

Shut up and get in the car.

—Where are we going, Dix?

—To the pictures.

—What? Are you serious? They'll see us there for sure.

—Let 'em. I don't care anymore.

—Where's the Professor? I thought you were picking him up.

—He's not coming.

—Dix! How can we go through with this? The Professor had the plan, he knew every angle, he studied—

—Forget about him! We're improvising from here on. If you don't have the stomach for it – get out.

—What about Tony, the gunsel? Is he out, too?

—I'm picking him up in ten minutes. South Street and Third. He'll be there.

—Dix, what happened to the Professor? Is he alright? You two were so close, you'd been together so many years–

—Leave it alone, Doll.

—He taught you so much, Dix. You always said you felt like a small time chiseler until the Professor taught you about your – what did he call it? Your... manifest destiny! And what about all that French poetic realism, and Jacobean tragedy, and Expressionism! You used to love to listen to his theories — why isn't he here, Dix? Wh–

—*Because I killed him! I couldn't stand it anymore!* I couldn't take another minute of his blather about Judeo-Christian patriarchal systems and structuro-semiological judgments. My head was going to explode!

—My God, Dix — *what did you do?*

—Let's just say I deconstructed him.

—You've finished us, Dix. I hope you know that. We're doomed.

—What else is new? Everybody dies. In the meantime, we'll be able to live again, like real people, not like little symbols on his big blackboard.

—And you think you can pull off this job without him?

—Did the Professor step up for me when Pete Hurley tried to kill me that night in Jefty's saloon? Was he in the car when I had to crash that roadblock upstate? Did the Professor have to tell me where you liked to be kissed?

—Give him his due, Dix. He was a great thinker.

—Thinking's overrated.

—Turn here.

—Shut up.

—Don't tell me to shut up...I just might kill you.

—Let me see it coming, that's all I ask.

—There's Tony! See him? Sitting on the running board?

—This stinks. It's all wrong.

—Why doesn't he see us? Why doesn't he look over?

—Could be that bullethole in his forehead, but it's just a hunch.

—What are you going to do now, Dix?

—We're gonna keep moving, Doll. Once a deal gets queered, that's when things get interesting.

—You're not going back to Dark City, are you? They'll kill you for sure.

—Well, I'm not running away. I'm through with that. What about you? You in or out?

—What else can I do? I've taken so many wrong turns I'm right back where I started. I may as well play it out.

—You could find yourself a rich guy. Break him. Drag him around until his knees are bloody.

—And leave you?

—I didn't say that.

—So it's back to the city, huh? No clear blue ocean, no boozy fruit drinks, no waiters in white?

—Later. I've got some housecleaning to do. Can I drop you someplace?

—Shut up, Dix. Just shut up and drive fast.

Welcome to Dark City

Lights down, curtain up, voice-over: Observe the mighty beast, mankind's riskiest experiment. A sprawling, soaring monster with a steel skeleton and a concrete overcoat. Some brilliant Frankensteins learned how to pump electricity through its arteries; now it lurchs and crackles and spews non-stop. On its daylight streets you'll witness the most courageous of human endeavors: the will to co-exist. But when the curtain of night falls, you'd better head for home. Or learn first-hand about our truly ingrained trait: the desire to devour.

A few years back, the eminent philosopher Lewis Mumford came to Dark City. He was a bright guy, little full of himself, in town to lecture on his book *The Culture of Cities*. He climbed out of a cab in front of the downtown auditorium and gazed up at the buildings looming around him. A knockout brunette who'd been hanging there rushed up to him.

"Spectacular, isn't it?" she gushed, ogling the skyscrapers with him. Even Mumford felt the blood rush a guy gets from a dishy dame.

"The city arose as a special kind of environment, favorable to cooperative association," he nattered. "It was a collective utility that ensured order and regularity in the comings and goings of men, that diminished the force of nature's random onslaughts, and reduced the menace of wild animals and the more predatory tribes of men. Permanent settlement meant not only continuity but security."

"Do tell," she breathed, nuzzling up to him.

"The big city becomes the prestige symbol for the whole civilization," he pronounced. "Life in all the subordinate regions is sacrificed to its temples of pleasure and towers of pecuniary aspiration."

The dame nodded. A guy jumped from behind a parked car, rapped Mumford's dome with a sap, and nailed his wallet before the philosopher hit the pavement.

Like a real trouper, Mumford gave his lecture that night, but skipped the intro he'd rehearsed. He got right to the point, delivering it with much feeling:

"It is impossible here to go into all the perversions and miscarriages of civic functions because of the physical spread and the congestion and misplanning of the mass city... the physical drain, the emotional defeat, of these cramped quarters, these dingy streets, the tear and noise of transit — these are but the most obvious results of megalopolitan growth...For what the metropolis gives with one hand, it takes back with the other: one climbs its golden tree with such difficulty that, even if one succeeds in plucking the fruit, one can no longer enjoy it."

Mumford probably got the shakes when he watched film noir. One way or another, noirs are all about people's struggle to survive in what he calls the "megalopolis," and in most cases the square-off is short, nasty, and brutal. Urban omnipotence casts long shadows over the genre. Its power cowed some filmmakers, who slavishly began their stories by paying obeisance to the city itself: cameras swooping over rooftops, prowling labrynthine streets, or simply displaying, with fearful reverence, the overwhelming skyline. It was a ritual, a genuflection. You make a hasty sign of the cross when confronted by the immensity of the cathedral.

In *City That Never Sleeps* (Republic, 1953) the metropolis, with the slight echo indicative of God's voice, narrates its own tale (channeled through scriptwriter Steve Fisher): "I am the city. Hub and heart of America. Melting pot of every race, creed, color, and religion in humanity. From my famous stockyards to my towering factories, from my tenement district to swank Lake Shore Drive, I am the voice, the heartbeat, of this giant, sprawling, sordid and beautiful, poor and magnificent citadel of civilization. And this is the story of just one night in this great city. Now meet my citizens..."

The City promptly introduces us to some of its regulars: jaundiced cop, corrupt businessman, psychotic crook, scheming wife, lovelorn loser, sweet-natured stripper. The apostles.

In this film, as in every noir, these characters will carom through a storyline in which the structure resembles the city itself. Unexpected intersections. Twisted corridors. Secrets hidden in locked rooms. Lives dangling from dangerous heights. Abrupt dead ends. The blueprint for noir scripts seemed to have been drafted by a demented urban planner. Down in the catacombs of the Dark City Department of Urban Development lived a wretched hermit who tried like hell to con-

jure diagrams for a perfectly functional metropolis. Problem was, he sought to account for human nature in his designs. His dementia swallowed him whole when he ran up against the inevitable truth: there's too many rats in the cage, and no bond issue or blue ribbon civic panel was going to bail us out.

His serpentine outlines served no useful purpose — until screenwriters made that murky basement a downtown local stop on their nocturnal visits to Dark City. They fleshed out his tortured guidelines, and the results were projected into the national psyche: *Whispering City, City of Fear, Cry of the City, Captive City, Naked City. Street of Chance, One Way Street, Terror Street, No Way Out.*

A FEVER DREAM OF MODERN LIFE erupted from these motion pictures. Something dreadful had crept into the social fabric, especially at the most bustling hubs of urban activity. Over at *The Sentinel*, the city's largest newspaper, the sold-out publisher pits his hot-shot scribblers against each other in a sensational campaign to capture the "Lipstick Killer," who murders women *While the City Sleeps* (RKO, 1956).

Across the street, at the *Express*, the city's biggest *Scandal Sheet* (Columbia, 1952), circulation zooms as the paper sponsors the hunt for "The Lonelyheart Murderer." Wouldn't you know? The culprit is the paper's own managing editor (Broderick Crawford), who is eventually hunted down by his star investigative reporter and protegé (John Derek).

At *Union Station* (Paramount, 1950), a regular Joe (Lyle Bettger) has gone off his nut and kidnapped a blind girl. The pitiful guy thinks he can leverage a ransom that will solve all his big city problems. The cops pursue him through the maze of train tunnels and exterminate him, finally freeing hordes of cheesed-off commuters.

Even the city's massive monument to mercy, the general hospital, isn't immune from the spreading societal cancers. The cops have to send in an undercover man, Fred Rowan (Richard Conte) to probe the brutal demise of several doctors. *The Sleeping City* (Universal, 1950) won't rest any easier when it learns what happens on the hospital's night-shift. Rowan discovers that head nurse Ann Sebastian (Coleen Gray), whom he was falling for, is the linchpin in a drug smuggling ring.

The Sleeping City was filmed on location at Manhattan's Bellevue Hospital in 1949, at the height of Hollywood's fascination with brooding crime melodramas. Prior to its release, New York's Mayor O'Dwyer pressured Universal executives to attach a prologue, delivered by Richard Conte, advising viewers that the story had nothing to do with the reality of big city hospitals, in New York or anywhere else.

This dichotomy — between overripe imagination and disingenuous denial — was the yawning cultural fissure upon which the foundations of Dark City were laid. Many of the stories you'll encounter here are a tantalizing blend of fact, fiction, and myth. Cinematic cocktails, if you will, in which a jigger of creative license and a dash of bitters put a dreamy edge on material rooted in ugly realities both contemporary and timeless.

Sorting through the facts and fictions of this place can be tricky. It pays to watch your step. Consider the film *Frightened City* (Columbia, 1951; a/k/a *The Killer That Stalked New York*), in which the threat of a disease contaminating the urban organism became grist for film noir. *Frightened City* is a more noirish treatment of the spread of a modern plague than *Panic in the Streets*, the heralded Elia Kazan-directed film released the previous year.

In *Panic*, the unsettling notion of the metropolis being infected with "foreign bodies" was made explicit: the disease is carried into the city from a merchant ship filled with foreigners, one of whom is slain on leave by local crooks, who contract the virus and rapidly spread it through the city's underworld.

The Sleeping City: undercover cop Fred Rowan (Richard Conte) learns from Pop Ware (Richard Taber) of a drug conspiracy in the city's general hospital.

In *Frightened City*, screenwriter Harry Essex threaded a crime narrative through the fact-based story of a smallpox outbreak that threatened New York in 1946. Sheila Bennet (Evelyn Keyes) and her husband Matt (Charles Korvin) run a diamond smuggling operation. Sheila mails the gems back to the States from Cuba, but unwittingly carries back with her the smallpox virus. While they wait for the diamonds to arrive, Sheila infects everyone she touches, including a young girl who later dies. Full-scale panic grips the city, as the national guard is called in to help set up an emergency inoculation program. A crusading health inspector spearheads a manhunt for the source carrier of the disease.

The story plays fast and loose with the actual "epidemic" that gripped New York, which was brief, well-controlled, and not very sensational. It's a choice example of how "the truth" was often bent, stretched, and artfully manipulated on the production lines of Hollywood's picture factories, for the sake of a more exciting story. The old "based on a true story" pitch always lent authenticity to the hyperbolic proceedings.

But the blurring of reality and imagination sometimes got so extreme, it created another half-world, in which the truth swings endlessly between what you think is real and what is merely a projection.

Fourteen Hours (20th Century-Fox, 1951) is another urban drama based on a true story. On July 26, 1938, John Warde held downtown New York spellbound for more than half a day as he perched on the 17th floor ledge of the Gotham Hotel, threatening to jump. The first man at the scene, sympathetic traffic cop Charles Glasco, valiantly bonded with Warde — talking to him for an anguished fourteen hours — but in the end he couldn't save the troubled young man, who leaped to his death.

The film version (written by John Paxton, directed by Henry Hathaway) exemplifies what you'll be encountering on your journey through Dark City. It's a tense depiction of one man's personal despair amid the teeming concrete indifference of the modern city. As Robert

Cosick (Richard Basehart) teeters on the verge of suicide, cabbies in the throng below wager on the hour he'll jump. A pair of young lovers meet in the glare of searchlights. A wife filing for divorce in the attorney's office across from the hotel is inspired to reconcile with her husband.

And in every shot of the distraught Cosick, the sky-scrapers of Dark City loom above him and the endless avenues stretch out to the horizon — the city's immensity mocking the insignificance of the young man's confusion. Despite the gallant effort of Officer Dunnigan (Paul Douglas) to talk him down, Cosick falls to his death. In the picture's final shot, a sanitation truck, moving like a leth-argic antibody, washes away the remnants of Cosick's splattered, trivial remains, while the budding lovers walk past, arm in arm.

At least that's what audiences saw when the film premiered. That same day in New York, the daughter of 20th Century-Fox executive Spyros Skouras killed herself in a leap from the eighth floor of Bellevue Hospital. Skouras was so devastated he immediately pulled *Fourteen Hours* from distribution. The resourceful Darryl F. Zanuck rounded up several actors (Basehart not among them) and a skeleton crew and hastily re-shot a new ending, in which Cosick is rescued at the last moment and whisked to safety.

This confounding waltz between fantasy and reality will be a leitmotif of our tour.

As we travel, be sure not to focus just on the major landmarks. Some of the best stories emanate from the transients' hotels in the town's tenderloin, within cramped rooms clammy with the residue of spoiled hopes. Where wallpaper sweats from the radiator's steam heat and neon buzzes incessantly outside the window. Here, lifetimes are squeezed into eighty taut minutes.

Somebody checked out earlier than expected; there's a vacancy on the third floor, ready for another story.

This page: Richard Basehart resists rescue in *Fourteen Hours.*

Opposite: Charles Korvin flees the deadly touch of Evelyn Keyes in *Frightened City,* a/k/a *The Killer That Stalked New York.*

Force of Evil

Up there in the diamond bracelet of penthouse lights champagne corks pop, feckless women squeal, and power courses mercilessly among the insulated "businessmen." Down here, forty floors below, their clerks prowl the selling floor, wholesaling fear and muscle without any conscience. But there are climbers among the minions. One day the boss will slip and fall in the trail of blood money, and one of his loyal boys will ease through the side door and finally be up there, on the inside, looking down.

Sinister Heights

When these images and motives flooded America's movie screens there was no such animal as film noir. Cinéastes hadn't yet bestowed the academic nomenclature. At the picture factories in Los Angeles, and in the boardrooms of the Wall Street underwriters, these movies were known simply as "crime dramas." Accurate, if not as highfalutin. For if there's a common denominator in film noir, it's crime. In Dark City, laws, and hearts, are trampled daily.

As popular as crime dramas were after World War II, they were also unnerving to great suburban segments of the filmgoing public. In Monroe, Michigan, theater owner J. R. Denniston, a "small exhibitor in the sticks," declared in the March 10, 1951 issue of *Showmen's Trade Review:* "In order to get our theater programs in proper balance I would suggest that the production of all crime pictures be discontinued by all producers, and that those they now have on their shelves be withdrawn from the market."

No doubt emboldened by the patriotic search-and-destroy mission of the House Un-American Activities Committee, Mr. Denniston requested that Hollywood produce "Great romances written about business, industry, farming, medicine and education." In keeping with the Stalinist overtones of his wish list, he concluded, "To get these things we will probably have to have a new set of writers, because the people who write the stories must know and understand what they are writing about."

The theater owner's diatribe, it must be noted, was motivated by dwindling audiences, not love of country. Better box office surely would have eased his mind. But Denniston's Babbittism shouldn't be dismissed merely as the whining of an exhibitor crying poor-mouth. He knew his clientele, and in the heartland citizens were truly horrified by the barrage of movies that depicted urban corruption as a spreading cancer.

During the Depression, the era in which noir germinated, Hollywood fed the public a glamorous vision of gangsters as renegade cowboy bandits. The Cagneys and Robinsons ran wild until the strong arm of our newly-civilized society ran them to ground. Audiences loved their flamboyant crooks, even if the bad guys did have to end up face down in the gutter.

Post-WWII criminals were far scarier. They weren't after the living wage the Depression robbed them of, they were after power. They didn't buck the system, they took full advantage of it. Crime dramas of this era borrowed the trappings of traditional gangster pictures to present a vision of urban America in which the Have-Nots — vulgar and angry and determined — battled the Haves for control of the gears and levers that operate the modern city.

In noir, crooks are shaved, shined and high-toned. They've learned how to fold their rackets into the straining seams of the capitalist economy. Aspiring to the heights, they work their way from the dark edges of society toward the light of "legitimacy." They'd laugh at their scrappy twenty-year-old ancestors, knocking over banks with guns blazing. The noir crime boss had the bank president, and the police chief, in his pocket.

No film traced this transition more clearly, or more artfully, than *Force of Evil* (MGM, 1948). Adapted by Abraham Polonsky from Ira Wolfert's keenly-researched journalistic novel *Tucker's People*, the movie was originally going to be called *The Numbers Racket*. In Polonsky's hands, though, it became much more than an indictment of racketeering. It drew stark parallels between organized crime and big business, and painted a bleak picture of America, its industrial might festering with institutionalized corruption. Crime was defined, in the words of Wolfert, as "the grease that makes things run."

"I wanted to be a success, to get ahead in the world, and I believed there were three ways to do it," explained protagonist Joe Morse in an opening voice-over Polonsky cut from the film prior to release. "You could inherit a fortune, you could work hard all your life for it, or you could steal it. I was born poor and impatient."

Sylvia Morse (Georgia Backus) watches her husband Leo (Thomas Gomez) suffer the hard sell of his brother Joe (John Garfield). Joe wants to convince Leo there's nothing to lose by joining Tucker's combination in Abraham Polonsky's *Force of Evil*.

Joe Morse is a partner in a Wall Street law firm with clients on both sides of the line. He craves the fortune he'll reap from transforming the "policy racket" into a legal lottery. He and his golden goose, gangster Ben Tucker, plan to break the small freelance neighborhood policy banks by fixing the July 4th number, 776, to hit — paying off a multitude of superstitious bettors, and leaving the penny-ante policy boys financially vulnerable. Tucker will then bail them out if they agree to be absorbed into one all-encompassing "combination" under his control.

The snag in the plan is Joe's guilty conscience. His brother Leo runs a tiny numbers bank, and has no desire to be consumed by the capitalist juggernaut. He likes his policy set-up personal and communal; he won't follow Joe to "an office in the clouds." Leo's intransigence strains Joe's partnership with Tucker. Doris, Leo's secretary, further weakens Joe's materialistic resolve by spurning his cocky advances. "You're a strange man. And a very evil one," she tells Joe when he tries to impress her with a bouquet.

"I didn't have enough strength to resist corruption," Joe says, "but I had enough strength to fight for a piece of it." Joe spirals into spiritual and ethical purgatory, culminating with Leo's death. His resultant moral reawakening is one of the most unsatisfying — yet apt — conclusions in film history; Joe limps to the authorities with all the confidence of a lone man facing down the force of evil.

In both content and style, *Force of Evil* was pivotal. Its treatment of a formulaic storyline — ghetto kid takes a crooked road to the top only to learn the error of his ways — transcended or undercut Hollywood cliché at every turn. The moral agony faced by the characters was suffocating; Polonsky's script refused to opt for easy answers to complex questions. And its prescient dissection of the ground shared by free enterprise and racketeering invites present-day viewers to connect the dots between Ben Tucker and the corporate raiders and merger pirates of contemporary Wall Street.

"I do not write stories which attempt to sell a certain morality to the audience," Polonsky has said. "I accept the world and our place in it and I know we have to deal with it. I also know that if we have certain concerns about our nature in it, we're going to pay the price for that. The point of *Force of Evil* is that the price for stealing is Joe's destruction of himself, his brother, and everything else. If you're not willing to pay that price, then you can't live in that world. That's the soldier's attitude: that's how you survive a battle."

Polonsky, like producer-star John Garfield, was a Jewish street kid from New York, his head full to bursting with the intellectual fervor of the New York art scene of the 1930s. Both had survived the rugged road out of the Depression, through the war, and into the rarefied air of Hollywood. "However appalled as I was by the industry and its product," Polonsky said, "the medium overwhelmed me with a language I had been trying to speak all my life."

Stylistically, he was the first Hollywood filmmaker to attempt a type of concentrated cinematic poetry, using imagery, dialogue and narration in three-part harmony. Revelatory, stylized speech seems to erupt, unconsciously, from the characters. Scenes are framed and lighted with the brooding melancholy of Hopper paintings. The editing is often daringly abrupt. Despite the existential bleakness at the film's core, the storytelling was fueled by pure creative adrenaline. Polonsky's approach wasn't brazen, like Orson Welles, but it did inject more self-conscious artistry into a crime drama than anyone had previously thought necessary.

Ben Tucker (Roy Roberts) tries to convince Joe Morse (Garfield, *left*) to stay in the combination. "You were a gunman and a killer before we became partners," Joe snaps, "and I showed you how to hide your business from the police... But I'm not going to end up on the rocks in the river, like my brother."

Neither Hollywood, nor the public, was receptive. At the same time Garfield and Polonsky were seeking to slip their world view into the rushing stream of Hollywood pabulum, many studio heads were slavishly reading a booklet entitled *Screen Guide for Americans*, concocted by the doyenne of social Darwinism, Ayn Rand. Published by the Motion Picture Alliance for the Preservation of American Ideals, and distributed with the imprimatur of the House Un-American Activities Committee, the guide instructed studio heads: "Don't Smear Industrialists," "Don't Smear the Free Enterprise System," and "Don't Smear Success." Rand advocated the disposal of any script that implied villainy on the part of money-making industrialists.

Imagine Rand's reaction to Leo Morse's blustering anti-business tirade: "Living from mortgage to mortgage, stealing credit like a thief. And the garage! That was a business! Three cents overcharge on every gallon of gas... two cents for the chauffeur, and a penny for me. A penny for one thief, two cents for the other. Well Joe is here now. I won't have to steal pennies any more. I'll have big crooks to steal dollars for me."

Parallels connecting the studio system and the rackets depicted in crime dramas such as *Force of Evil* are too rich to ignore. As Harry Cohn, the boss of Columbia Pictures, admitted: "This isn't a business, it's a racket." Its direct link to the Mob was a wiseguy named Willie Bioff, a roly-poly racketeer from the same Windy City streets that produced Al Capone, Frank Nitti, Johnny Roselli, and Sam "Momo" Giancana. Bioff teamed up in the early '30s with George Browne, the Chicago head of the International Alliance of Theatrical Stage Employees (IATSE), to help the working man – and get rich in the process.

John Garfield and Lilli Palmer in *Body and Soul.*

They started by hustling John and Barney Balaban. The brothers ran a Midwest theater chain, and during the Depression they drastically cut the wages of IATSE projectionists. Bioff taught Browne Capone-style tactics, demanding $50,000 from the Balabans. When they begged off, projection rooms had unexplained electrical fires, equipment broke, reels were shown out of order. The theater owners coughed up twenty G's. Bioff and Browne were on their way.

They took their grand scheme of conquering the movie business to Nitti, "The Enforcer," who'd taken control of the Chicago rackets after Capone was sent up. Nitti turned out the vote for Browne, electing him national president of IATSE in 1934 (he'd eventually become a vice-president of the American Federation of Labor). Bioff was named his international representative. They roadshowed the extortion act coast-to-coast.

Nicholas Schenck, president of Loew's, the exhibition overlord of Metro-Goldwyn-Mayer, met Bioff and Browne in a Waldorf-Astoria hotel room with a fifty grand payoff wrapped in a paper sack. Schenck waited while Browne counted out the dough. Sidney Kent, president of 20th Century-Fox walked in, dumping another fifty large on the bed.

Before long, the dynamic duo had a sweet deal set up in Lotus Land. They assumed control of the craft and stagehand unions, convincing members a 10 percent wage hike would be extracted from the studios. But first the rank and file would have to donate two percent of their paychecks to a union war fund, in case of strikes. That money was funnelled straight to Nitti and the boys.

While workers waited for the day they'd get a fair shake, Bioff and Browne were paid tribute by the studio bosses to ensure there'd be no costly walkouts. Bioff envisioned a future in which every Hollywood union was in his fold.

"We had about 20 percent of Hollywood when we got in trouble," Bioff testified, once his shakedown flamed out in 1941. "If we hadn't got loused up, we'd have had 50 percent. I had Hollywood dancing to my tune."

The Feds nailed him, in large part due to a private investigation launched by Screen Actor's Guild president Robert Montgomery. Faced with a stint at Alcatraz, Bioff ratted out the Nitti gang: Louie "Little New York" Campagna, Phil "The Squire" D'Andrea, Paul "The Waiter" Ricca, Charlie "Cherry Nose" Gioe, and Frank "The Immune" Maritone. Nitti promptly shot himself in the head in a Chicago railyard.

Joe Schenck (Nick's brother), president of 20th Century–Fox, and the Motion Picture Producers Association, was convicted of paying the mobsters a $100,000 bribe, and sentenced to three years in the can. Bioff and Browne pulled longer stretches. It was all largely symbolic. The trade papers played it as though Hollywood's respectable businessmen had been the prey of ruthless extortionists. But as journalist Otto Friedrich notes in his study of Hollywood in the Forties, *City of Nets:* "Bribery and extortion can turn out to be pretty much the same thing. Money is paid in exchange for a service; both sides agree on a price and a service; the only question is who is corrupting whom."

The deal the mob had with studios was simple: bribes were shelled out to keep the unions docile and relatively powerless. A ruling in Chicago tax court later stated that studios "knowingly and willingly paid over the funds and in a sense lent encouragement and participated with full knowledge of the facts in the activities of Browne and Bioff." Payoffs to the pair, it was estimated in court papers, saved the studios as much as $15 million in wages.

After leaving prison, Bioff changed his name to Bill Nelson and moved to Phoenix. But the garrulous gangster couldn't keep his profile low. He hooked up with the Riviera in Vegas – which was tied to the very mobsters he'd set up. He made showy contributions to Barry Goldwater's first Senate campaign. One day in 1955 he was blown apart by a car bomb.

MOST MOVIE MOGULS, LIKE GANGSTERS, were poorly educated, ostentatious, vulgar, power-hungry, insecure, and obsessed with being publicly respected. They ran Hollywood with a ruthlessness that Dutch Schultz would have envied. Their job was to make money for the investors; their mission was to get power and hold it. Art was rarely invited to their parties. It had to crash the gate.

In 1947, as soon as John Garfield was free of his contractual obligation to Jack Warner's stable, he used his newfound wealth to bankroll Enterprise Studios, an independent production company dedicated to challenging the status quo. Any rogue operator is considered a threat, and Garfield and company were no exception. To Hollywood's racket bosses, he was a brash upstart, cutting himself too big a piece of pie.

To the artists Enterprise recruited, moviemaking presented a moral quandary akin to Joe Morse's in *Force of Evil:* was success worth anything if it came at the expense of truth? Garfield set the tone, refusing to turn his back on where he'd come from, and demanding that his movies reflect the reality of the world beyond the sound stage. That's why he had a kinship with Abe Polonsky, whose passion for social justice was tempered by deep doubts about society's ability to ever achieve it. To them, it was imperative to fight the good fight, and damn the consequences.

So it was only fitting that Enterprise's first big hit was *Body and Soul* (UA, 1947), about a tough Jewish kid from the Lower East Side, Charlie Davis, who fights his way to the top, but loses his soul along the way by throwing in with racketeers. Polonsky called his script "a fable from the

Body and Soul: Shorty Polaski (Joe Pevney) is killed after challenging his boyhood pal, boxer Charlie Davis (John Garfield) to break away from corrupt promoter, Roberts (Lloyd Gough). Everybody knows Roberts had Shorty killed, but only Peg (Lilli Palmer) has the integrity to walk away from the high life and easy money.

Empire City," and it was given vivid life by the aggressive direction of Robert Rossen, the visual poetry of cameraman James Wong Howe, and most vitally, the bristling performance of Garfield.

Beneath the emotionalism of the story, however, was a depiction of crime central to the development of film noir: there are no characters crusading against the mob's infiltration of boxing. The corruption, as in the subsequent *Force of Evil*, is too deeply entrenched.

As Polonsky was writing *Body and Soul*, a Senate probe was seeking to expose the reach of racketeers like Frankie Carbo into New York boxing rings. Polonsky's script intimates that such efforts are ultimately futile. Government committees may selectively squeeze some token miscreants out of the system's bloodstream, but a true clean-up is impossible. In Polonsky's view, the notion of a God-fearing G-Man setting things straight — the reliable Hollywood "square-up" — was at best laughable, at worst fascistic.

Body and Soul and *Force of Evil* both chronicle a world in which it's far too late to isolate corruption and root it out. The challenge for conscious people, which Charlie Davis and Joe Morse eventually become, is to live with personal dignity in a society where the cancer is inoperable.

Body and Soul was the vision of a realist more than a pessimist. Robert Rossen, an Enterprise rebel with far less subtlety than Polonsky, wanted to end the film with Charlie Davis murdered by the racket boss he's betrayed, gunned down in an alley in a lingering, sickening image of futility. Polonsky fought tooth and nail to maintain his original, and now famous, ending: After winning the fight he was ordered to lose — and blowing the small fortune he and his boss wagered on the opponent — Charlie defiantly sneers at his overlord, "What are you gonna do, kill me? Everybody dies." Die he might, minutes after the fade-out, but at least he's regained his soul.

If horseracing was the sport of kings, boxing was the sport of knaves. Several other fight films followed closely in the wake of *Body and Soul*, solidifying the notion that the sweet science was corrupted, either by its very nature, or by criminal maneuvering in its ranks. Some were created with strokes broad enough for audiences to see the ring as a metaphor for the win-at-all-costs struggle of modern life.

In *The Set-Up* (RKO, 1949), Robert Ryan portrays Stoker Thompson, a journeyman heavyweight on the backside of his career, whose only cherished possession is the belief that he can still win a title. His manager sells him out, assuring local gangsters that Stoker will tank that night's bout. When he gets wise to the set-up, Stoker wages the fight of his life, finally battering his younger rival into submission. For his trouble, Stoker has his hands crushed, so he can no longer earn a living.

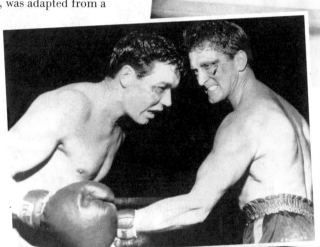

The picture, written by former sportswriter Art Cohn, was adapted from a poem by Joseph Moncure March, and directed by Robert Wise in real time — the 72 minutes before, during and after the fight that constitute the solar plexus of Stoker Thompson's life. The film remained the personal favorite of both Wise and Robert Ryan. *The Set-Up* is noir boiled down to its existential essence: this is the way the world works, make your choices and be prepared to live, or die, by them.

Champion (UA) was also made in 1949, and until a lawsuit sorted things out, it too was called *The Set-Up*. In the film, based on a 1916 short story by Ring Lardner, the savagery of fighter Midge Kelley (Kirk Douglas) is never ennobled. Midge is a rotten son-of-a-bitch throughout. He has no compunction about letting the mob grease the wheels for him, cynically discarding his wife and brother when they try to reform him. It's a relief when he finally dies of a brain hemorrhage in the locker room. The Mark Robson-directed film is scathing in its depiction of the public and the media, which conspire to make Midge a hero, even though he's a thug.

Top to bottom:
John Garfield rises to the top in
Body and Soul,
Kirk Douglas deals punishment
in *Champion,* and
Robert Ryan fights for his
dignity in *The Set-Up.*

Robson also directed Budd Schulberg's *The Harder They Fall*, released in 1956, a loose account of the absurd career of early Thirties heavyweight champion Primo Carnera, a lumbering circus strongman from Italy who was ushered to the title by conniving promoters. Once his backers had earned sufficient lucre from their freak attraction, he was left on his own to be cruelly exposed: Max Baer knocked him down 11 times in their title fight. Schulberg, who always wrote with great moral indignation, centers his story around jaded sportswriter Eddie Willis (Humphrey Bogart, in his last performance), who sells his soul to gangster Nick Benko (Rod Steiger) by taking a flak job for an operation he knows is completely crooked. The film ends with Willis shaking off the dirt and calling for the abolition of boxing.

By the time Martin Scorsese made *Raging Bull* (UA, 1980), Schulberg's notion of "exposing" corruption in the sport was passé. Instead, Scorsese's grainy operatic coda to the noir boxing genre concentrated on how Jake LaMotta's personal demons made him an easy mark for the gangsters controlling the New York prize ring. Despite his jailhouse whimperings — "I'm not an animal" — Jake was crippled carrion, ripe for the vultures. More than thirty years separated *Body and Soul* and *Raging Bull*, but the philosophical left hook remained the same: you can't control the way the world works, only how you choose to live within it. It may well be the noir credo.

One of the most famous films to wrestle with sports rackets was *Night and the City* (20th, 1950). Its protagonist wasn't a boxer, but he was a scrappy combatant nonetheless. Harry Fabian, an expatriate Yank living in London (it's easy to imagine him having fled from stateside loansharks), longs for his piece of the action, and hatches a plot that pits him against Kristo, the kingpin of professional wrestling. Despite all his frenzied promoting and emoting, cajoling and button-holing, Fabian meets the fate that Charlie Davis and Stoker Thompson escaped: he's murdered and dumped in the river.

Harry Fabian is noir's most pathetic character. Unlike the fighters, he doesn't even have the potential to physically transcend humiliation with his fists. His grab for power comes solely through crafty, low-rent schemes. But Harry's not cut out for it. He's a stunted child, not ashamed to rifle his girlfriend's purse for money. Richard Widmark, one of the true noir artists, suffuses Fabian with a maniacal intensity that makes his headlong rush to hell uncomfortably exhilarating; it's like watching a human pinball careering explosively off the bumpers only to suddenly and silently drop down the chute. Game over. No replay.

In most crime pictures, Harry Fabian would be a supporting character, a petty climber, the type played by Elisha Cook, Jr. Kristo might have patted Harry's cheek and dismissed him offhandedly: "Kid, you've got moxie. I like that." But Harry's naked desire is so wretched that it repulses the crooks who aspire to respectability. He's ultimately disposed of not because he's a threat, but because he's an embarrassment to the successful criminals who have cloaked the desperate wanna-be inside them with threadbare sophistication. Fabian is executed for the offense of making everybody else look bad.

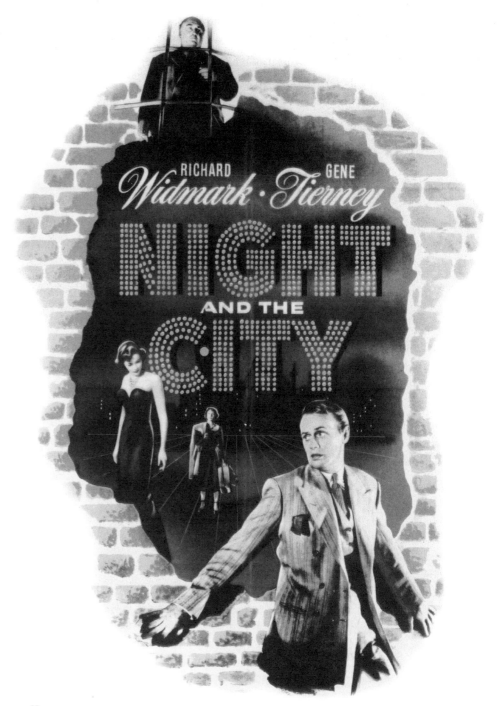

Richard Conte (center) displays the essential élan of the well-heeled mobster. For the noir criminal, the purpose of acquiring power is to show it off in glittery public venues. The ultimate satisfaction is to force his moral "superiors" to watch him enjoy the spoils of corruption. From *Under the Gun* (Universal-International, 1951).

Two years earlier Widmark had played a crooked fight promoter named Alec Stiles in *The Street With No Name* (20th, 1948). Stiles was who Harry Fabian might have become if he'd had a little more personal discipline. He's mightily impressed with himself because of his ability "to build an organization along scientific lines." The first order of business is to dress and act the part. He tosses a wad of bills at his new lieutenant (actually an undercover fed) and instructs him: "Buy a closet full of new clothes. I like my boys to look sharp."

Stiles was given edgy life by Widmark, who had shot to fame with his twitchy, keening portrayal of a psychotic killer in *Kiss of Death* (20th, 1947). Alec Stiles's resplendent suits can't camouflage his pathological hypochondria. He's terrified of drafts ("You open that window and I'll throw ya out it!"), the first of a long line of allergy-plagued punks who snort blasts of sinus medicine from nasal inhalers. Stiles is a cheap chiseler with an overpowering need to be perceived as devilishly stylish – a common goal for most of the residents of Sinister Heights.

In terms of vanity, these men were more married to their mirrors than Norma Desmond. Most mobsters fled the squalor of the slums. They were compulsive about displaying panache around the swells who'd made their piles legitimately.

That's why nightclubs figure so prominently in Dark City datebooks. Fronting the typical City speakeasy was a boy born to the booze business, who'd missed last call at the recruiting office but emerged on the other side of the war with an up-and-up establishment, well-equipped to host victory parties. Welcome to Slim Dundee's Round-Up, The Sanctuary Club, The Blue Dahlia, or The Kit Kat — ask about our veteran's two-for-one special.

The club owner's juice within the city's power structure was built on savoir faire and seating strategy. A discreet booth for the shady contractor buying a highball for the district alderman. A stage-side table for the judge who likes an unobstructed view of the seductive chanteuse. It's all show biz. The bistro boss and his maître d' are choreographers of a nightly mating dance in which lowlifes and upper crust mingle, their schemes and secrets spilling out amidst the top-shelf bourbon and the torchy ballads.

The proprietor snaps his fingers. A table is reset, a kneecap is shattered. It's easy to see how these nocturnal entrepreneurs believed their well-connected customers could be bent to suit alternative agendas.

The nightlife impresario is a fixture in noir: Peter Lorre in *Black Angel* (Universal, 1946), Robert Alda in *The Man I Love* (WB, 1946), Morris Carnovsky in *Dead Reckoning* (Columbia, 1947), Dan Duryea in *Criss Cross* (Universal, 1949) are but a few memorable examples of the barroom brotherhood. The symbolism of the potentially dangerous night spot is crucial. It marks the halfway point in the criminal's rise from illicit to legitimate business.

If they can dazzle the city's crème de la crème, no one will notice the deal-fixing and arm-twisting going down in the back room.

Sartorial superiority is essential to crook Alec Stiles (Richard Widmark). Undercover underling Gene Cordell (Mark Stevens) helps dress the boss in *The Street With No Name*.

This gray area between old-school hoodlum and the new "organization man" was fertile turf for noir fables. *The Racket*, released by Howard Hughes's RKO studio in 1951, was a remake of the second film that Hughes produced, back in 1928. Its central figure, Nick Scanlon (Robert Ryan, in another seething performance), is a Prohibition-style enforcer, all grease and muscle and boiling rage. He's a thorn in the side of the cops (represented, in true melodrama fashion, by his boyhood pal), and a liability to the boardroom boys who have slickly moved from running numbers to buying judges and fixing elections.

While he delights in intimidating people, Scanlon's deeper motives are familial. His younger brother must be given the opportunity to make it in legitimate endeavors. "I even kept him out of the rackets," he explains to his nemesis, Capt. McQuigg (Robert Mitchum). "He could marry anybody in this town — society people even!" Emulating the snooty gentry they despised was a full-time job for mob bosses.

Scanlon lives in an apartment that McQuigg describes as "the lobby of the Palace Theater," has an English butler, and

Robert Ryan as Nick Scanlon in Howard Hughes' *The Racket.*

gloats to McQuigg that "My taxes would pay the salaries of ten guys like you — public servants!" His suits are tailored, his Homburg perfectly blocked, his personal barber always on call. Lest anyone think he's just a knuckle-busting poseur, Scanlon likes to bark: "I was running this town when you cheap crooks were still eating in diners" — a withering insult to any social-climbing hooligan.

Scanlon has a spiritual kinship with Shubunka, a self-made racket man played by Barry Sullivan in *The Gangster* (Monogram, 1947). Shubunka runs a protection dodge in a nameless beachfront district. A puffed-up peacock presiding over his two-bit territory, Shubunka believes he's the second coming of Scarface. In truth, he's a paranoid psychotic, his judgment clouded by obsessive jealousy over his beautiful mistress. As

the encroaching syndicate puts the screws to him, Shubunka's insecurities come spewing out: "I came up from the sewer. Out of the muck and the mud, I came up by myself. I went to work when I was six — six years old! I was doing jobs for gangsters when I was nine. Bootlegging on my own when I was fourteen. Did anybody worry about me? Did anybody cry his eyes out over me? What do you want me to do — worry about the world?

Let 'em rot, every one of them. They don't mean a thing to me. Don't flinch at me, don't you dare look down at me. I'm no crumb — I made something out of myself and I'm proud of it!"

Shubunka is confessing not to the chief of police, but to a teenage girl whose condescending gaze rips him apart. Like Scanlon, he'll be dead before the night is out, "removed" by the neater, tidier businessmen parceling out his turf.

VIRILITY IS EVERY BIT AS CRITICAL to Dark City's crooks as respectability. In *The Big Combo* (Allied Artists, 1955) the gangster picture is distilled into a sexual battle between the saturnine, sensual Mr. Brown (Richard Conte) and dogged but frustrated flatfoot Leonard Diamond (Cornel Wilde). Both men covet the appetizing Susan Lowell (Jean Wallace), whom Diamond has been stalking for months as part of his investigation of Brown's illegal Combination.

The themes are insinuated from the start: David Raksin's score bumps and grinds like a burlesque band summoning a stripper. Susan flees a boxing match, pursued through shadowy alleys, and finally collared, by Brown's henchmen. The scene is a pure visual expression of Brown's sexual dominance. Possession of a beautiful woman is at the root of his quest for power.

Brown and his yes-man, McClure (Brian Donlevy), visit the dressing room of Brown's boxer, Benny, who's lost his bout. Brown gives Benny his philosophical crash course, using the whipped McClure as his case history. "We eat the same steak, drink the same bourbon. Look — same manicure, cufflinks. But we don't get the same girls. Why? Because women know the difference. They got instinct. First is first and second is nobody....What makes the difference? Hate. Hate is the word, Benny. Hate the man who tries to kill you. Hate him until you see red and you come out winning the big money. The girls will come tumbling after. You'll have to shut off the phone and lock the door to get a night's rest."

Brown then slaps Benny across his already bruised face. When the fighter takes it, Brown says, "You should have hit me back. You haven't got the hate. Tear up Benny's contract. He's no good to me anymore."

From then on, *The Big Combo* becomes a different kind of noir boxing film, with Brown and Diamond, twentieth-century cavemen, slugging it out for possession of the trophy blonde. Diamond may genuinely want to staunch the spread of Brown's corruption, but he'd rather castrate than incarcerate him. Sexual perversity runs rampant. Susan is suicidally seduced by Brown. She's sacrificed her personal ambitions, held captive by the way he lavishes his bankroll, and his tongue, on her. Brown gets an erotic charge out of bracing her in a secret room filled with money and munitions. Brown's enforcers, Fante (Lee Van Cleef) and Mingo (Earl Holliman) appear to be homosexual lovers who use beatings and torture as foreplay. Rita, the cop's girlfriend, gives him the lay of the land: "Women don't care how a man makes his living, only how he makes love." Brown scores points against Diamond even by proxy.

"You'd like to be me," Brown flatly tells Diamond. "You'd like to have my organization, my influence, my fix. You think it's the money. It's not — it's personality." He also dominates the verbal sparring match. Brown clips off some of the best racketeer chatter ever, courtesy of screenwriter Philip Yordan:

"That's *Mister* Brown to you. Only my friends call me Brown."

"I'm gonna break him so fast he won't have time to change his pants."

"You're a little man with a soft job and good pay. Stop thinking about what might have been and who knows — you may live to die in bed."

"If they take you to police headquarters, shoot yourself in the head. It'll make things simpler."

Aside from its snappy patter, Yordan's tale was the most stripped-down rendering of gangsterism yet. It benefits no end from the austere direction of Joseph H. Lewis, who plays it like Robert Bresson, if Bresson was swinging a shot-loaded sap. The poverty of the production values is artfully masked by the stark photography of John Alton. The three were obviously having a good time toying with the genre conventions, and pushing the limits of what was permissible on-screen. In one scene, Conte laps at Jean Wallace's shoulders, then sinks out of the frame, leaving the strong suggestion of oral sex. When the buddy-buddy button men are in hiding, Fante tries to get his stir crazy roomie to eat something. "I can't swallow no more salami," mumbles Mingo, subtly enough to evade the censor's radar.

"It was for her I began to work my way up. All I had was guts. I traded them for money and influence. I got respect from everybody but her...

"This is my bank... we don't take checks, we deal strictly in cash. There isn't anybody I'd trust with so much temptation – except myself. Or maybe you."

— Mr. Brown (Richard Conte) to
Susan (Jean Wallace)
in *The Big Combo*

CRIME DRAMAS PRODUCED IN THE YEARS immediately following WWII projected a political battle onto the nation's movie screens. The hot-button on the dashboard of every crime screenplay was the Haves versus the Have-Nots. The distribution of wealth in America was an unresolved bête noire from the Depression, and a chief ingredient in noir after the war.

The "naturalist" school of writing took hold in Hollywood. Its politics were knee-jerk leftist, steeped in the Utopian Socialism that swirled around New York's influential Group Theater of the 1930s. Crime stories that emerged from this creative cauldron saw the hapless criminal as the product of a flawed system.

No artist exemplified the "naturalist" approach more than John Garfield. While directors and cinematographers are routinely lauded for developing the noir ethos, it was actually Garfield, more than anyone else, who gave early noir its defiant face and voice. One of his first star turns was in the aptly titled *They Made Me a Criminal* (WB, 1939).

On screen, Garfield shone as the first true rebel. Despite his being cast in dreck that tried to bleach his ethnicity and drain his raw power, audiences could feel that his motivations were straight from street level, that he was a new dose of reality. Here was a Bowery boy who took no guff, who hit with the impact of boxing heroes Benny Leonard and Barney Ross.

Born in 1913 as Jacob Julius Garfinkle, John Garfield would become for another underclass the kind of larger-than-life symbol Jimmy Cagney was for the shanty Irish. He brought with him to Hollywood a fiery desire to Make a Difference. Trailing him was a caravan of writers, directors and actors from the New York stage. If the initial wave from Ellis Island who developed the movie business were dedicated to making money, the second wave, of which Garfield was the point man, were committed to making art. The ideological and economic clash that ensued was like a

gangland turf war. Backstabbing was par for the course — and don't think it wasn't an influence on the angry, pessimistic screenplays that line the library shelves of film noir.

As a Warners contract player, Garfield began to comb Dark City's limits with offerings such as *Out of the Fog* (1941) and *The Postman Always Rings Twice* (on loan to MGM, 1946). But it was his attitude, his way of struggling with moral ambiguity, that would prove most influential on the genre. Once he was operating as an independent, Garfield's projects adopted a darker hue, and a heavier weight: the previously cited *Body and Soul* and *Force of Evil* were followed by *We Were Strangers* (Columbia, 1949), a politically-charged miscalculation about 1930s Cuban revolution that riled Communists and capitalists alike; *The Breaking Point* (WB, 1950), a wrenching rendering of Hemingway's *To Have and Have Not*,

JOHN GARFIELD: He Ran All the Way

grimmer and more emotional than Howard Hawks's flippant 1946 version; and best of all, *He Ran All the Way* (UA, 1951), an overlooked noir classic that features Garfield's best performance.

It's a crime drama that effectively cauterizes its bleeding heart. Nick Robey (Garfield) is one of Dark City's lost souls, still living with his spiteful shrew of a mother, unable to lift himself above a life of petty crime. When a cut-and-dried robbery gets scrambled, Nick panics and shoots a cop. He hides out among the sweltering masses at a public swimming pool, where he latches onto Peg Dobbs (Shelley Winters). Nick charms her into taking him home, where he'll be safe from the manhunt.

Nick tries to ingratiate himself with Peg's folks, but before the night is out, he goes berserk again and takes them hostage at gunpoint. While the Dobbses sweat out whether they'll survive, Nick veers between envy and derision of their complacent family life. He tries on roles as patriarch, big brother, benefactor and, ultimately, Mr. Right for Peg. He gives her the holdup cash, so she can get them a car in which they can elope/escape.

But the plan goes haywire. Upshot is, Peg winds up with the .38 and has to choose between her Dad and Nick. Tough, because Peg really likes Nick. But she shoots him, and he staggers back out to the gutter to die.

He Ran All the Way was Garfield's last film. It's fitting that he made it — almost defiantly — with screenwriters Hugo Butler and Guy Endore, and director John Berry, all of whom would be hounded out of Hollywood by the HUAC witchhunt. But of all the Hollywood artists unjustly tarred by the blacklist, John Garfield suffered the most.

Abraham Polonsky vividly explained Garfield's triumph and tragedy in his introduction to Howard Gelman's *The Films of John Garfield*: "Garfield was a star who represented a social phenomenon of enormous importance for his times and, perhaps, ours too. He lived as a star without contradiction in the imagination of those who loved him for something that lay dormant in themselves, and this was tuned to the social vigor of the time that created him. Naturally, when those times became the political target of the establishment in the United States, Garfield, whose training, whose past were the environment of the romantic rebellion the depression gave birth to, became a public target for the great simplifiers."

Those simplifiers, Joe McCarthy, Roy Cohn, J. Edgar Hoover, J. Parnell Thomas, and the rest of the HUAC crew, were convinced that Garfield was helping commie vipers infiltrate Hollywood. Garfield, who was never a fellow traveler — and had done more than any other Hollywood actor to aid the war effort on the homefront — was invited to clear his red-stained reputation by publicly turning fink before the committee. He ratted out no one.

As a result, his Hollywood star was irreparably tarnished and he was exiled to the New York stage that spawned him. Angry and embittered, Garfield died of a heart attack in New York at the age of 39. Abe Polonsky, who would also lose his career, if not his life, to the blacklist, says that Garfield "had defended his streetboy's honor and they killed him for it."

Opposite: In *He Ran All the Way,* Nick (Garfield) both infatuates and terrorizes Peg (Shelley Winters) with dreams of escaping the slums.

Right, top: Garfield had aged enough to perfectly play Hemingway's Harry Morgan in *The Breaking Point* (WB, 1950).

Right, bottom: In *He Ran All the Way,* every day is a waking nightmare for Nick Robey. His mother (Gladys George) is about to freshen him up with a slap in the face.

THE POLARITY BETWEEN THE LEFT- AND RIGHT-WING responses to crime received its fiercest treatment in *Brute Force* (Universal, 1947), the most explosive example of the "prison movie" subgenre of noir. (Others: *Canon City, Caged, The Story of Molly X, Riot in Cell Block 11*).

The film at first appears to be a liberal vilification of the fascist state. Its message-mongering is broad enough that the picture can be read as a radical polemic against Hitler, Franco, or any totalitarian regime. (At the time, resilient Nazism was still a greater public fear than nascent Marxism.) But within a few short years, the director, Jules Dassin, would have his Hollywood career snuffed out by the Napoleonic tactics of the House Un-American Activities Committee. He'd never have missed the parallel between Sen. McCarthy and Capt. Munsey, *Brute Force*'s scarily institutionalized chief operating officer.

The prisoners of Westgate Penitentiary are the recipients of inhuman cruelty, Gestapo style, dispensed by Munsey (Hume Cronyn), a small, miserable man who finds fulfillment in a uniform, and the license it gives to abuse power.

Richard Brooks's script paints Munsey as the archetypal crypto-Nazi, just doing his job to maintain order: "I really want to help the warden. It's just that he's confused. He doesn't know that kindness is actually weakness. And weakness is an infection that makes a man a follower instead of a leader." Munsey even listens to Wagner while he wields the truncheon in his interrogation room: "There's no reward for bringing them back alive."

Vengeful Joe Collins (Burt Lancaster) is determined to lead his cellmates in a breakout, even though he has to know it will ignite a full-scale riot.

Hours tick off toward the bust-out.

The climax of *Brute Force* displayed the most harrowing violence ever seen in movie theaters. *Opposite:* After discovering that Freshman (Jeff Corey) is an informer, Collins (Lancaster) straps him to the front of a railcar and sends him out of the prison tunnel to be ripped apart by the guards' machine gun fire. Soldier (Howard Duff) and Kid Coy (Jack Overman) die almost instantly. Collins murders the guards and makes it to the tower, where he battles the sadistic Capt. Munsey. Despite the seemingly Christ-like benediction Munsey bestows on Collins, he's about to be thrown to his death amidst the doomed, rioting mob. As he watches the prison erupt in flames, Dr. Walker (Art Smith) sighs: "No one escapes. No one ever escapes."

Flashbacks reveal how each man in Cell R17 came to be trapped in his personal hell. In the type of pat, by-the-numbers writing that characterizes the worst of film noir, each man's transgression revolves around a woman.

Their bogus rationalizations — and the standard-issue plea for understanding and compassion — turn steadily darker. It becomes sickeningly clear that there is no escape, no hope, for anyone. The petty schemes that led to their arrests wither beside the full-throttle hatred that consumes all the men, on both sides of the bars.

The only lemmings opting out of the rush to destruction are the warden, a useless and feeble administrator, and the prison doctor, Walker (Art Smith), a pie-eyed pinko who has the ignominious chore of regularly underlining the film's themes. "That's it, Munsey, that's it," he says, after finally provoking the top bull into hitting him. "Not cleverness, not imagination, just force. Brute force. Congratulations. Force does make leaders. But you forget one thing. It also destroys them."

The jailbreak runs off-track immediately when Collins uncovers an informer in his crew. "What's the plan now?" he's asked. "The plan's a flop. You're on your own. It's a million to one." Regardless, the prisoners surge ahead with a violent, fatal determinism unrivaled until *The Wild Bunch*, but devoid of any suggestion of heroism.

Brute Force is the blackest of film noirs. By the time it ends, any trace of political posturing has been burned beyond recognition by its searing nihilism.

IF IT TAKES A "SOLDIER'S MENTALITY" to survive in a dangerously corrupt world, as Abe Polonsky maintains, then it's Samuel Fuller who produced the basic training manual for Dark City's dogfaces.

Fuller, more than any other writer or director, espoused a coherent philosophy for coping with the creeping venality that, in his view, stretched well beyond City limits. During the prime years of film noir, 1948-1952, while other directors were exposing the tender underbelly of our urban nightmare, Fuller made westerns and war films that revealed the same criminal element thriving on the frontier and the front lines. Crime was nothing new to Fuller; it was just another depraved aspect of human nature. Civilization was a pretense: society is constantly at war, and war, Fuller says, is "organized lunacy." The real issue is how to survive in the crossfire.

"Strip him of everything we can use, wrap him in a blanket, bury him, mark him," is the mantra of hard-bitten Sergeant Rock (Gene Evans) in Fuller's noirish war drama *Fixed Bayonets* (20th, 1951). Whether it's Omaha Beach or Omaha, Nebraska, if you don't keep moving, your fate may be sealed.

Tolly Devlin (Cliff Robertson, top, with Beatrice Kay), sentences to death the gangsters who killed his father, then drowns crime boss Connors (Roger Emhardt), in Sam Fuller's *Underworld USA*.

Sinister Heights is just one more battleground to Fuller. His ultimate noir gangster picture is *Underworld USA* (Columbia, 1961), which presents the Feds and mob as warring clans of equal resources, firepower, and ruthlessness. Fuller offers no moral judgment, just bitter irony: the hitman who murders a witness's child is also the lifeguard at a public swimming pool the mob runs for PR purposes. As Connors, the syndicate boss, says: "There'll always be people like us. As long as we keep the books and subscribe to charities we'll win the war. We always have."

Fuller's real concern is for Tolly Devlin (Cliff Robertson), his vengeful protagonist. As a teen, Tolly sees his father murdered by a group of small-time hoodlums. Orphaned, he falls into a life of petty crime and ends up in prison, where he connives to meet one of his father's killers, and squeezes from him the names of the others. Once free, Devlin embarks on a crusade to execute them all.

By this time, the hoods are pillars of the community — and syndicate directors. Tolly manages to infiltrate the mob and manipulate the Feds, using each to his own advantage. Spreading disinformation, he sows paranoia among the mobsters. He escorts his father's killers to death, while keeping his own hands clean. Mission accomplished.

But when Connors orders Tolly's girlfriend roughed up, the plan is junked. Tolly bursts into the big man's lair, throws him in the swimming pool, and stands on him until he's dead. Connors's button man shoots Tolly, who winds up dying in the same alley as his father. Love, fatefully, has loused up the mission.

Fuller spins this saga, as he does all his stories, in the bombastic cinematic equivalent of tabloid journalism — lurid, punchy, and sensational — ideas and emotions smacking the viewer in 200-point type. It's a style Fuller understood early, as a teenage crime reporter for the *New York Graphic*, Manhattan's pre-eminent "scandal sheet" during the Roaring Twenties. It was there Fuller learned to deliver hard facts with the added thrill of "creative exaggeration."

Fuller followed the lead of other successful newshawks (Ben Hecht, Charles MacArthur, Gene Fowler, Herman Mankiewicz, Allen Rivkin) to the picture studios of Hollywood, but he was drafted before he really established himself. Service as a "doggie" in the First Infantry Division was the baptism of fire that forged his world view.

In 1960 Fuller declined an offer from John Wayne to produce Fuller's dream project, a war film called *The Big Red One*. His reasoning reveals the "soldier's mentality" at the heart of noir: "[Wayne] is a symbol of a kind of man I never saw in war. He would have given it a heroic touch that I hate in war movies. In real combat situations, everyone is scared, everyone is a nervous animal. You can't determine the heroes from the cowards in advance.

"A lot of those John Wayne-type characters came through in combat and a lot of them fell apart. The ones you didn't expect anything from, you'd be surprised what they could do in that situation, when you're *cornered*. I saw things men did – they might have been called heroes later, but we didn't call them that. You were doing your job. Or you were saving your ass. If you got spotted — an officer has to be one of your witnesses — you got a medal... if you weren't spotted – nothing."

That credo of self-preservation, seasoned with a dash of fatalistic existentialism, got a full airing in *Pickup on South Street* (20th, 1953), Fuller's first full-fledged crime drama, and one of the best ever produced. It's another war story — this one a battle between America and under-cover communists — and again, Fuller's loyalties lie with the grunts who are trying to survive in the margins while the ideological loonies struggle for power.

Skip McCoy (Richard Widmark) lives literally on the periphery of society — in a shanty teetering over New York harbor, content to eke out a meager living picking pockets and pilfering purses on the subway. One day he unwittingly lifts stolen military microfilm off Candy, a luscious tart being used, unknowingly, as a courier by her commie boyfriend (Richard Kiley). Just like Tolly Devlin, Skip McCoy relishes playing both ends against the middle in frantic bidding for the prized strip of celluloid. When a federal agent grills Skip, accusing him of treason, he gets a hearty laugh and a "Who cares?" in response.

Skip winds up aiding the FBI, but it's out of love and loyalty to Candy, not patriotism. In the subculture of grifters and operators with which Fuller empathizes, allegiance to the other doggies in the trench is all that matters. When his compatriot, the elderly grifter Mo, is killed by a communist agent, Skip retrieves her plain pine coffin from a barge headed for Potter's Field, and pays for a proper burial with his own hard-stolen money. No unmarked graves for Fuller's valiant footsoldiers.

Under the watchful, but enthusiastic auspices of Darryl Zanuck and 20th Century-Fox, Fuller shot the 70-minute *Pickup on South Street* in ten days. Within those time and budget limitations, he packed more story-telling pizzazz than some directors could muster in a lifetime. In one scene Widmark knocks Jean Peters cold with a right cross, then revives her by pouring beer over her face. She comes to, and as he's fingering the bruise

on her lips, they embrace as kindred lovers. In the climactic subway fight, Widmark yanks Richard Kiley down a flight of stairs, banging his chin on every step. Love scenes or fight scenes, Fuller gave them all the lurid gusto of someone born to the crime beat.

And, like a good muckraking journalist, he stirred up controversy. FBI boss J. Edgar Hoover was mortified at the film's disdain for flag-waving ideology. At the same time, from the opposite corner, Fuller was criticized for joining the anti-Communist Hollywood bandwagon, which

Candy (Jean Peters) and Skip (Richard Widmark) are made for each other, a pair of hard-shelled grifters who know how to get along in the tight margin society affords them in *Pickup on South Street.*

was reeling out such titles as *I Married a Communist*, *The Red Menace*, and *I Was a Communist for the FBI*.

Sam Fuller was the Hollywood equivalent of Skip McCoy: scuffling in the marginal world of "B" program-fillers, picking his marks carefully, striking quickly, light on his feet, living to work another day. And, like Skip, Fuller faced the brutalities of the world with a cynical laugh and an eagerness to keep forging ahead, one foot in front of the other.

Fuller never shrugged off the nihilism of his vision: he charged right into it, robust and uproarious, fists flying. He proved to be the ultimate noir survivor, making crazy, independent potboilers into his eighties, all of them loudly proclaiming: The world is a madhouse, but *goddamn* it's a thrilling ride.

T he captain's stack of unsolved cases topples off the desk, into the dead Christmas tree. He'll deal with it next year. Four hours left on this shift; the coffee's burned blacker than tar. He tries not to think of the new folders being created this minute, tomorrow, always. The wife wants to dance in the New Year at the Glass Slipper. He wants to spend the night busting the mobbed-up owner and knocking that slimy smile off his face. Come midnight he'll be dreaming the usual: open house in the weapons room, and a free day in the streets to settle up.

The Precinct

The chore of riding herd on Dark City's crime rate fell to either harrassed, burned-out cops, or clean-cut, impossibly upright federal agents. Distinctions between the two went deeper than their shoeshines and expense accounts. The local boys were only trying to keep their heads above water until the pension kicked in. The Feds were on a political crusade.

Any picture that involved the actions of the Federal Bureau of Investigation had J. Edgar Hoover, figuratively, as its executive producer. He'd been installed as the Bureau's acting director in 1924, and in his early days he presided over an obscure, unarmed agency that did little more than chase car thieves who crossed state lines. Then, in 1932, national obsession with the Lindbergh baby kidnapping upped the profile of the FBI forever. Fear of kidnappers and bank robbers roaming the country led, in 1933, to a broadening of the FBI's activities and its arsenal. The tommy gun was soon as synonymous with the "G-man" as it was with Pretty Boy Floyd.

Hoover was a better propagandist than he was a crimebuster. He often stooped to rewriting facts to bolster the image of the FBI — and that of himself as the nation's most fearless lawman. Melvyn Purvis, the field agent whose tenacious lone pursuit of John Dillinger finally resulted in the post-matinée execution of Public Enemy Number One, was extricated from all official accounts of the story. In the sanctioned version, a loyal army of G-Men drew the noose ever tighter on Dillinger, all under the guidance of General Hoover. Purvis quit the bureau in disgust.

Hoover obsessively mythologized the FBI to counteract the outlaw folk legends retold in tabloid newspapers and on the silver screen. His right-hand man, publicist Louis Nichols, helped J. Edgar hone his image as the rock-hard, unbreakable eunuch of justice, able to resist every temptation but one: using the latest technical gadgetry — surveillance cameras, wiretaps — to lay bare the life of any suspected wrongdoer.

For many years, Director Hoover withheld his

imparimatur from crime movies. He wouldn't grant the Bureau stamp to *G-Men* (WB, 1935) solely because undercover agent Jimmy Cagney patronizes a nightclub. After Hoover saw Hollywood's impact on the WWII propaganda machine, however, he earnestly recruited filmmakers to aid his mythmaking.

Louis de Rochemont had produced the successful *March of Time* documentary series, and he came with the solid financial backing of 20th Century-Fox. Hoover figured that de Rochemont's facility with factual material would add an authentic patina to the bureau's product.

The resulting collaboration, *The House on 92nd Street* (20th, 1945), was the first film to take a semi-documentary approach to crime drama. Based on several authentic cases in which Nazi spies were undone by undercover FBI tactics, the film was shot on actual locations, often using the same type of clandestine camerawork that is celebrated in the film. The bureau proudly loaned director Henry Hathaway the same covert surveillance vehicles it employed in the field.

Throughout the film, the FBI demonstrates its innovative use of hidden cameras and microphones, two-way mirrors, and microphotography. Americans saw, for the first time, the immensity of the Fingerprint Collection that Hoover hoped would one day contain the thumbprints of every American. Reaction was, to say the least, mixed. Some citizens marveled at this new level of security. Others saw the foundations of a fascist state. One didn't have to squint too hard to see Hoover, a notorious anti-Semite, as a fledgling Goebbels.

De Rochemont had to be nimble in concocting the film. As it was readied for release in 1945, the Allied triumph in Europe seemed imminent. To stay current, he transformed the Nazi spy ring into a band of nebulous subversives, who could easily be interpreted as the nation's next enemy *du jour*, the Communists. The secret at the script's core, Project 97, wasn't explicitly identified, but when A-bombs were dropped on Nagasaki and Hiroshima weeks before the film opened, the soundtrack was altered to refer specifically to the patriotic atom-smashing scientists who had developed those bombs.

The ersatz-documentary approach to crime would influence other pictures such as *Call Northside 777, Boomerang, Walk East on Beacon*, and *Walk a Crooked Mile*, the latter pair finally getting around to calling a Red a Red.

More central to the development of film noir was a series of low-budget films produced by Eagle-Lion Studios (an outgrowth of the former Producers Releasing Corporation), which thrust government agents from Hoover's land of straight-arrow righteousness into a shady nightworld devised by director Anthony Mann and cinematographer John Alton.

The most schizophrenic of the federal-agent noirs is *T-Men* (1948), in which two Treasury agents (Dennis O'Keefe and Alfred Ryder) are sent undercover to bust a ring of counterfeiters. It opens with a Treasury offical reciting — with startling ineptness — statistics proving the effectiveness of the department's crime-busting tactics. Viewers expecting the typically stiff Federal dog-and-pony show were about to be surprised.

As the narration (courtesy of stentorian gasbag Reed Hadley) drones on about the courage and dedication that the T-men display for the people of these United States, the agents descend into an underworld of horrifying brutality unlike anything Hoover's G-men had faced on-screen. When O'Keefe, who's infiltrated the ring's inner circle, has to stand by silently and watch his partner murdered, the crime film hits a new level of cold-blooded discomfort. Mann and Alton were so adept at capturing the undercover agents' life of loneliness and dread that the jingoist narration comes off as disrespectful and insulting. It's about as believably sincere as the pep talk of a desk-bound colonel sending troops into combat.

The surprising success of *T-Men* apparently influenced the FBI. Its next officially-sanctioned film, *The Street With No Name* (directed by William Keighley, who'd also done *G-Men*), eschewed the documentary look for more stylized noir elements, but kept the bogus narration and *92nd Street*'s Lloyd Nolan as a federally-funded father figure.

Later that year Alton and Mann (uncredited) collaborated on another influential Eagle–Lion quickie, *He Walked by Night*. Richard Basehart is a psychotic killer who uses his brilliance with electronics to evade police detection. The battle of wits ends, after 79 minutes of shadowy foreboding, with Basehart killed like a rat in the city's sewers.

Playing a small role as a dogged police technician was Jack Webb, who would co-opt much of *He Walked by Night* to create *Dragnet*, the archetypal police procedural that combined the righteous attitude of the crusading Feds with the daily grind of a lowly flatfoot.

All these films shared a Republican view of crime, totally at odds with the Democratic, Garfield-style film that sympathetically saw crooks as wayward offspring of a corrupt environment. Whenever the Feds were heroes, criminals were rogue parasites, hunted down and exterminated to protect taxpayers from further infection.

Now step into authentic noir terrain, by considering this: *T-Men*, *He Walked by Night* and *Canon City* were all financed by a silent partnership between Joe Breen, the head censor of the Hays Office, and Johnny Roselli, who had started his show business career as a liaison between the Chicago mob and the Hollywood craft unions. Roselli had worked in the Hays Office, and reunited with Breen after a federal stretch for extortion. He'd been sent up the river by Willie Bioff and George Browne, former heads of the corrupted IATSE union, who, as noted back in Sinister Heights, enjoyed several lucrative years taking studio payoffs to ensure no strikes by the union membership.

Roselli left Hollywood to help the Chicago boys establish their foothold in Vegas. He later was a middleman in negotiations between the Mafia and the CIA to assassinate Fidel Castro. His show business career ended on a yacht off Miami, when he was butchered, stuffed into an oil drum, and set adrift by hoodlums who'd seen too many Charles McGraw movies.

Charles McGraw, who had previously made a striking, but brief, impression as a hitman in *The Killers* (1946), raised movie cruelty to a new level as Moxie, the counterfeit ring's torpedo, in *T-Men*. Whether threatening to break off Dennis O'Keefe's fingers, or nonchalantly frying Wallace Ford in a steambath, McGraw's ruthlessness plumbed frigid depths. Here he impassively menaces Dennis O'Keefe, who's being throttled by Jack Overman.

The Feds only trooped into Dark City on the heels of interstate racketeers, or other footloose miscreants deemed a threat to national security. Solving the load of crimes perpetrated in the burg itself was typically left to local lawmen, who didn't have Hoover's juice to help cut through the rotgut of corruption.

By the early 1950s, the city's station houses were lousy with disgruntled detectives, embittered that their decision to patrol the straight and narrow was earning them less than a hundred bucks a week, paltry benefits, and a calloused heart. The proud police academy cadet had become Sisyphus with a service revolver.

Jim Wilson (Robert Ryan), protagonist of *On Dangerous Ground* (RKO, 1951) was once a decent cop. Eleven years on the beat have hardened him into a marauding thug, doling out fierce punishment to Dark City's denizens – who crave his vengeance in a sick, sado-masochistic way. His uncontrollable violence threatens both the department's image and his career.

"So I get thrown off the force," he barks. "What kind of job is this anyway? Garbage, that's all we handle. Garbage!...How do you live with yourself?"

"I don't," his more level-headed partner responds. "I live with other people. This is a job just like any other. When I go home I don't take this stuff with me. I leave it outside."

Wilson doesn't have a home, or a family, or the promise of one. His contempt for the easily corrupted is so strong that he acts as solitary judge, jury, and — if he doesn't get straight — executioner. Sensing that Wilson's a bomb with a smoldering fuse, his boss sends him upstate to "cool off," and meanwhile bring some city savvy to a manhunt in the sticks. In the course of tracking down a young girl's murderer, Wilson meets his doppelganger: the victim's father, Walter Brent (Ward Bond), a vengeful ignoramus bent on vigilante justice.

The trail leads Wilson to the isolated farmhouse of Mary Walden (Ida Lupino), a blind spinster devoted to her mentally ill brother, Danny — who is the killer. Wilson sees in Mary a brighter reflection of his lonely soul, but one not encrusted with bitterness. In her trust and faith, he glimpses a shard of hope. He promises Mary that he'll protect her brother from Brent. But Danny falls to his death in the climactic chase, and Wilson and Brent are shaken to learn the mad-dog killer is just a whipped pup of a boy. Wilson guiltily tries to reconcile with Mary, but she sends him away, back to Dark City. Tearlessly she asks, "What difference does it make?"

On Dangerous Ground introduced Eastern philosophy to the cop drama. The duality of nature, both physical and spiritual, is the theme of A. I. Bezzerides' script. To find any connectedness to life, the unbalanced destroyer must shed his impenetrable shell and accept the vulnerability of compassion. Although Mary, the nurturer, spurns him, Wilson returns to duty with a more Zen-like perspective.

At least that was writer Bezzerides' original, ambiguous, version of things. RKO encouraged Ray to tack on a new ending in which Wilson wheels around and races back to Mary, who suddenly embraces him at the fade-out. Romance and revenue, not spiritualism, were the studio heads' answer to all moral conundrums.

A deeper crisis of faith — and a worse fate — confronts Detective Jim McLeod (Kirk Douglas) in *Detective Story* (Paramount, 1951). Like Jim Wilson, McLeod has been made a heartless bastard by police work (and no one, not even Robert Ryan, played a bastard as viciously as Kirk Douglas). He presides over his precinct like a courthouse judge, meting out punishment to everyone in his jurisdiction, crooks and suspects alike.

He reserves his most hateful third-degree for a suspected abortionist. The doctor's attorney turns the tables on McLeod, however, declaring that the cop is on a personal vendetta: McLeod's wife, it's revealed, had received an abortion from the doctor the previous year. Devastated, McLeod clings to his righteousness, refusing to forgive his wife. Instead, he commits suicide by walking into the firing line of a scared punk trying to escape arrest.

In *Where the Sidewalk Ends* (20th, 1950) cop Dana Andrews beats a suspect to death, then tries to pin the murder on a gangster he despises. During the early Fifties, dozens of film noirs would show the police as not only fallible and fatigued, but as bust-out sociopaths. By 1955, the cinematic battle between the cops and the crooks had gotten so brutal that Sen. Estes Kefauver launched yet another of his high-profile Congressional "investigations," declaring that such movies were turning children into violent delinquents.

Two decades later, the deranged cop would reemerge in Dark City, unrepentant, as "Dirty" Harry Callahan. By then there were twice as many rats in the cage, and the film-going public, pissed-off and powerless, embraced him. Where film noirs typically treated psychopathology as a sad human condition, by the 1980s Clint Eastwood's character was worth millions: hate franchised as heroism.

The Big Heat (Columbia, 1953) is the ultimate angry cop noir, its tale of vengeance rendered with almost tantalizing perfection. Uptown critics dismissed it at the time as just another crime potboiler, signifying Fritz Lang's demise as an A-list director. They missed the cold brilliance that electrified genre conventions, and the exhilarating union of brooding Germanic fatalism and Wild West ass-kicking.

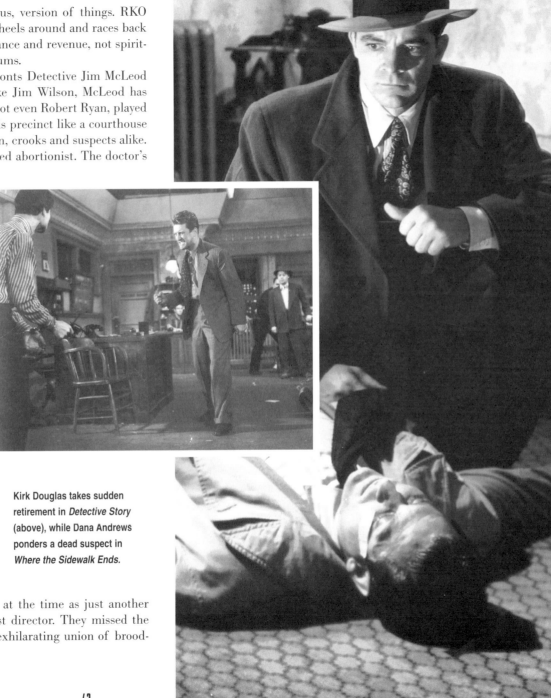

Kirk Douglas takes sudden retirement in *Detective Story* (above), while Dana Andrews ponders a dead suspect in *Where the Sidewalk Ends.*

The Big Heat : With a shot heard, one hopes, in all the barrooms and brothels of Dark City, Debbie Marsh (Gloria Grahame) settles a score for all the town's B-girls. Confronting the corrupt Bertha Duncan, who's living high on the hog off Mike Lagana's blood money, Debbie informs her that "You know, Bertha, we're sisters under the mink." She then lets Bannion's borrowed revolver finish the thought.

Seconds after the fade-in, corrupt cop Tom Duncan blows his brains out. His suicide note exposes the death-grip gangster Mike Lagana (Alex Scourby) has on the city's power elite. Duncan's wife finds the body and stashes the note, safekeeping it to blackmail Lagana and keep herself in a style she never enjoyed as a cop's wife. Sgt. Dave Bannion (Glenn Ford), a blue-collar bulldog, gets suspicious and turns up Duncan's mistress, Lucy Chapman, a B-girl who knows where the bodies are buried. Next thing Bannion knows, Lucy's one of those bodies.

Despite warnings from his bosses to back off, Bannion barges into Lagana's palatial mansion. There's art, servants, music: it sickens Bannion. "Cops have homes, too. Only sometimes there isn't enough money to pay the rent, because an honest cop gets hounded off the force by your thievin' cockroaches for tryin' to do an honest job." He personally vows to bring the big heat down on Lagana.

Insulted, Lagana returns to his roots: his thugs plant a bomb in Bannion's car, which kills the cop's wife, Katie. When his boss doesn't pursue Lagana, Bannion flips off his badge and loads up his .38; "That doesn't belong to the department," he seethes. "I bought it."

Locked and loaded, *The Big Heat* gallops into the concrete frontier: there

The Big Heat: Incorruptible cop Dave Bannion (Glenn Ford) calls out sadistic thug Vince Stone (Lee Marvin).

are showdowns in saloons, rustlers biding time with endless hands of poker, a robber baron devouring territory while tin stars look the other way. And most critically, there's the whore with the heart of gold.

Debbie Marsh (Gloria Grahame) is the moll of Lagana's troglodyte torpedo, Vince Stone (Lee Marvin). She's a sexy, smart-mouthed material woman, hopelessly lost amid the macho posturing and power plays. After Vince, in a jealous rage, scars her face with a pot of boiling coffee, Debbie throws in her lot with the honest cop. Bannion, true to his moral superiority, never gives in to his murderous temptations. But Debbie, already in the gutter, redeems herself by laying waste to their tormentors. First she blows the lid off Lagana's empire by blasting Mrs. Duncan — allowing Bannion to retrieve the incriminating suicide note. Feeling her

oats, Debbie settles up with Vince, administering her own hot java facial.

Debbie dies in the climactic shoot-out. As she longingly looks to Bannion for love and approval, he eulogizes his dead wife. In the epilogue, Bannion is back on the force, frontier marshal in Metropolis, waiting for the next Lagana to ride into town.

The film's power is mainly due to the talents of two men: screenwriter Sydney Boehm, a former crime reporter responsible for more crackerjack noir scripts than anyone else, and Lang, whose work is almost synonymous with noir. His early German films, *Metropolis* and *M*, etched the first blueprints of Dark City: omnipotent external forces dictating the fate of innocent people, and uncontrollable internal urges leading to self-destruction.

Lang himself fostered the legend that he had stared the demon in the face in 1933, when Hitler and Goebbels annointed him as the "the man who will give us the big Nazi pictures." He claimed to have immediately fled Germany, his riches later repatriated by the Reich. Later research revealed Lang to be a master of embellishment: he had, in truth, displayed little resistance to the Nazis during their rise to power. It was the promise of Hollywood opportunity — mixed with a nagging fear that the Nazis would betray him due to his mother's Jewish heritage — that led Lang to surrender his preeminence in the German film industry. Ensconced on Hollywood production lines, Lang became the movie industry's official Minister of Fear, almost gleefully dusting his studio confections with the doom he felt was at the heart of the universe.

With *The Big Heat*, Lang shook off several desultory years, inspired by the crisp geometry of Boehm's script — and perhaps by its ferocious outrage. Accounting for the film's popularity, Lang said, uncharacteristically, that "Deep down... in every human being is the desire that good shall conquer evil. Could it be that people see in [Bannion] a symbol of hope in these days of taxes, insecurity, and the H-bomb?"

Only Fritz Lang could extract equal dread from government taxation and nuclear annihilation.

ON THE OTHER SIDE OF THE STATION HOUSE from upright, uptight cops like Bannion and Wilson was another kind of lawman. Brogans propped on the desk, worrying a toothpick, figuring his angles. This guy could easily be one of the perps cooling his heels in the holding cell. He's from the same neighborhood scrap heap. He just figured the badge was a better percentage play. Somewhere along the line he saw the game was rigged, leaving him a flatfooted schmuck holding all the low cards.

So he decided to fix his own game, determined to beat the house. By virtue of his vice, he was as corrupt as the crooks he was paid to collar.

"So I'm no good," snaps Webb Garwood, one of the dirtiest boys in blue. "But I'm no worse than anybody else. You work in a store you knock down the cash register; a big boss, the income tax; ward heeler, you sell votes; a lawyer, you take bribes. I was a cop – I used a gun."

Webb (Van Heflin) is rationalizing the selfish Machiavellian scheme he perpetrates in *The Prowler* (UA, 1950). It begins when he answers a distress call from an affluent married woman reporting a peeping tom. Webb's more interested in the richness of her home and body.

Pretending it's in the line of duty, Webb insidiously ingratiates himself into the life of Susie Gilvray (Evelyn Keyes). They have an affair, while her popular disc jockey husband does his nightly broadcasts. (The voice is that of uncredited script doctor Dalton Trumbo.)

This page and opposite: **Van Heflin and Evelyn Keyes in** *The Prowler.*

Susie's no femme fatale. She's level-headed but lonely, unable to resist the cocky advances of the handsome, attentive cop. When Webb learns she's depressed because her husband is sterile, he hatches a nefarious plan. He reappears as the prowler, coaxing Susie's husband out of the house. He murders him, arranging it to look like a tragic accident.

An inquest upholds Webb's version of events, but Susie's convinced he's a murderer. Her derision doesn't deter him: Webb has big plans for their future. He quits the force and methodically sets out to win Susie's trust, convincing her he's a decent guy who just never got a break in this world. He's eager to marry her and give her the baby she desperately wants. In exchange, he'll be able to tap her late husband's hefty life insur-

ance windfall, so he can buy a little newlyweds' motel out in tax-free Nevada, and escape the rat race.

Susie caves in and marries Webb, who squires her away to his dusty little dream resort. She stuns Webb, however, by announcing that she's four months pregnant. Webb realizes that the timing of the baby's birth will cast suspicion on him, for it's proof of their affair, and it gives him a motive for killing Gilvray.

In a perverted mockery of the domestic bliss they craved, Webb and Susie set up bizarre domicile in a desert ghost town, so the baby can be born in secrecy. Delivery complications force Webb to bring in a doctor. Susie finally turns on Webb when she realizes he'll kill the doctor to preserve their secret. She slips the doctor the car keys, and her newborn. Webb's in hot pursuit, but the cops are already on their way. His former brethren corner Webb and waste him like a wild dog.

Webb Garwood was significantly different from other loony lawmen: his wild scheme was based more on an impatient, selfish desire for middle-class ease than a need to set the world straight. A swaggering sports hero in high school, Webb figured himself for a world-beater. He'd done everything by the book, but the book turned out to be a cheap, crappy paperback. If his badge couldn't give him a leg up on a better life, what the hell good was it?

In his first features, *The Boy with Green Hair* (RKO, 1948) and *The Lawless* (Paramount, 1949), director Joseph Losey avidly attacked social ills, particularly bigotry and prejudice. He'd been honing a vigorous social conscience since the 1930s, when he'd worked in the decidedly Red-hued Federal Theater project in New York. In Hollywood he cut his teeth directing shorts for MGM's FBI-sponsored *Crime Does Not Pay* series (one of which, *The Gun in His Hand*, was the genesis of *The Prowler*).

He maintained his theatrical chops as well, directing the 1947 world

premiere of Bertolt Brecht's *Galileo*. The combustible mixture was typical of many artists who'd laid out the streets of Dark City: gritty crime mixed with a "subversive" intellectualism.

(Parallels between Losey and noir compatriot Nick Ray are, in fact, eerie: both were born in La Crosse, Wisconsin, were the same age, went to the same high school, moved to New York and worked on the Fed Theater's Living Newspaper project, made a living writing radio scripts, and came to Hollywood at the same time from New York.)

In 1950-51, Losey worked exclusively in noir, cranking out a remake of *M* that transposed the cloistered criminal underworld of Berlin to Los Angeles, and *The Big Night*, a film that treats a young boy's passage to adulthood as a noirish nightmare. But it was *The Prowler* in which Losey's political antagonists saw an insidious anti-American suggestion: pursuit of the perfect middle-class nuclear family could lead to derangement. (The film's working title, *The Cost of Living*, made the allusion obvious. Today, the "subversive" messages seem barely discernible. The modern Garwood equivalent is just a garden-variety nutcase, as played by Ray Liotta in *Unlawful Entry*, an Eighties cop-from-hell redo of *The Prowler*.) To Hollywood's anti-communist crowd of 1951, the film's subtext was anything but subtle: its makers were trying to undermine American values.

Screenwriter Hugo Butler (who also penned *He Ran All the Way*) and Losey were both named as communist sympathizers — "comsymps" in the hardboiled argot of the day — and blacklisted. Losey's incrimination oddly paralleled that of *The Prowler*: his career was derailed by an ass-covering informer who, Losey learned later, once had an affair with his wife. His last memory of Hollywood was hiding in his darkened house to avoid being served a HUAC subpoena.

Can anyone argue that Hollywood, between 1947-1952, was not the daily double of Dark City?

WEBB GARWOOD'S PLAN TO USE HIS BADGE as a shield for murder was directly echoed in a 1954 film, named, appropriately enough, *Shield for Murder*, also released by UA. Based on a novel by veteran crime writer William P. McGivern, the story reverberates with many of the same motivations found in Losey's film.

Barney Nolan (Edmond O'Brien, who also co-directed) desperately wants to swap his roller and revolver for a two-car garage and backyard barbecue. Realizing it will take years of saving — and that he might stop a stray bullet in the meantime — Barney opts for an easier route: he kills a bagman carrying a $25,000 payoff and pockets the loot. All in the line of duty, he testifies, neglecting to mention the dough. What busts his play is the old mute fellow who witnessed the alleyway murder and sucks up the guts to report it. Nolan assigns himself the investigation, and ends up murdering the guy to cover his tracks.

Barney Nolan (Edmond O'Brien) gets threatening in *Shield for Murder*.

All the sweaty, frantic Barney wants is a tidy suburban oasis for him and his fiancée, Patty (Marla English). Is that too much to ask? While Nolan is conning his peers, gangster Packy Reed is tracking his missing 25 G's. Soon, Barney is on the lam from both the crooks and his colleagues. After shooting his way out of a public swimming pool, Barney hides out in the empty tract home he covets, and ends up riddled with police slugs, dying face-down on the yet-to-be-planted front lawn.

While *The Prowler* is subtle and complex, unwinding with a seductive rhythm, *Shield for Murder* is a drum solo by a club-footed spastic. Thematically, however, they are virtually identical. Both are about policeman abusing power, and each contrasts the puniness of middle-class aspirations with the oversized compulsion to achieve them.

There were lots of other dirty cop noirs, from high-profile studio product like *Rogue Cop* (MGM, 1954), in which Robert Taylor plays a bull who'd rather take mob payoffs than get dirty solving crimes, to mellers like *The Man Who Cheated Himself* (20th, 1951) and *Pushover* (Columbia, 1954), about cops abandoning their ethics for erotic prizes (Jane Wyatt and Kim Novak, respectively).

One of the best was *Private Hell 36* (Filmakers, 1954), in which the bond between two cops (Howard Duff and Steve Cochran) comes unglued after Cochran steals a dead gangster's strongbox of counterfeit money and swears Duff to secrecy. Cochran wants to launder the swag in Mexico and then hightail it to the good life with his torch-singer girlfriend, played by Ida Lupino (who also produced and co-wrote the script).

When the dead gangster's partner tries to blackmail them, the pair decides to pull the money from the trailer where it's hidden (the trailer-park slot of the title). It turns out the blackmailer was actually their suspicious boss, and Cochran is gunned down after wounding his partner, who he thinks has ratted him out.

THE MOST UNSCRUPULOUS COP in Dark City, though, wasn't unearthed until 1957. By then most noir had been whitewashed and transplanted to television shows like *The Line Up* and *Dragnet*. But lying low on the outskirts, wallowing in his own foul fiefdom, was Hank Quinlan, whose twelve-year reign as the local "police celebrity" of Los Robles, a pestilent little bordertown, is tainted by a *Touch of Evil* (Universal-International).

The film, starring and adapted by Orson Welles (from Whit Masterson's novel *Badge of Evil*) follows the final day of Quinlan's life, when the car-bomb murder of powerful contractor Rudy Linnekar explodes long-buried conspiracies. Passing through town when the fireworks start is Miguel Vargas (Charlton Heston), an incorruptible narcotics investigator from Mexico City, on honeymoon with his American wife, Susie (Janet Leigh). Vargas, much to Quinlan's chagrin, takes an interest in the Linnekar bomb case, since the victim had crossed the border from Mexico. Meanwhile, Uncle Joe Grandi (Akim Tamiroff), Los Robles' drug-running crimelord, frantically plots to ruin Vargas, who plans to send Grandi's brother to prison in Mexico.

Vargas is appalled by Quinlan — a 300-pound pustule of hubris, arrogance, and racism, ready to rupture. Part of the big man's duty has been to absorb the sins of those around him, namely the district attorney and the police chief. Quinlan does their dirty work, leaving them clean and dignified, while he

Howard Duff (left) and Steve Cochran grapple in *Private Hell 36.*

These are night faces...

Living on the edge of evil and violence!

FILMAKERS Present

PRIVATE HELL 36

Starring

Ida **Lupino**
Steve **Cochran**
Howard **Duff**
Dean **Jagger**
Dorothy **Malone**

"Touch of Evil"

bloats with venality. In exchange, they surround him like a covey of quail, marveling at his intuitive powers, chuckling in bemusement at his every affront to proper police procedure.

Vargas realizes that Quinlan plans to frame a Mexican suspect for the car-bombing. Outraged, he digs into Quinlan's record and exhumes a history of frame-ups. The Vargas threat makes allies of Quinlan and Joe Grandi, who conspire to discredit Vargas and his wife by planting evidence that they're junkies. Quinlan's a more creative schemer: he murders Uncle Joe and makes it appear as if Susie Vargas is the drug-addled culprit.

All the stray plot lines, tangled double-crosses, and lurid tortures of Susie Vargas by the Grandi clan are embellishments to the core story: how Vargas drives a fatal wedge into the relationship of Hank Quinlan and his partner, Pete Menzies (Joseph Calleia). The cops are like ruined old queens who've loved each other longer than either can remember. Pete's always doted on Hank, who's never forgiven himself for failing to catch his wife's killer. Hank once stopped a bullet for Pete, and claims that it's his game leg that helps him divine solutions to crimes. Out of loyalty to Hank, Pete was accomplice to years of bogus police work, helping plant evidence, and buying into Quinlan's rationalization that "I never framed anybody — unless they were guilty."

Vargas manages to hook his idealism into Menzies' last vestige of self-respect. When Menzies discovers Quinlan's cane in the hotel room where Susie supposedly killed Joe Grandi, he realizes how far Quinlan has sunk. He grimly agrees to wear a wire and coax Quinlan into exposing his guilt. Quinlan tips to the set-up, however, and outraged by Menzies' betrayal, he shoots him. As Quinlan is about to kill Vargas — his next frame-up already formulated — Menzies shoots his best friend with a last dying spasm.

In the rogue's gallery of rotten cops, Hank Quinlan is the most pathetic. He didn't betray the badge for money or social station, like Webb Garwood or Barney Nolan. He justifies his corruption by *not* accepting the spoils, preferring to look down his nose at the DA and police chief, as he provides them with fast, efficient convictions that keep the voters happy. As he and Menzies pass through the shadows of Los Robles' pumping oil derricks, he reminds his friend how rich he could have been, amid all that

Janet Leigh and Charlton Heston navigate the treacherous terrain of Los Robles.

black gold, if he'd really been corrupt. "Instead, all I've got to show for my thirty years is that lousy turkey farm."

Touch of Evil is film noir as three-ring circus. There are highwire acts (the dazzling three-minute traveling camera shot that opens the film), sleight-of-hand tricks (the complex single-take interrogation of Manolo Sanchez), outrageous clowns (Akim Tamiroff and Dennis Weaver), scary animal acts (the Grandi boys' torture of Susie) and clever disguises (Joseph Cotten, Mercedes McCambridge, Zsa Zsa Gabor and Marlene Dietrich all have costume dress cameos). Welles capably plays both ringleader and elephant.

Welles pulled out all the stops to prove he was still a viable artist and commercial filmmaker. After years of self-destructive shenanigans and a series of creative stutter-steps, it was this lowly "B" thriller that cleared the genius a path back to the movie business. Here was a man whose first film, *Citizen Kane*, forever changed the grammar of motion picture storytelling and set the cinematic syntax for film noir: the shadowy quest for the truth in morally ambiguous terrain, the cynical take on the corrupting influence of power, the daring, off-kilter visual style. With *Touch of Evil*, the most influential director of modern times had ended up working for Albert Zugsmith, who would move on to such masterworks as *Sex Kittens Go to College* and *The Incredible Sex Revolution*.

After spending most of the Fifties in European exile, Welles had returned to America paranoid, alcoholic, and with the IRS on his heels. He worked as an actor solely for survival pay. Zugsmith offered him the Quinlan role, and Welles, jockeying for a comeback within the major studios, said he'd rewrite and direct for nothing more than his actor's salary. He turned what was meant to be a starring vehicle for Charlton Heston (fresh off *The Ten Commandments*) into a grotesque auto-excoriation.

Quinlan's debasement mirrors Welles's own fall from grace. Like Quinlan, Welles made a career of half-baked convictions, in which wild intuition and flagrant grandstanding were passed off as determined, well-crafted work. Like Quinlan, he surrounded himself with toadies who worshipped his brilliance, no matter how jerry-rigged. Like Quinlan, he made up outrageous lies about anyone who dared criticize his working methods or personal habits.

Watching *Touch of Evil* is like drinking vintage wine not long before it turns to vinegar. The headiness, the pungency and the uniqueness are there, but so is a queasy aftertaste. The filmmaking is intoxicating, at times magnificent, but as the coda of Orson Welles's Hollywood career, it leaves a painful hangover. Welles could have been the most original talent of the century, but his uncontrollable ego and appetites left his ability squandered in exhilarating but disappointing productions. He was a hell of a man, but then, what does it matter what you say about people?

"C'mon, read my future for me."
"You haven't got any."
"Whatd'ya mean?"
"Your future is all used up."
— Former flame Tanya (Marlene Dietrich) tells Quinlan (Orson Welles) the bad news in *Touch of Evil*.

WHENEVER A COP OR CROOK NEEDED SOLACE OR A PAID DATE, he'd troll The Retreat, a bluesy nightspot in the red-light district where a guy could savor thirty-five-cent beer and visions of more exotic diversions. In the back, in the red leather booth, forever waiting for a kept promise, sat the fallen queen of this demimonde.

There's something flinty in her eyes, a regal jut to her chin. She couldn't possibly be available. But that's just part of her come-on. The guy who works past that will be treated to the brittle laugh and the sharp wit. Sadly, most run scared once she lets them feel the genuine heat of her longing.

That fallen queen was Gloria Grahame, in the movies and in real life. Born Gloria Hallward in Los Angeles in 1923, she was descended from both British and Scottish royalty. In 1944 Louis B. Mayer bestowed the new name upon her, perhaps hoping to recast her in the same regal realm as Greta Garbo. Such haughtiness was either beneath or above her. Gloria preferred to be an accessible empress.

In *Blonde Fever* (MGM, 1944) she was introduced with the prophetic line, "You're destined to make wise men foolish." Her early specialty was sultriness, tempered by a silly streak. She learned her Shakespeare chapter and verse, but if they wanted her to swing her hips and bat her vampish eyes, why not?

Her initial foray into Dark City came in *It's a Wonderful Life* (RKO, 1946), the first and only time sunny director Frank Capra set foot inside the city limits (if only for a frightened 15 minutes). She played Violet Bick, a sweetly sexy girl, who, in Jimmy Stewart's angel dust–inspired nightmare, becomes the dark whore of Pottersville. She left a vivid impression, for better and worse.

She secured her position — as actress and B-girl — with an Academy Award nomination for *Crossfire* (RKO, 1947), as a lonely call girl ensnared

Gloria Grahame displays her specialty in *Human Desire* (Columbia, 1954).
Opposite: As a nightclub singer hiding out in a border town, she tempts another renegade cop, Sterling Hayden, in *Naked Alibi* (Universal, 1954).

in a murder investigation. Director Edward Dmytryk described her as "a serious kind of kooky." You'd be kooky too if you had training in classical theater, a wicked sense of humor, a ravenous intellect, and a longing to portray Lady Macbeth — but always ended up in a crib with greasy wallpaper.

Gloria's ticket out of Dark City was a deal to play the coveted role of Billie Dawn in Columbia's version of the hit Broadway comedy *Born Yesterday*. It fell through when Howard Hughes, tinkering around as the head of RKO, refused to release her from her contract. Judy Holliday won an Oscar for the role; Gloria settled for the part of a slinky gambling house girl in the debacle *Macao* (RKO, 1950).

Although she had success with supporting parts in major films such as *The Bad and the Beautiful*, *The Greatest Show on Earth*, and *Oklahoma!*, the breakthrough leading role eluded her. Dark City became her permanent address: *A Woman's Secret*, *In a Lonely Place*, *Sudden Fear*, *The Big Heat*, *Human Desire*, *Naked Alibi*, *Odds Against Tomorrow* — a gallery of screwloose but seductive women, all aching to break out of the conscripted margins of a man's world, but trapped by their own compulsions and insecurities.

In her personal life Grahame pursued the kind of rugged, self-determined men that she clung to in the movies. But every relationship exploded when the men turned out to be equally insecure. She was married and divorced four times, with a list of lovers longer than her film credits.

George Englund, a producer and an early suitor of Gloria's, explained her promiscuity as untamed: "Have you ever seen a litter of kittens feeding at their bowls? There's always one who lifts her head and looks around at the other bowls in curiosity, nudging her head into them to see different things they might have to offer. That was Gloria."

Real life began to take on the noirish overtones of her films, and vice-versa. Her first starring role, opposite Humphrey Bogart in *In a Lonely Place*, should have made her a front-line star. But in Hollywood, the performance was secondary to the strangeness surrounding its creation. Her marriage to the film's director, Nicholas Ray, was disintegrating, and to preclude production problems, Grahame had to sign a contract stipulating that she would accede to all of Ray's on-set demands. The finished film, a bitter meditation on doomed relationships, was a thinly-veiled portrait of their hopeless union.

Their relationship came crashing down in 1951 when Gloria's feline curiosity resulted in a sexual liaison with Anthony Ray, her husband's 13-year-old son by a previous marriage. Fallout from the incident gave her a reputation for being professionally engaged and personally unhinged. (In his early twenties, Tony became Gloria's fourth and last husband, although the knot came quickly undone.)

Even winning an Oscar (Best Supporting Actress of 1952, for *The Bad and the Beautiful*) had its pitfalls. In the ceremony's first-ever national broadcast, Gloria stumbled badly on her way to the stage. To the rumor-mongering public, her image was confirmed as a lovable *drunken* whore.

As producers during the Fifties continued to trade on her sex appeal, she became increasingly insecure about her looks. She had numerous plastic surgeries on her upper lip, obsessively trying to enhance the lush pout that she thought was essential to her allure. She lifted weights in the hope of enlarging her breasts, which, unlike her mouth, she refused to have surgically altered.

Despite her best efforts, time took its toll. The boys prowling The Retreat started passing her by for younger game. She staved off the inevitable on the stage, but by the 1970s she was discounting the remnants of her sexiness in tawdry horror films.

During her last years she battled cancer in her own holistic, narcissistic way, refusing any treatment that altered her physical appearance. She died in 1981, at the age of 56, from septic shock suffered when a doctor punctured her bowel trying to drain fluid from her cancerous stomach.

It was a sad life, but not a tragic one. In the Dark City district she inhabited, she left a unique legacy, including the most heartbreaking lines in film noir (from *In a Lonely Place*):

> I was born when you kissed me
> I died when you left me
> I lived a few weeks while you loved me.

Gloria Grahame and Glenn Ford
in *Human Desire*.

Hot winds shake the sycamores. Leaves dance on the dry lawn. Dad sits at the wheel of the Hudson, staring at their dream house. Room 619 of the Embassy, that's his dream house now. He can feel her heat on his fingertips. His lips still ache. How can he go back? Mortgage, insurance, scrimping for some new thing, always more *things*. The ball 'n' chain is waiting inside with her list. He checks his eyes in the rearview: she'll never know. Mom sees him through the kitchen curtains, coming up the walk. She thumbs the edge of the blade: it's good and sharp.

In Dark City, crime isn't solely the province of professionals. Between the picket fences and manicured box hedges of the city's residential enclaves, death is sown daily. Little white lies sprout into guilty deceit, then grow into dreadful secrets, and finally bloom into fateful gunblasts or knife slashes. But in this part of town, it's passion, not profit, that's at stake.

When dark deeds were done by amateurs, as was usually the case on Hate Street, the tales were known in the trade as "murder dramas," distinct from the "crime dramas" that belonged to the crooks and cops. Murder dramas weren't as male-dominated. In fact, they were a noirish subgenre of what exhibitors called "women's pictures." The distinction was as much one of geography as of gender. Crime dramas took place in the streets and offices where men fought to conquer the city. Murder dramas unfolded in bedrooms and gardens and kitchens, where conquests happened one at a time, and women wielded their own weapons.

During the hardscrabble Thirties, Holly-wood gamely sold American women an ideal of domestic complacency and economic security. Hang tough, girls: the perfect man, the right neighborhood, and two darling kids were the answer to any soul-searching question that might toss and turn you in your sleep. Men had cops and crooks and cowboys to distract or inspire them. For women, films of the 1930s were Sears catalogues of middle-class gratification.

Noir tore the catalogue apart. It showed that domestic bliss could be a suffocating trap. Somewhere amid the folded laundry, polished silverware and accordion file of cancelled checks, life's passion had been snuffed out. Noir was about what happened when people reignited the fuse. When the devoted husband took a new woman in his arms. When the bored wife admitted that the vapid dreams she had cherished would never satisfy her; when her hope chest became Pandora's Box.

Over at the Precinct, and in Sinister Heights, the root causes of lawlessness were debated, and issues of guilt, innocence and

accountable for their actions – and everyone was guilty.

If you want to hold one man responsible for screwing up Hollywood's master plan for matrimonial harmony, blame James M. Cain. In his tales the sacred conjugal bed is soaked with the sweat of illicit sex. Before long, the gleaming white kitchen tiles will be spattered with blood. For Cain, death and sex were inseparable.

Cain helped lay some of the major foundation work for Dark City in 1934, when Alfred Knopf published his first novel, *The Postman Always Rings Twice*. A fierce tale of adultery and murder, it scored an immediate critical and popular success. Its bluntness and desperation tapped deep into Depression-era consciousness. The prose was so spare and vivid it demanded critical appraisal. Its popularity was primarily based on two factors: sex more raw than anything previously offered in a mainstream novel; and a terse style that compressed a complex story into a

and easily hide in a purse or bureau drawer.

RKO and Columbia both saw sparks jump from Cain's manuscript when it was in galley form. But the newly rejuvenated Production Code Administration — Hollywood's censorship entity — quickly provided a cold shower. Chief censor Joseph Breen vowed that *Postman* — or any Cain book — would never reach the screen. Undaunted, MGM bought the rights to the novel. Nothing came of it. No screen writer was able to tame Cain, so tightly was the depravity woven into his plots.

Cain followed up his initial success with a serialized story in *Liberty* magazine called *Double Indemnity*. Five studios panted after the story, driving the price up to $25,000 – even though the PCA office warned that such amorality would never see the light of a carbon-arc projector. Meanwhile, Cain kept hammering away. In 1937 he released *Serenade*, an even more unfilmable concoction of rough sex, homosexuality, murder, and opera.

It wasn't until 1943 that European import Billy Wilder, working for Paramount, found a way to raise Cain onto America's movie screens. After his usual writing partner, Charles Brackett, begged off handling such tawdry material, Wilder adapted Cain's story with popular mystery novelist Raymond Chandler. The duo dealt the PCA a miraculous hand of three-card monte, earning approval for the script by cutting some of Cain's more debased notions, substituting wicked innuendo in place of Cain's smash-mouth sex, and stressing that the moral of the story was that even the "perfect crime" will not go unpunished.

Double Indemnity marked the first time a Hollywood film explicitly explored the means, motives, and opportunity of committing murder. Like every story from Hate Street, it's about people throwing away their established lives on the one big risk they think will transform their mundane existence.

Insurance salesman Walter Neff (Fred MacMurray) takes his big risk with Phyllis Dietrichson (Barbara Stanwyck), a client's dangerously sexy wife. She involve

Double Indemnity: **Walter and Phyllis flee after staging her husband's "accident."**

him in a plot to murder her husband and trick the insurance company into paying out double on the "accidental death" clause in his life insurance policy. Neff dives right into Phyllis's black pool, intoxicated by her glossy lips, tight white sweaters, and little flesh-pinching anklet.

But Neff isn't just being led around by his libido. Under the cavalier manner and playboy patter lurks a terrorist, eager to shed society's rigid structures. Neff wants to refute the constipated world-view of his mentor, claims investigator Barton Keyes (Edward G. Robinson), a man who believes that every human emotion and action is reducible to statistical demographics and empirical probabilities. So Neff coldly commits murder — just to throw a wrench into the big gambling wheel over which Keyes proudly stands watch.

Walter Neff is a sharp, amoral fellow. But he's a potzer compared to Phyllis. She's working on a much larger canvas. Turns out she killed the previous Mrs. Dietrichson and slipped smoothly into the big stucco mansion on the hill. She's already seduced a back-up to Walter: her step-daughter's boyfriend, Nino Zachetti. And she's got plans to kill Walter and pin the whole thing on him, should the authorities decide her husband's death was foul play.

Realizing he's in over his head, Walter strikes first. He plans to kill Phyllis in her house and frame Zachetti for both murders. Phyllis gets the drop on him, and wounds him. But she can't bring herself to kill Walter. Instead, she clutches him to her, professing genuine love. Walter looks into the eyes that once beguiled him. "Goodbye, baby," he chirps, before letting her have it, point-blank.

Neff confesses all the sordid details into an insurance office dictaphone, a bitter last laugh at Keyes, who was prepared to pin everything on the innocent Zachetti. Keyes shows up, and is stunned almost speechless by his disciple's betrayal. Neff tries to escape, but collapses.

The film's critical and commercial success was due to Wilder's wizardry in coordinating brilliant collaborators. Chandler goosed Cain's clipped dialogue into whip-crack sass traded by the provocative stars: There's a speed limit in this state, Mr. Neff — forty-five miles an hour / How fast was I going, officer? / I'd say about ninety / Suppose you get down off your motorcycle and give me a ticket / Suppose I let you off with a warning this time / Suppose it doesn't take / Suppose I have to whack you over the knuckles / Suppose I bust out crying and put my head on your shoulder / Suppose you try putting it on my husband's shoulder / That tears it.

MacMurray and Stanwyck handled the banter, and the dangerous glances, with indelible panache. Through them, Wilder achieved something unprecedented: He made murder wickedly entertaining. The PCA may have accepted that *Double Indemnity* was about the punishment of immoral people, but Wilder knew that its appeal was in the vicarious excitement of participating in a murder, then stepping out of the killer's shoes and watching the noose slowly tighten around his neck. This double-barreled structure would become essential to film noir.

Double Indemnity influenced not just the development of noir, but movies in general. It broke new ground

"Goodbye, baby." Walter chooses his own neck over Phyllis's ankles.

in the treatment of adult themes. The first-person narration, relating the entire story in flashback, became a standard film device (although it was never equalled). John Seitz's moody cinematography turned sunny Southern California into a landscape of shadowy dread, a transformation that would influence writers and directors for decades to come.

"That gloomy, horrible house the Dietrichsons lived in, the slit of sunlight slicing through those heavy drapes — you could smell that death was in the air, you understood why she wanted to get out of there, away, no matter how," Barbara Stanwyck later reflected. "And for an actress, let me tell you the way those sets were lit, the house, Walter's apartment, those dark shadows, those slices of harsh light at strange angles — all that helped my performance. The way Billy staged it and John Seitz lit it, it was all one sensational mood."

Stanwyck, Wilder and company had turned Cain's slender novel into the primer for dozens of future film noirs. *Double Indemnity*'s hit status also rejuvenated sales of Cain's earlier books, and solidified his erroneous reputation as a leading practitioner of the "hard-boiled" school of novelists. His incredible success as an author was a twist worthy of one of his credulity-stretching plots.

JAMES M. CAIN WAS REARED IN THE AFFLUENT UPPER-MIDDLE CLASS ENVIRONS of Maryland. His parents were Irish Catholics, and despite his lapsing at age 13, vestiges of sin, guilt and retribution remained. It formed the backbone of his books. Opera, not literature, was Cain's primary love. His mother, a coloratura whom he worshipped, dissuaded him from a singing career. She had, in the tenor of the times, quit her own career to marry a successful businessman. Cain had little regard for his father, perhaps explaining why he'd end up writing stories about ambitious, vengeful women who murder their way out of unfulfilling marriages.

During the Teens and Twenties, Cain flailed at both work and marriage. His wife, Mary Clough, was too highbrow for his taste, and he cheated on her regularly. He claimed God's voice directed him to be a writer, although by his own admission he had little aptitude for it. He caught on as a newspaperman, which is how he'd describe himself for the rest of his life. In 1924, his writing career kicked in, with H. L. Mencken's acceptance of an article for *The American Mercury*, the witty, caustic journal of American letters.

Cain divorced his wife, moved to New York, and hobnobbed with luminaries like Mencken and Walter Lippmann, kings of elite journalism. He had a passionate affair with a Finn, Elina Tyszecka, whom he would call "the great love of my life." Once they married, in 1927, the flame died out: "It was gone, that old black magic we had." Recapturing the heat of passion would be a core motivation for Cain's characters, and by extension, for many of Dark City's dwellers.

After jockeying around Manhattan's magazine scene for a few more years, Cain moved to Hollywood with Elina. In L. A. he made boatloads of money as a script doctor, without ever being able to float a coherent, saleable script of his own. In fact, he hated movies. But the bare-boned discipline of screenwriting, and the sultriness of Southern California, had a profound effect on his writing.

Bar-B-Q, the manuscript that would become *The Postman*, was lashed out in a blast of May-September desperation, before Cain moved back East. It was as if he was unconsciously spewing out his demons in a to-hell-with-it kiss-off of his literary ambitions.

Sparking his imagination were impure thoughts he had about a "bosomy-looking thing" who pumped his gas at a local filling station: "Commonplace, but sexy, the kind you have ideas about." Cain gave those ideas free rein, and used his reporter's savvy to shoehorn in details from the case of Ruth Snyder, who in 1927 had murdered her husband and then tried to poison her lover/accomplice.

Almost unwittingly, Cain had become the surveyor and architect of Hate Street. The terrain is morally unstable and there is no outlet. Residents wind up murderously delusional or cynically corrupt. When they grab their darkest wish, choosing ecstasy over civility, their lives literally climax. But then the world — like Cain's plots — breaks in half. Guilt, suspicion, and fate slam the lovers head-on into the big black cul-de-sac. You can only hope the sex was worth it.

After *Double Indemnity*, Hollywood finally figured out how to translate Cain's brand of forbidden lust to the screen. The thorny branches were pruned from his gnarled plots and the gamier parts of his characters' sexuality were cloaked in vague allusions. Warner Brothers' glossy melodrama *Mildred Pierce* (1945) and MGM's version of *The Postman Always Rings Twice* (1946), were tamed Cain —

and hugely profitable. He became so identified with sexually charged murder dramas that he started to believe Hate Street was his exclusive domain. In 1946, despite his disdain for any kind of political activism, Cain led a campaign within the Screen Writers Guild to create the American Authors' Authority, a writers' union which would own its members' work, negotiate better subsidiary deals, and guard against copyright infringement.

Cain believed that *Postman* and *Double Indemnity* clones were multiplying like crazy, and that he deserved credit and remuneration. He was right, of course. (Monogram Pictures' *Apology for Murder* [1945] was an uncredited carbon copy of *Double Indemnity*. Today, video store shelves are crammed with "erotic thrillers" that all owe him some debt.) But there was no way Cain could corner the market on murder. Despite the imminent perception that the Writers Guild was swarming with communists, Cain's socialist notion of safeguarding work was rejected; most writers preferred to compete privately for the best deals they could get, their colleagues be damned.

So Cain left Hollywood, bitterly, at the height of his renown, returning to Maryland. He unfortunately forgot to pack his knack for terse, exciting storytelling. None of Cain's later work came close to matching the four novels he produced in California. He bloody-mindedly worked against the very qualities that made him successful, trying to neuter his later books, shake the pall of death that clung to his characters, and expand his storytelling scope through third-person narration.

Hollywood wanted none of that. Once Billy Wilder showed the way, the movies did Cain better than Cain himself. The almost surreal Technicolor noir, *Slightly Scarlet* (RKO, 1956) is far more entertaining than the Cain novel it's based on, *Love's Lovely Counterfeit* (1942). When Jerry Wald adapted *Mildred Pierce*, he went straight to the original template: a murder (not in the book) kicks off the tale, which is related entirely in flashback. Although the sex was watered down in both *Mildred Pierce* and *Postman*, the power of the female protagonists was undiluted. The focus on Joan Crawford and Lana Turner, respectively, led to these films being tagged as "women's pictures."

The label was apt. One of Cain's major contributions to noir was his treatment of women. They're powerful, almost elemental, forces of nature. Cain's men place their faith in these women the way the devout place theirs in God. It's a toss-up as to whether they'll be life-givers or death-dealers.

THE FILM VERSION OF *MILDRED PIERCE* unveiled one of the legendary dames of Dark City. People came from miles around to strap on the feed bag at her bustling diner, where she served heaping portions of All-American chow.

John Garfield and Lana Turner plot dark deeds in Cain's *The Postman Always Rings Twice.*

Some guys — if they looked useful to her — got the special dessert, after hours. Mildred (Joan Crawford) was an impoverished woman obsessed with conquering the material world. She'd dig her high heels into anyone's back to gain purchase in the social register. Just like the gangsters of Sinister Heights, Mildred wanted to ensure that her offspring — especially spoiled princess Veda — would be welcomed in the swankest salons.

In her rise from hash-slinger to cutthroat capitalist, Mildred milked her kitchen and bedroom skills, but left a succession of husbands and lovers emasculated. Her only true love was Veda, for whom she'd make any sacrifice. In the novel, Veda showed her gratitude by stealing Mildred's husband, following her bliss to a successful opera career, and leaving her mother with the solitary crush.

On-screen, Veda didn't run away with lecherous Monty Beregon; she killed him (for spurning her matrimonial desires). This allowed Mildred to be the ultimate matriarchal martyr, taking the rap for her precious daughter.

Cain loved Crawford's version of Mildred, inscribing a leather-bound copy of the book "To Joan Crawford, who brought Mildred to life as I had always hoped she would be and who has my lifelong gratitude."

Crawford deserved the credit, and how. But her Oscar-winning portrayal of this hydra-headed woman — mother, moneymaker, homemaker, whore — only tapped a few drops from the dark vein that ran through Crawford herself.

JOAN CRAWFORD WAS A CLASSIC HOLLYWOOD rags-to-riches story — as written by Cain. Born dirt poor in San Antonio, Lucille Fay LeSueur was abandoned by her father in childhood. She changed her name to Billie Cassin after moving to Kansas City with her remarried mother.

After toiling as a phone operator, launderer and waitress, she won a Charleston contest that earned her a spot in a Springfield, Missouri chorus line. She danced her way to New York stages, then to Hollywood, parlaying her big eyes and shapely legs into a series of "flapper" roles in silent pictures.

Like Mildred, she was ruthless in her quest for the brass ring. She trained diligently to improve her body, mind, acting, and savoir faire. A nation-wide publicity campaign staged by Louis B. Mayer changed her name to Joan Crawford, signifying MGM's commitment to her career. She was, almost literally, reborn. Columnist Louella Parsons said that "She is the only star I know who manufactured herself... She drew up a blueprint for herself and outlined a beautiful package of skin, bones and character and then set out to put life into the outline. She succeeded, and so Joan Crawford came into existence at the same time an overweight Charleston dancer, born Lucille LeSueur, disappeared from the world." If this sounds suspiciously like the plot of a film noir, wait — it gets thicker.

Crawford's ascension from chippie to princess culminated in marriage to Douglas Fairbanks, Jr., scion of the most famous and wealthy acting family on earth. Joan's mother-in-law, Mary Pickford, was the biggest star of the silent era. (Joan never spoke of her marriage to New York sax player James Welton, whom she left when Hollywood called.) Soon Crawford was coronated herself, able to pick plum leading roles and leave that cheap party girl Lucille behind forever. Joan's wide-shouldered costumes, exclusively tailored by Gilbert Adrian, started fashion trends; she demanded approval of her close-ups; she refused to work during her period, claiming she didn't photograph as well. She controlled her career, and stood up to the biggest shots with a tough-talking demeanor Mildred Pierce would have envied.

Such ball-breaking bluntness proved a rough go for her husbands. Crawford blurred the line between home and career. She required that her husbands walk two steps behind her in public, and in private she often made them submit to her on their knees. Once she gained entrée to the Dream Factory firmament, she dropped Fairbanks. She had affairs with many of her leading men, most famously Clark Gable, but she picked stage actor Franchot Tone as Husband #3. Then one day she caught him in his dressing room, rehearsing with a young extra. She demanded to know how long he'd been cheating. "It happens every day," he replied. "I have to prove to myself that I am still a man, before I go home to you."

Husband #4, Phil Terry, was functional. "I knew what kind of marriage it was going to be when she walked on the set," recalled John Wayne. "First came Joan, then her secretary, then her makeup man, then her wardrobe woman, then finally Phil Terry, carrying the dog."

Crawford had had an abortion in the late 1920s, so as not to derail her accelerating career. Once she wanted children, things got difficult: she had seven miscarriages while married to Tone. By 1939 she had abandoned hope of conceiving. One attempt at adoption was pure noir: she secretly ordered a newborn from a Tennessee "baby mill," but when the child's mother learned who had adopted her, she showed up at Crawford's house, angling for more money. Instead, Joan just gave the baby back.

She adopted a baby girl who endured infancy as Joan Crawford, Jr., before Mother gave her a break and renamed her Christina. That was the last break the kid got. The maternal Joan Crawford careered out of Dark City into horror film terrain. She'd beat Christina and her three adopted siblings, lock them in closets, publicly humiliate them, lash them to their beds all night — a form of psychotic motherly domination that would have challenged the world's finest headshrinkers. Years later, Christina would exact her revenge, penning the poison memoir *Mommie Dearest*.

When *Mildred Pierce* came along, Crawford was on the skids. MGM had soured on her, convinced that her big, brassy style was tarnished by encroaching "middle age" (she was in her early forties). She needed a hit. Badly. Moving to Warner Bros., she forsook the glamor roles, and went for a harder, tougher, more self-revelatory persona. Despite the airs she affected, Crawford had a gutter mouth and always toted a short dog of Canadian Club in her velvet clutch. Noir was a perfect fit for her; it let some of Lucille LeSueur resurface.

"From *Mildred Pierce* onward, a show of innocence was impossible," wrote her biographer, Bob Thomas. "Her portrayals could no longer be complementary to men, they were competitive with men. She sought to destroy them, not to entice them."

In *Possessed* (WB, 1947) she destroys Van Heflin, even though he's the love of her life. The film opens with Crawford wandering catatonic through Los Angeles at dawn, asking strangers if they've seen "David." Taken to a hospital, she is induced — through "narcosynthesis" — to relate her story (in tried-and-true flashback fashion): Joan is, yet again, a poor working woman, nurse Louise Howell, who falls in love with engineer David Sutton (Heflin). She cares for rich industrialist Dean Graham's bedridden wife, Gretchen. She introduces David to her employer (Raymond Massey), who gives him a job – in Canada. Louise is crushed. Gretchen imagines her husband and Louise are having an affair; she commits suicide. Now Graham does make a play

A cop (Gary Owen) gives incredulous consideration to the ultimate Cain woman: cutthroat capitalist, smothering mother, calculating slut, and culinary goddess. Joan Crawford as *Mildred Pierce*.

for Louise. Having lost true love, she opts for security. But David shows up at the wedding reception, this time more interested in Louise's stepdaughter, Carol (Geraldine Brooks).

Confused and jealous, Louise has a mental breakdown. Thus impaired, she murders David.

Possessed is a classic example of a "women's picture" tinted noir by the application of murder, madness, and the brooding expressionistic direction of Curtis Bernhardt. It was also the first time that Joan's huge eyes displayed more craziness than sexiness. She was nominated for another Oscar, but her career had passed a point of no return. The oddly masculine animus that lurked beneath those fine cheekbones came pouring out.

The Damned Don't Cry (WB, 1950) came closest to Joan's own noir verité soul. She plays Ethel Whitehead, white trash sharing an oil field shack with a bitter husband. After the death of her young son, she takes off for a new life in New York as a dress model. She quickly learns there's faster cash in private fittings with the buyers. She lures a naive accountant, Martin Blackford (Kent Smith), into doing her bidding, even arranging for him to handle the books of a syndicate boss, George Castleman (David Brian).

Once Castleman realizes Ethel's eggs are as brassy as his own balls, he takes a cue from Louis B. Mayer, transforming her into "Lorna Hansen Forbes," his high-society mistress. Martin is left high and dry. Castleman sends her to Nevada to spy on Nick Prenta (Steve Cochran), a regional crime boss who's getting mutinous. She falls for Prenta, and all kinds of double-dealing and gunplay erupt amid the ranch houses and saguaro cactus. Lorna lams to Ethel's old oil field shack, still swaddled in her cherished mink. Castleman hunts her down, looking to terminate their contract.

The film was entertaining, but not a huge

hit. The public may have been catching on to the Wald-Crawford formula. Once again the climactic murder opened the proceedings, and the story spilled out as a "where did I go wrong" confession of a tough, cast-iron golddigger.

Joan's big-screen luster dimmed for a couple of years, but in 1952, noir rescued her again. In *Sudden Fear* (RKO) she played Myra Hudson, a successful playwright who is romanced by Lester Blaine (Jack Palance), an actor whom she's rejected for her latest play. He may be flaccid on the boards, but in the sack he's just the ticket. They marry. This being Dark City, Lester's really interested in Myra's will. He's got a greedy little gal (Gloria Grahame) on the side and together they script an accidental final curtain for the wealthy playwright. The lovers concoct the plot, however, in Myra's study, where a built-in dictaphone records them. Myra cunningly counterplots their demise. *Sudden Fear* was a big hit, and earned Crawford her third noir-etched Oscar nomination.

That was Joan's last hurrah. She clung tenaciously to her imperiousness, but producers, trying to fend off the challenge of television, looked elsewhere for box-office allure. When the big contracts dried up, she married husband #5, Alfred Steele, an executive with Pepsi-Cola. Joan became a board director and touring ambassador for the soft-drink company, and she and Al lived the high life on Pepsi's tab for four years. When he died suddenly of a heart attack in 1959, it was a one-two punch for Joan: after debts and taxes were tallied, Steele had died flat broke.

Joan went back to work, but now, as she approached true middle age, the parts offered parodied her former image. She and Bette Davis picked themselves to pieces in Robert Aldrich's horrific black comedy *Whatever Happened to Baby Jane?* By the 1960s, Crawford was a monstrous joke, bulging her famous eyes in

Top: *Possessed* **Bottom:** *The Damned Don't Cry*

horror shows such as *Strait-Jacket*, *Berserk*, and *I Saw What You Did*. She was treading whiskey by the time she did her last picture, *Trog*, in 1970.

After that, most of her public appearances were boozy, bleary, and embarrassing. Pepsi distanced itself from its most famous stockholder. A serious fall almost killed her, but scared her into drying out. Unfortunately, her withdrawal induced paranoia. She spent her last years a virtual prisoner in her apartment, afraid to venture out for fear that she'd be murdered. By May, 1977, she'd withered to a shell of her once vital self, bedridden, attended by two nurses. But she had one great Joan Crawford moment left. When she overheard one of the nurses praying for her soul in her final moments, she raised her head and seethed: "Damn it — don't you *dare* ask God to help me!"

The perfect Dark City exit line.

ONE BALMY EVENING IN THE MID-THIRTIES you'd have sworn Hate Street was really Bristol Avenue, a tony boulevard in the exclusive L.A. enclave of Brentwood. It was the night Joan Crawford's neighbor, Barbara Stanwyck, scrambled over the wall separating their palatial homes, fleeing the punches of her drunk husband, Frank Fay. Crawford knew where Stanwyck was coming from. She often used a thick base to hide the bruises doled out by her own tanked-up spouse, Franchot Tone. For both men, the booze was just a lubricant — envy of their wives' broader power and renown is what fueled their violent rage.

Lousy husbands weren't all the two stars had in common. Both had been chorines in New York. Both survived bleak, impoverished childhoods. Both ranked career over marriage, and played second fiddle to no man. Neither could bear children. Both chose to adopt; both proved to be atrocious mothers. Between them, they left an indelible impression — a new cinematic image of iron-willed, independent women.

If any actress came to epitomize film noir, it was Barbara Stanwyck. Her memorable turn as the scheming temptress in *Double Indemnity* was only her initial contribution to a legacy of "murder dramas." During noir's heyday, Stanwyck reeled out an array of ferocious females, both "good" and "evil," slugging their way through the riskiest neighborhoods of Dark City, and the existential void beyond. Real life had offered Stanwyck plenty of experience to draw from.

Born Ruby Stevens in Brooklyn, 1907, youngest of five kids, she was three when her mother, stepping from a streetcar, was killed by a drunk. Her devastated Dad abandoned the children and fled to Panama, where he found work as a ditch digger. When Ruby ran away from foster homes, her siblings always found her in the same place: on the stoop of the old house on Classon Avenue, waiting for Mom.

Joan plots vengeance in *Sudden Fear*.

At fourteen Ruby was on her own, supporting herself with menial jobs and foregoing a formal education. She had no illusions about the world and her place in it. She was wounded and angry, and talented and disciplined. The perfect soldier. (A pity she and Sam Fuller only made one picture together, the loaded-for-bear western *Forty Guns.*)

By sixteen she had found a home in The Deuce, hoofing in the chorus of the Strand

Stanwyck and Kirk Douglas in *The Strange Love of Martha Ivers*.

Roof nightclub, her first of many shake-and-shimmy venues. Working the roaring all-night shift, she no doubt rubbed shoulders with fellow jazz baby Lucille LeSueur in one glittery speakeasy or another. She became tight with Oscar Levant, the piano-playing Pied Piper of Manhattan's smart set.

Broadway impresario Willard Mack gave Ruby, at 19, her big boost to the legit stage, with a showcase role in his production of *The Noose*,

starring Rex Cherryman. He also changed her name to Barbara Stanwyck. "Ruby Stevens sounds too much like a stripper," Mack said.

Wise to the ramble, but still unschooled in affairs of the heart, Stanwyck fell in love with the rakish Cherryman. Simultaneously, their careers got legs: Stage work and film offers poured in. They talked of marriage, once things settled down. Suffering from exhaustion, Cherryman was advised by doctors to book a restorative voyage to Europe. Barbara bid him adieu on the New York wharves, pledging her love. Cherryman didn't need the round-trip ticket. He died aboard ship, from septic poisoning.

The lonely orphan learned a lesson. From then on she would be invulnerable.

Levant introduced Stanwyck to vaudeville superstar Frank Fay, New York's King of Comedy. His Irish bluster and roguish arrogance were the wedge that split open the Big Apple for her. Stanwyck would later say that Frank was like the father she never had. One month after Cherryman's ill-fated cruise, Stanwyck and Fay were married. Louis B. Mayer, in town to find performers who had voices he could exploit in those newfangled talkies, provided the next plot twist: after seeing, and hearing, Stanwyck in the stage show *Burlesque,* he offered her a screen test.

The fortunes of Frank Fay and Barbara Stanwyck progressed in opposite directions. In Hollywood, Stanwyck rose to prominence, while Fay's pugnacious brand of tomfoolery fizzled. Their rocky relationship served as the basis of the regularly remade *A Star is Born.*

Stanwyck was always different. She projected a steely self-reliance that had as much to do with her ingrained identity as it did with acting ability. Without formal training, Barbara

Stanwyck quickly became the most reliable, protean actress in the business. She appeared in a number of challenging films by Frank Capra and William Wellman, waded to an Oscar nomination in the tear-drenched soap opera *Stella Dallas* (UA, 1937), and was a smashing comedienne in two classics, *Ball of Fire* (RKO, 1941), in which she played slang-spewing Sugarpuss O'Shea, and *The Lady Eve* (Paramount, 1941).

Although she could deliver vulnerable maidens as convincingly as any doe-eyed ingenue, Stanwyck had spine to spare in her personal life. In 1933 she founded Athena National Sorority, an organization that sought to advance the careers of young businesswomen. Stanwyck was a good role model, since she acted as her own boss. She eschewed long-term studio contracts, opting astutely to pursue, as a freelancer, the juiciest roles. Her on-screen naturalism appealed to both men and women, and distinguished her from more mannered contemporaries. What stood out most strongly in her screen persona was toughness. Even playing a victim, she'd never quit without a fight.

Stanwyck feared her first descent into Dark City, *Double Indemnity*, would cold-cock her career, pushing her hardness to the extreme — remorseless murder. To her surprise, audiences relished her cruelty. Mrs. Dietrichson became legend. In 1944, the Internal Revenue Service revealed that the former dime-a-dance dame was the highest paid woman in the United States, outworking and outearning her nearest rival, Bette Davis.

After some lightweight wartime fodder, Stanwyck found a permanent parking spot on the shady side of Hate Street, as the black heart of the meanest murder drama ever, *The Strange Love of Martha Ivers* (Paramount, 1946).

Written by Robert Rossen, *Martha Ivers* is a delirious "women's picture," in which the fear and guilt of youth plague the protagonists through their adult lives.

Walter O'Neil's a witness as orphaned Martha kills her evil aunt. Martha's cover story blames the killing on a robber, and she gets Walter to back her up. Walter's father, a greedy lawyer, realizes that Martha stands to inherit her late father's fortune, so he uses her fraudulent testimony to frame an innocent man, who is executed for the murder. Walter and Martha then marry, bound forever by conspiracy. They end up dominating Iverstown: Martha (Stanwyck) as a hard-charging industrialist, Walter (Kirk Douglas, in his movie debut) as the Scotch-sodden district attorney.

The hateful, guilt-edged union turns into a volatile triangle when Sam Masterson (Van Heflin) comes home. Sam had been Martha's childhood chum; they were supposed to run away together the same night Martha iced her aunt. Now a nomadic ne'er-do-well, Sam rekindles Martha's deferred desires, provoking jealousy and suspicion in Walter. He's convinced Sam is out to blackmail them, and hires some local muscle to work over his former pal and deposit him beyond the city limits.

But Sam won't quit. He's determined to uncover the secret that's lashing the mismatched couple together. He also wants to humiliate Walter by flaunting Martha's attraction to him. It works.

"You know what's on my mind, Martha? About Sam, I mean," says Walter. "I think I do," she responds. "And that's where it will stay. On your mind. Unless, of course, I tell you differently."

Definitive Barbara Stanwyck.

After Sam and Martha consummate their passion, the guilt rains down. Walter confronts Sam with self-loathing fury, but tumbles down the master stairway, plastered and impotent. Sam is stunned when Martha implores him to finish off her unconscious husband, so they can be "free." But just like he did twenty years earlier, Sam bolts from the house — this time taking their secret with him.

In a feverish finale, Walter embraces and forgives Martha. "I love you," he tells her, as she watches Sam, her true love, walk away. "And don't cry. It's not your fault... It's not anyone's fault. It's just the way things are. It's about what people want, and how hard they want it. And how hard it is for them to get it."

Martha and Walter kiss, and she vows that they'll start over, "Just like nothing ever happened." Walter pulls the gun from his

Van Heflin looks suspicious succumbing to Stanwyck's feral allure in *Martha Ivers*.

pocket and plants it against Martha's waist. He hesitates, still looking for her to lead. She guides his trigger finger. At last, an end to all her fear and loathing. Walter then obliterates his own pain with a single shot to his heart.

WHILE THIS GRIM FAIRY TALE was concocted on Paramount's painted sets, real-life dramas flared outside the lot. A power struggle between rival labor unions, the entrenched IATSE and the growing Conference of Studio Unions (CSU) erupted in chain-swinging melees. The CSU, promising to chase racketeers out of Hollywood unions, had loosened IATSE's grip on a number of craft unions. Pressing its advantage, it threw picket lines around several major studios, trying to intimidate IATSE members into defecting. Studio heads, caught in the middle, called in the cops — and mob-sponsored goon squads — to break things up. This street warfare was ground zero in the coming anti-communist frenzy. Hollywood honchos and IATSE bosses would preserve their uneasy alliance by casting the CSU as a communist-front organization, thereby marshalling federal forces behind them. (There was more than a tinge of pink to the fledgling conference, but it was cleaner than graft-tainted IATSE.)

Lewis Milestone, director of *The Strange Love of Martha Ivers*, often ceded the helm

Stanwyck in the rare role of victim: *Sorry, Wrong Number.*

to assistant directors Robert Aldrich or Byron Haskin while he attended CSU strategy sessions at a restaurant across the street. Milestone would be among the first group of "unfriendly" witnesses targeted by the original HUAC hunting expedition in 1947.

Barbara Stanwyck had no qualms about crossing picket lines. She disdained the political battle raging around her. It was simple: trample anyone who tried to cheat her out of work. She had long ago traded political and religious beliefs for career compulsion. It was as if she'd evaporate if she couldn't recreate herself with each new role, disguising her intense insecurity in a parade of commanding characters. When the witchhunt

burned through Hollywood, Stanwyck swung far to the right, aligning herself with those who'd safeguard her career.

The "real" Stanwyck was a legendary cipher. She was obsessively private and had a very small circle of friends. Her second marriage, to actor Robert Taylor, was a studio-arranged union that many people suspected was "lavender": intended to camouflage both partners' rumored homosexuality. Although Taylor's later affairs with Ava Gardner and other ingenues proved him at least bisexual, Stanwyck remained loyal, steadfastly propping up the facade of "the perfect Hollywood marriage."

Throughout the twelve-year arrangement with Taylor, which ended in divorce in 1951, Stanwyck was actually closer to her veteran publicist, Helen Ferguson. Their personal and professional bond spawned decades of rumors that Stanwyck was Hollywood's most famous closeted lesbian.

While the innuendo swirled, Stanwyck marched on. She forced herself to be a trouper, submerging loneliness in a torrent of work, much of it emanating from that nasty residential cul-de-sac in Dark City.

In *Sorry, Wrong Number* (Paramount, 1948) she was wealthy invalid Leona Stevenson, who through crossed telephone wires overhears the planning of a woman's murder. Confined to her bed, Leona is terrorized when she realizes she is the intended victim. Scenarist Lucille Fletcher fleshed out her famous 22-minute radio play to feature length, infusing it with a theme endemic to many noirs of the period — the resentful underclass scheming to undermine the rich. In this case the culprit is her dim-wit husband (Burt Lancaster), rebelling against his wife's mental and monetary domination.

The File on Thelma Jordon (Paramount, 1950), placed Stanwyck back in Cain territory. She lures gullible district attorney Cleve Marshall (Wendell Corey) into an affair, so she can use him in a complex plot to rob and murder her rich aunt. Although her sleazeball lover, Tony Laredo

(Richard Romer), actually hatches the crime, Thelma's arrested and tried. Hopelessly in love with Thelma, Cleve intentionally loses the case, expecting to win her devotion. He is stunned when the acquitted Thelma dumps him to run away with Tony. But Thelma, displaying the sudden remorse that tends to overwhelm people in Dark City, yanks the steering wheel from Tony as they're leaving town, plummeting them over a cliff.

No Man of Her Own (Paramount, 1950), may be the ultimate "women's noir." Mitchell Leisen, a wizard at "weepies," directed this adaptation of Cornell Woolrich's novel *I Married A Dead Man*, fashioning a soapy and sinister combination of tear-jerker and back-stabber. A pregnant woman (named Helen Ferguson, in honor of Barbara's close friend) is dumped by her cad boyfriend and tearfully heads cross-country, seeking a fresh start. She's befriended on the train by another pregnant woman, traveling with her husband. The train crashes and Helen, through a wild fluke (a Woolrich hallmark), is mistaken for the other woman and eventually accepted into her "late husband's" affluent family. Needless to say, her past creeps back into the picture, threatening her newfound happiness.

Clash by Night (RKO, 1952), based on Clifford Odets's play, was, like most of his work, a verbose variety of noir. Mae Doyle (Stanwyck) returns to her hometown and takes a shot at complacency by marrying a sweet, simple fisherman (Paul Douglas). But even motherhood can't ease her angst; she ruins herself by having an affair with her husband's scary pal, Earl (Robert Ryan). By the tenth self-revelatory Odets monologue you're itching for somebody to grab a gat and start blasting.

Jeopardy (MGM, 1952) featured the queasy spectacle of Stanwyck allowing herself to be raped by escaped con Ralph Meeker, in exchange for his helping save her drowning husband (Barry Sullivan). *Witness to Murder* (UA, 1954) was a distaff *Rear Window*, beating Hitchcock's gem into theaters, but lacking all its brilliantly polished angles.

Stanwyck's last saunter down Hate Street came with *Crime of Passion* (UA, 1957). A feisty San Francisco newspaper advice columnist, Kathy Ferguson (!), shows up a pair of out-of-town cops by using her

Stanwyck and Raymond Burr commit a *Crime of Passion*.

column to reel in the fugitive they're pursuing. Lt. Bill Doyle (Sterling Hayden) falls for her, and they get hitched. Kathy abandons her career and moves to the drowsy suburbs of Los Angeles. The thrill of the newsroom is replaced by an endless succession of parties where the men talk pensions and the wives blather about clothes and canapés. Her suddenly mundane existence induces psychosis: she foists all her thwarted ambition onto her passive husband, and competes to win him the promotion that will hoist them above their detested peers.

Unfortunately, her scheme involves sex with Tony Pope, chief of Homicide (Raymond Burr). When Pope balks at naming Bill his successor, Kathy swipes a gun from the precinct's evidence room and gives Pope six good reasons why he should have promoted her husband. Bill swiftly pieces things together, collars his wife, and carts her off to jail.

Jo Eisenger's script isn't bold enough to portray Kathy as much more than a sociopathic harpy, but it clearly suggests that she was better off as a career woman than as an unhappy homemaker. Stanwyck's transformation from tart-tongued, streetwise reporter to a human lapdog lost in her own house was a none-too-subtle condemnation of women's subordination, trapped in a curt, conventional murder drama. It was a solid, if unspectacular, finale to Stanwyck's reign as the Queen of Noir.

Shamus Flats

Half the rye in the bottle had disappeared since I'd sat back to watch the sun drop behind the rooftops. It was no time to hear footsteps echoing in the corridor. Especially jangling footsteps, like some cowboy forgot to doff his spurs. I saw a hulking shadow on the pebbled glass. The door slowly swung open. Beneath the Stetson, his face was cracked like shoe leather. Decades of prairie dust clung to him. He drew his Colt, spun it twice, and slapped the butt in my open palm. "Your turn," he whispered. Then he folded over, deader than last night's four-star final.

Somewhere in the mid-Forties, the lonesome rider on the range passed the iron to a new icon of macho American independence — another cynical, alienated, yet incorruptible lone wolf: the private detective.

Here was a guy without roots who knew all the ins and outs of Dark City. Typically a former cop, he became a thorn in the side of the boys at the Precinct when he decided to go solo. Most of his clients drove downtown from Hate Street, seeking some street-wise savvy to locate a lost relative or stray sibling. Without fail, the trail led to Sinister Heights. The retainer: twenty-five bucks a day plus expenses. The latter probably shocked his clients. For all the getting around this guy did — especially during wartime rationing — the gas bill must have been a doozy.

Our man was born in *Black Mask*, in the early Twenties. You can paddle around in the dark waters of Edgar Allan Poe panning for artistic antecedents to film noir, but you needn't venture further back than this rough-edged maga-zine of "pulp" fiction. It was created in 1920 by H. L. Mencken and George Jean Nathan, as a low-brow bookend for the pair's witty and urbane *Smart Set*. They sold their interest in the book prematurely, not anticipating the mother lode of significant popular fiction that would run through the tawdry little publication. Joseph T. Shaw, "The Captain," took over as editor in 1926, and became the leading prospector of what would become known as "hard-boiled" fiction: spare, pull-no-punches fantasies of city-dwelling masculinity and moxie.

In its pages the philosophical and stylistic underpinnings of noir first took root, principally in the work of Dashiell Hammett. Like most writers of this period who slashed verbiage to its lean essentials, Hammett would be compared to Ernest Hemingway. No sale. Hammett was his own man, and a decidedly original writer. His stories crackled with an unmatched aura of immediacy that was perfectly targeted to a new type of urban reader. His prose snapped straight at the

THE OFFICE was empty again. No leggy brunettes, no little girls with slanted glasses, no neat dark men with gangster's eyes.

I sat down at the desk and watched the light fade. The going-home sounds had died away. Outside the neon signs began to glare at one another across the boulevard. There was something to be done, but I didn't know what. Whatever it was, it would be useless.

—Philip Marlowe
from Raymond Chandler's *The Little Sister*

Dick Powell as Marlowe in *Murder, My Sweet* (1944).

proles, headed to work on the subway or slogging through a killer shift. Terse tales for laborers with little leisure time. An instinctive storyteller, Hammett never failed to entertain. But he also had a gift for weaving a world-view into the narrative flow, without waxing didactic.

His tales of crime and detection weren't delicate diversions penned by the "classic" authors of drawing-room intrigues. In old-fashioned mysteries, egghead investigators engaged in games of clever reasoning: find the liar. In Hammett's world, deducing truth was a war of attrition, in which the detective had his work cut out for him outlasting all the liars. No one spoke the truth. Solving a case was the mission, but keeping your balance and retaining a shred of integrity was also a priority. Although there wasn't much "realism" in Hammett's contrived plots, readers responded to his authentic voice and his cold, clear vision.

Hammett's protagonists could have been descendants of Cooper's Natty Bumppo or Twain's Huckleberry Finn. Loners on a quest, small men in a sprawling landscape seeking private vindication in the wilderness, telling their tales in rugged New World vernacular. By the 1920s, the vast frontier had been squeezed off, paved over, forever cheapened. The pathfinder was relegated to a spare third-floor office in an anonymous downtown walk-up. Randomness, not destiny, became the overriding theme, and a code of honor, however quixotic, was all that kept the "hero" afloat. The hard-boiled gumshoe became a soldier of discipline in a one-man army.

Hammett's background added weight to his writing. He'd left home in Maryland at fourteen, scuffling through his "tender years" as a stevedore, railyard freight agent, stock clerk and cannery worker. In 1915 he answered a cryptic classified ad in a Baltimore tabloid, taking a job with the local branch of the Pinkerton National Detective Agency. By twenty-one, he was adept at tradecraft, shadowing suspects, packing heat and using it. (The long knife scar on his leg, and the indentation of a brick in his skull, were lasting mementoes of some slipshod techniques that helped spur his imminent career change.)

Pinkerton's clients were a far cry from Brigid O'Shaughnessy. The agency was mostly involved in industrial work, protecting corporations from internal employee conspir-

acies. Pinkertons were frequently hired as moles and strikebreakers. In a pivotal event in his life, Hammett was assigned to infiltrate the ranks of the Industrial Workers of the World, which was trying to unionize Anaconda copper miners in Montana. At first, Hammett exhibited the same professional zeal and buried conscience that he'd later give his nameless shamus, the Continental Op. He'd adopt alternative identities and pull information out of duped "colleagues." But when Hammett was offered five grand by an Anaconda official to kill IWW union organizer Frank Little, he quickly developed a firm, if situational, code of ethics. Little was murdered anyway — by a company-supported lynch mob — and Hammett's world-view snapped into focus. (So did his politics: Hammett would become, for better and worse, a staunch Communist supporter.)

Hammett was diagnosed tubercular when he volunteered for military duty in WWI. For the next several years he checked in and out of hospitals before finally settling down in San Francisco, marrying one of his nurses, Josephine Annis Dolan. It was by the Bay, during the Twenties, that the fragile, alcoholic Hammett would hammer out a small but influential body of work.

The Continental Op stories for *Black Mask* were vigorous exercises in which Hammett seemed to be limbering up for a big vault. His first novel, *Red Harvest*, serialized in *Black Mask*, was a fast-paced, thrilling exposé of political corruption that drew heavily on his experience with the Montana copper miners' uprising. The style remains so fresh it reads tonight like it was written tomorrow. Its follow-up, *The Dain Curse*, didn't coalesce its serialized origins quite as well.

The third book, *The Maltese Falcon*, was the McCoy. The stuff legends are made of.

Amazingly, for a book deemed emblematic of a whole genre, *The Maltese Falcon* is more a character study than a typical whodunit. It revolves around Sam Spade's entanglement with a gaggle of double-crossing dervishes, all pursuing the elusive, jewel-encrusted "black bird." Plot takes a back seat

Det. Tom Polhaus (Ward Bond) confronts Sam Spade (Humphrey Bogart) in John Huston's faithful adaptation of Dashiell Hammett's *The Maltese Falcon*.

to Hammett's exploration of deceit and avarice. The question of "Who done it?" is moot (the murder of Spade's partner, Miles Archer, kick-starts matters and casts a menacing pall, but Archer's already forgotten fifty pages in).

Most detective stories that emerged from Dark City followed this pattern. They had less to do with intricate plots and feats of deduction than they did with the tarnished chivalry and jaundiced attitude of the detective. This was a character trait Hammett made immortal when he penned Spade's callous kiss-off to the desirable but duplicitous Brigid, or Ruth, or whoever she was that day: "I won't play the sap for you... If I send you over, I'll be sorry as hell — I'll have some rotten nights — but that'll pass" Sam Spade lived a long way down a dark street from the likes of Philo Vance.

Depression-era Hollywood was incapable of capturing this cold world. Warner Bros. paid $8,500 for the movie rights to the *Falcon*, and mustered only a pair of smirky "B's" from Hammett's masterwork: *Woman of the World* (a/k/a *Dangerous Female*, 1931) and *Satan Met a Lady* (1936). The industry in the 1930s was more in tune with the author's final novel, *The Thin Man*, which he cranked out for the paycheck before consigning his gifts to a lifelong flood of alcohol. The slim *Thin Man*, full of the boozy banter Hammett exchanged with paramour Lillian Hellman, generated a remarkably lucrative franchise: comedy capers starring William Powell, Myrna Loy, and a spunky terrier. (The novel is as overserved as Hammett; downing it in one gulp can induce a contact high.)

In 1940, when screenwriter John Huston told Jack Warner he wanted to remake *The Maltese Falcon* as his directorial debut, the first spark in a cultural phenomenon was struck. Huston and screenwriter Allen Rivkin decided not to tinker with a good thing: the director's secretary broke the novel down into script form without any major changes, and Huston sent it to the big boss for approval. Although he'd twice demanded tangled reworkings of the same material, Warner now inexplicably commended Huston on "a great script."

For the first time, Hammett's words were in the care of someone who felt an affinity for them. "The story was a dramatization of myself, of how I felt about things," Huston said. "Hammett's mentality and philosophy were quite congenial to me, and I implicitly accepted Hammett's writing." By hewing faithfully to the writer's crisp and caustic exposition, Huston would craft the first example of hardboiled film noir.

No small measure of the film's success can be attributed to the ego of actor George Raft. As Warner's top gangster star, Raft got right of first refusal on all tough-guy roles. He disdained doing *Falcon* because it was a remake, unbecoming a star of his magnitude. He also begged off because the budget was paltry and Huston was a tyro. Only four days before the cameras were to roll, Warner told Huston he'd have to settle for a leading man from the second tier: Humphrey Bogart.

Bogart. Spade. Huston caught lightning in a bottle. Bogey'd been waiting for a role like this his whole career. He'd managed to transcend his blue-blood birthright by playing menacing gangsters in an assortment of Thirties' melodramas, but he'd always been to the left of center, leering in the shadow of Cagney, Robinson, and Raft. And he always died, snarling, at the finish. Spade was his first bona fide starring role. Any limitations he had as an actor didn't matter. They were swept aside by a stolid, evocative posture and attitude, spiced with cruel humor. The fit was so right, Bogart kept up the act for the rest of his life.

By the time *The Maltese Falcon* wrapped, Bogart had crafted the persona he'd inhabit for the rest of his life.

In his critical reappraisal of Bogart, *Take It and Like It*, Jonathan Coe put his finger precisely on the spot at which Hammett and Bogart meshed to create a new archetype. "What the audience senses here is not an absence of feeling, but a distant suggestion of feelings so complex that Spade sees no point in bringing them to the surface." Beneath that, Coe notes, was "a deeper tension, fundamental to the Bogart persona, between an ironic fatalism (his belief that life does not count for much) and an indisputable courage (his will to persevere at all costs, nevertheless)."

John Huston cut Bogart a wide swath through which his Spade could swagger. Much of it involved keeping producer Hal Wallis at bay. Throughout production Wallis complained that Bogart had "adopted a leisurely, suave form of delivery [that has] a tendency to drag down the scenes and slow them up too much. Bogart must have his usual brisk, staccato manner and delivery, and if he doesn't have it, I'm afraid we're going to be in trouble." Mary Astor, like Huston, was thrilled by Bogart's approach. "He kept other actors on their toes because he listened to them, he watched them, he looked at them." She recalled that he "related to people as though they had no clothes on. If they grabbed at their various little hypocrisies for protective cover, his laugh was a particularly unpleasant chortle."

That sardonic laugh, and nasty bared-teeth grin, were part of the armor Bogart wore in real life, as well, where he was a regular at Dark City's watering holes. He and his third wife, Mayo Methot, had established residency on Hate Street by the time the *Falcon* flew in, and their combative relationship helped etch more weariness, and wariness, in Bogart's performances, live and filmed. Coming home late after yet another bender, Bogart encountered his wife crooning a few bars of "Embraceable You" — their private distress signal. Before she reached the chorus, Methot went at him with a butcher knife. Bogart hightailed it, but his back tasted the knife-tip several times. He survived, of course – one more lesson learned about dangerous females.

Just prior to its release, studio functionaries took one last crack at sabotaging the instant classic, changing the title to *The Gent from Frisco*. Hal Wallis redeemed himself then, asserting that *The Maltese Falcon* would do perfectly.

Even as the film launched Huston and Bogart on successful careers, Sam Spade's creator was virtually finished. Hammett lived off royalties from his novels and film adaptations, while illness and alcohol drained his creative well.

What little energy circulated in his tall, elegant frame was channeled into politics, not writing. Various directors offered him assignments, almost out of pity. But Hammett could no longer muster the muse. William Wyler handed him ten grand in 1950 to pass a blue pencil over Sidney Kingsley's play *Detective Story*, but Hammett, clinging to his ethics like a drowning man, returned the advance when he couldn't produce real work.

The McCarthy witchhunt provided Hammett with a stage for a final Spade-like stand. Haggard and spindly, he stood up to the inquisitors, declaring that "I don't let cops or judges tell me what democracy is." Found in contempt of Congress, he served six months at the federal pen in Ashland, Kentucky, where the old man was given light duty: cleaning toilets. Every Friday he'd gather with other inmates to listen to *The Adventures of Sam Spade* on the prison radio.

HAMMETT'S SUCCESSOR AS THE DEAN of the hard-boiled school had little in common with the founder. Raymond Chandler was a cranky, ill-tempered milquetoast, American-born but English-bred, who was a mid-level oil company executive until he was fired for problem drinking. At the late age of forty-five, Chandler took his first pecks at the typewriter keys, following Hammett's path through the pages of *Black Mask*. In a series of richly evocative short stories, Chandler molded the Golem-like alter ego who would avenge all the humiliations of his life.

Murder, My Sweet

Philip Marlowe was a more romanticized vision of the private eye. To Chandler he was a hero, not just a professional. His code of honor was far more rigid than Sam Spade's, and unlike Hammett's taciturn protagonists, Marlowe was inclined to erupt in florid soliloquy. Their respective gumshoes were mirror images of both men. While Hammett endured life's pain stoically, Chandler ranted over its indignities. If some of the energy he expended in bitchy letter-writing had been redirected to his fiction, Chandler's canon would have been even more impressive.

In the course of seven novels, Marlowe became Dark City's great soapbox orator. "We've got the big money, the sharp shooters, the percentage workers, the fast-dollar boys, the hoodlums out of New York, Chicago and Detroit...," he vents in *The Little Sister*. "We've got the flash restaurants and night clubs they run, and the hotels and apartment houses they own, and the grifters and con men and female bandits that live in them. The luxury trades, the pansy decorators, the lesbian dress designers, the riff-raff of a big hard-boiled city with no more personality than a paper cup."

Despite his contempt for the place, Chandler/Marlowe was helplessly in thrall to his perfumed and perverse city. Chandler's Los Angeles was an alluring *femme fatale* that kept crushing his heart each time he came back for more. His vision of the sprawling artificial paradise, in which moral corruption was covered by the glare of sunlight and neon and the fragrance of blooming jacaranda, was so vividly rendered that it would become the world's adopted perception of Los Angeles, long after the place had all the style leached out of it.

Hollywood could never translate the best of Chandler: the rhythms of his prose, the vulpine verbiage of his descriptive passages, his uncanny ability to paint moods at once invigorating and dreadful. Instead, adaptations of his books leaned on his flair for gaudy patter, while trying to cope with the shortcomings of his plot structures. (Chandler often assembled novel-length mysteries by cobbling elements from his short stories. His creaky plots had none of the narrative momentum of Hammett's. It was the seductive élan of his prose that made his novels compelling.)

The first two attempts to film Chandler were as bogus as the first two Hammett adaptations. RKO purchased Chandler's second novel, *Farewell, My Lovely*, to serve as source material for a film called *The Falcon Takes Over*, one of a series of hour-long programmers based on Leslie Charteris's effete investigator, the Saint. (The author groused so loudly about the lousy films made from his books that RKO finally changed the character's name to The Falcon, prompting a lawsuit by Charteris.) In 1942, Fox bought Chandler's *The High Window* to provide a storyline for *Time to Kill*, the last installment of its Michael Shayne detective series. Paying Chandler solely for his plots made as much sense as hiring Rita

Marlowe (Humphrey Bogart) has his hands full with the sexy Sternwood siblings, the enigmatic Vivian (Lauren Bacall) and her nymphomaniac sister Carmen (Martha Vickers) in Howard Hawks' cheerfully incoherent adaptation of Raymond Chandler's *The Big Sleep*.

Hayworth just to do voice-overs. Eventually someone had to recognize the distinctive vision Chandler had of Philip Marlowe and Los Angeles.

That turned out to be Adrian Scott, a theatrical producer from New York just beginning his film career at RKO. The studio already owned *Farewell, My Lovely*, so it didn't have to pay Chandler another cent. That prompted executive producer Sid Rogell to give Scott the green light. Enlisting the aid of fledgling screenwriter John Paxton, a crony from New York, and director Edward Dmytryk, a bulwark of the studio's "B" features, Scott set to work producing the first faithful Chandler movie.

Murder, My Sweet, released in early 1945, pruned Chandler's plot to within a mile or two of coherence, and smartly played up his strengths: attitude and ambiance. Dmytryk and cameraman Harry Wild established many of the visual motifs that would become noir standards: deep shadows cut by key light, unsettling angles (many lifted from *Kane*), a dreamy, hypnotic pace accelerating toward inevitable disaster. Scott and Paxton also understood that it was the reflective nature of the detective's first-person narration, weary with regret and resignation, that made these stories you could take personally. This is the essential distinction between the noir detective and other fictional sleuths. He may solve a case, but the answer to the big mystery, what he's really after, always eludes him.

Following hard on the heels of *Double Indemnity* (which Chandler scripted) *Murder, My Sweet* was the back end of a one-two punch that knocked filmgoers — and even more so, filmmakers — for a loop. After those two, things would be done a little differently around town.

Once *Murder, My Sweet* proved a hit, Jack Warner gave director Howard Hawks $50,000 to buy the rights to Chandler's first novel, *The Big Sleep*. Hawks called up Chandler and asked him if he'd like to see Bogart as Marlowe. Chandler was as tickled as a kid at Christmas, and Hawks paid him five grand for the book rights, pocketing the remaining loot most probably to underwrite one hell of a hunting trip. Chandler and Hammett, like their hard-boiled alter egos, were soft when it came to money. Hammett got a decent payday for the film rights to *The Maltese Falcon*, but then spent years legally wrangling to regain control of the character of Sam Spade, not wanting to believe he'd sold off the name forever. When Chandler signed on as a studio writer in the Forties, he was so overwhelmed by his weekly retainer it never dawned on him to ask for what other, lesser, writers were earning.

Although Dick Powell did a fine job in *Murder, My Sweet*, he couldn't quite conceal his bouncy, hoofer's energy beneath a rash of stubble and a rumpled suit. He came off more petulant than world-weary. Closer to the real Chandler, perhaps, but wide of the romantic ideal. On the other hand, "Bogart was the genuine article," Chandler bubbled in anticipation of his Marlowe incarnation.

Howard Hawks's production was not, however, as true to Chandler as Dmytryk's film. Blame Lauren Bacall. Both Hawks and Bogart were infatuated with the 20-year-old starlet, whom Hawks had Svengalied into a sexy, self-possessed woman of the world in her debut, *To Have and Have Not* (WB, 1944). It was Bogart who would Have, and Hawks who'd Have Not. Bacall fell hard for the man Bogart created on the set of *The Maltese Falcon*, and they lived out a romance that seemed to exist more in the Hollywood ether than in reality. (Mayo Methot was compensated for stepping aside; Bogart was lucky to escape with only flesh wounds.) Hawks overcame his envy of the lovey-dovey stars. His consolation prize was a long, successful marriage to the beautiful, adventurous Nancy Roe Gross — nicknamed Slim — a real life version of the take-no-guff dames Hawks made one of his silver-screen signatures.

While Bogart and Hawks lived large with women half their ages, Chandler doted on his frail wife Cissy, more than twenty years his senior. The code of honor the author ingrained in Marlowe had a wide streak of sexual repression. During his Hollywood years, Chandler was torn between loyalty to his elderly wife, and the temptations of beautiful young women who were bountiful as wild berries on the back lots. Chandler's libidinous conflicts often seeped into poor, unmarried Marlowe.

By contrast, breezy sexual byplay was the stock-in-trade of Hawks's men and women. *The Big Sleep* was made to cash in on the chemistry of its stars, and their sexual badinage became the core of the film. Chandler's supporting characters hung around the periphery while Bogey and Bacall swapped insinuating bon mots, scripted by William Faulkner and Jules Furthman. (Release of the film was delayed almost a year, when Warners decided it wanted even more innuendo tossed between the two.) When Bogart wasn't backchatting Bacall, he made time with various women who went into heat at the sight of him. This Marlowe would have snorted at the one in the novel — the one who tore apart his bed after Carmen Sternwood had the nerve to lay her nubile body on his pure sheets.

It's become legend now that no one involved in making *The Big Sleep* could make heads or tails of its byzantine plot, and that Howard Hawks couldn't have cared less. His intuition was dead on. Keeping pace with the P. I. as he puts his underpaid ass on the line in various dangerous settings is what detective fiction is all about. If it somehow hangs together, all the better. But this wasn't film noir. Howard Hawks was too cocksure a man, completely unfettered by doubt and anxiety, to give a damn about the cit-

izens of Dark City. *The Big Sleep* is a terrific piece of tomfoolery, a self-contained fantasy that has little to do with Chandler's vision of the world.

Just an aside: the actor most suited to the role of Marlowe was William Holden. As *Sunset Boulevard* and *Stalag 17* showed, he could be caustic and charismatic, and it's easy to picture him smoking a pipe and working out chess problems, like the Marlowe of the novels. In real life, Holden was as archly conservative as Marlowe, until the booze started fraying his tightly-stitched seams.

Instead, we're left with actor Robert Montgomery's wildly off-base homage to Chandler. Directing *The Lady in the Lake* (MGM, 1947) he attempted a visual corollary to Chandler's first-person narration by presenting the entire film from Marlowe's point-of-view. This led to numerous awkward scenes of actors playing to the camera's roving eye, while Montgomery, showing no flair for smart-mouth dialogue, tries

Robert Montgomery's Philip Marlowe had eyes for Audrey Totter in *The Lady in the Lake.*
A lugubrious exercise in subjective camerawork, the film was smug and jokey in ways
that the blithe *Big Sleep* avoided. Totter was its main attraction.

Every inch the noir icon:
Robert Mitchum in
Out of the Past.

cracking wise in voice-over. Cameras were cumbersome in 1947, which meant that everything unfolded slowly, a fatal flaw in a detective yarn. The lone advantage of Montgomery's folly was the amusing presence of Audrey Totter, whose character, Adrienne Fromsett, is beefed up from the novel. Totter gamely carries the whole affair with an apparently endless repertoire of facial expressions. Conforming to Hollywood scripture, Marlowe's ascetic pose is dropped for a happy holiday frolic with Miss Fromsett.

By the time Montgomery sank the *Lady in the Lake*, the tough-talking private dick had already veered into satire. *The Dark Corner* (20th, 1946) got some excitement, and laughs, out of contrasting the broadly-stroked character of gumshoe Bradford Galt (Mark Stevens) with the aristocratic snobbery of social gadfly Hardy Cathcart (Clifton Webb). The original screenplay by Jay Dratler and Bernard Schoenfeld was clearly an attempt to combine the private eye formula with the society milieu depicted in the popular *Laura* (1944), in which Webb played virtually the same character. Surveying the crowd at his gala, Cathcart remarks with practiced disdain that it's "a nauseating mixture of Park Avenue and Broadway – it proves I'm a liberal." Meanwhile, down in the flats, Galt tells his smitten secretary Kathleen (Lucille Ball), "If you're sharp you'll get out now. Fast. I got a feeling I'm behind the eight ball. Something's gonna happen. And when it does, you'll end up right in the corner pocket."

It had been only five years since John Huston put the first true hard-boiled dick onscreen, but *The Dark Corner* played like it was directed by Madame Tussaud. There would be one blast of transcendence, however, before the shamus passed into self-parody.

Out of the Past (RKO, 1947) burst some of the bonds of the P. I. formula, favoring a headlong plunge into the haunted, self-destructive psyche of its private eye. Daniel Mainwaring (writing as Geoffrey Homes) constructed an involuted tale that owned up to what most films in the genre only hinted at: these stories are about the protagonist's quest for solutions to his own problems, not his client's. *Out of the Past* spelled it out, and presented one of the sexiest, most bewildered, and vulnerable of detective heroes.

Jeff Markham (Robert Mitchum) is half of a two-man, nickel-and-dime detective agency. He's called up to Sinister Heights by glib gangster Whit Sterling (Kirk Douglas), who wants his girlfriend, Kathie Moffett (Jane Greer), tracked down. Seems she's lifted forty grand, leaving Whit a deposit of two low-caliber slugs. Markham tells his partner Jack Fisher (Steve Brodie) that they'll split the hefty skip trace fee, but he'll chase the skirt solo. The trail leads to Mexico, and as soon as Jeff spots Kathie, gliding from punishing sunlight into the languid dimness of La Mar Azul cantina, it's *hasta a vista*. The detective's code of honor is melted by sexual obsession.

Jeff sandbags Sterling, so he can saunter, slit-eyed, into the kind of erotic fantasy he hopes will make his crummy life worth living. "I went to Pablo's that night. I knew I'd go every night until she showed up. I knew she knew it. I sat there and I drank bourbon and I shut my eyes, but I didn't think of a joint on 56th Street. I knew where I was and what I was doing. What a sucker I was."

Kathie's wise to Jeff, figuring he's law come to arrest her. Confronting him, she's shocked to learn she only wounded Whit – and that Jeff's none too eager to extradite her for the boss. She claims she didn't steal Whit's dough. If Jeff provides her protection, she proposes, maybe they can parlay their affair into full-time bliss.

So Jeff gives Whit several bum steers, and he and Kathie hightail it to a new life. "I opened an office in San Francisco. A cheap little rathole that suited the work I did. Shabby jobs for whoever'd hire me. It was the bottom of the barrel and I scraped it. But I didn't care — I had her."

Their idyll comes to an end at the racetrack, when Jeff is spotted by his old partner, Fisher. "He just stood there with our lives in his pocket, because I knew if he ever saw her he'd sell us both for a dollar ninety-five." So the lovers split up, Jeff taking his shadow on a wild goose chase around Southern California. Once he shakes Fisher, he rendezvouses with Kathie at a cabin in the mountains above Pyramid Lake. Only problem: Fisher was bird-dogging her, not Jeff.

When Fisher walks in, angling for a cut of the stolen dough, Jeff tries to persuade his partner he's all wrong about Kathie. They promote rights and lefts off their respective chins. Kathie doesn't fancy long arguments: one pop from the handgun in her purse and Fisher's finished. While Jeff fires up a smoke to focus his thoughts, Kathie takes a powder, leaving her lover to bury the body and stew.

To slip the long reach of Whit Sterling, Jeff moves to a sleepy mountain town, calls himself Bailey, and opens a service station. He's eventually uncovered by Whit's henchman, Joe Stefanos (Paul Valentine), who summons him to a meeting with the gangster. Jeff reveals the whole sordid saga to his mousey surrogate love, Ann (Virginia Huston), on the drive to Whit's palatial retreat in Tahoe. He vows to face the music, break from his past, and start fresh with her.

As soon as Jeff crosses the threshold, the double-crosses start piling up. Kathie is back in Sterling's fold, too terrified of Whit to run anymore. Jeff's unmoved: "You're like a leaf that the wind blows from one gutter to another. You can't help anything you do." Whit coerces Jeff into stealing tax records from a former accountant, Leonard Eels, who's going to squeal to the Feds. "You see, Jeff, you owe me something, and you'll never be happy until you square yourself." Jeff figures it for a frame-up: they'll ice Eels and frame him for the murder. So it goes. But Jeff stashes the dead body and starts playing all ends against the middle.

Unfortunately for Jeff, Whit's a step ahead. He made Kathie ink an affidavit fingering Jeff as Fisher's killer. Kathie begs Jeff to forgive her. "I've never stopped loving you. I was afraid and no good, but I've never stopped. Even if you hated me. Did you?" "Yeah." "But you don't now."

Jeff melts into her arms. Maybe. Or maybe he's planning to play *her* for a sucker this time. Jeff steals the briefcase with the incriminating ledgers from Sterling's San Francisco nightclub. As ransom, he demands the affidavit branding him Fisher's killer.

The double-dealing boils over back at the lakefront lodge. Jeff turns Whit against Kathie by blaming her for the death of Sterling's loyal right hand man, Stefanos. Says Whit to his cowering paramour: "You dirty little phony — go on and lie some more. Tell me how you handled things in San Francisco….What a sucker you must think I am. I took you back when you came whimpering and crawling. I should have kicked your teeth in." Whit's ready to hand her over for the Fisher hit, but he doesn't act fast enough.

When Jeff returns with Whit's ledgers, ransomed for fifty grand, the gangster's stone-cold on the floor. Icy Kathie has her bags packed to run away with Jeff. "You can't make deals with a dead man," she reminds him. Jeff lets her think he's back in her web, but tips the cops by phone. When Kathie sees the roadblock, and realizes Jeff has slipped from her clutches, she empties her compact .32 in his gut. A machine gun blast finishes off little Miss Moffett.

Out of the Past was the most spellbinding film yet to emerge from Dark City. It reconfigured genre clichés by investing them with depth and style. Mainwaring's serpentine story is all about mood and movement. It plays like a long, unhurried jazz riff, dreamily winding its way around various locations, shifting rhythms, seducing the audience toward the black hole at its heart. It nailed the bullseye, and its reverberations linger after repeated viewings: guilt, duplicity, self-deception, and the lonely seeker's need to push it to the bitter end, tempting fate once too often.

For its top two behind-the-camera creators, director Jacques Tourneur and director of photography Nicholas Musuraca, *Out of the Past* would be a career high point. Tourneur was so ideally suited to this material it's a crime he made only one other bona fide noir, *Nightfall* (Columbia, 1957). Born in Paris but raised in the states, Tourneur was the son of eminent French director Maurice Tourneur, who'd made hundreds of films in both his homeland and Hollywood. Jacques grew up on sound stages, and by the early Forties he was given the directorial helm by innovative RKO producer Val Lewton. The duo produced a remarkable series of visually-inspired, low-budget horror films: *Cat People* (1942), *I Walked with a Zombie* (1943), and *The Leopard Man* (1943). The jungle was a short drive from Dark City, and Tourneur could have excelled at crime dramas. Instead, he was assigned an amazing number of forgettable costume pictures, such as *Stars in My Crown*, *Anne of the Indies*, and *Way of the Gaucho*.

In *Out of the Past*, Tourneur's fluency with *mise en scène* was extraordinary. No film better realized the swirl of shifting locations that made pulp fiction so intoxicating. New York to Mexico to Frisco to Tahoe. Ritzy penthouse to smoky cantina to moonlit beach to opulent apartment to roadside filling station to swank nightclub to lakefront lodge. With each new scene we share the rush of excitement drawing Mitchum deeper into limbo.

Nick Musuraca, who had photographed what many consider the first pre-*Falcon* noir, *Stranger on the Third Floor* (RKO, 1940), paints light and shadow on these settings with the touch of a master. Rather than cast stark swatches of light and dark, a noir convention, he used a subtle fill light to reveal the detail of the sets, and then played dramatically with the key lights. Each scene is visually engrossing — and distinct from those that come before and follow. The full monochromatic palette is used by Musuraca to achieve the richest chiaroscuro cinematography of any noir.

The actors also showed up to play. Kirk Douglas was never better than when his brash hamminess was channeled into nasty noir villains, and the character of Whit Sterling filled the bill. He electrifies whenever he appears, a squirmy portrayal of a man too rich, too young, too ruthless. Jane Greer's flashing, cunning eyes betray a depthless venality not apparent in her slightly plump, puckish face. She vamps her way into the ranks of cinematic Circes, second to none. (Greer was tight with a pair of Dark City's favorite daughters, Gloria Grahame and Audrey Totter — imagine the slumber parties!)

Then there's Mitchum, the slow, rolling piano theme beneath Kirk's insistent bass and Jane's sexy saxophone. He hit the set with fresh wounds from his own real-life Dark City dealings. Bob's business manager and "best friend," Paul Behrmann, had siphoned Mitchum's bank account down to fifty-eight bucks, while doling out a $20 per week stipend to his pedigreed stakehorse. Mitchum, whose bravado masked a timid streak, didn't press charges. When Behrmann was nailed for more fiscal malfeasance, he tried to hang the rap on Mitchum. Eventually Mitchum needed therapy, and assertiveness training. That passive pose onscreen was no act.

To medicate his woes, the toad-eyed tough guy started firing up more reefers — as if he needed to get more languorous. After his bust for possession in 1948, it looked like *Out of the Past* would remain Mitchum's most memorable star turn. At the booking he gave his occupation as "former actor." But RKO stood behind him, mainly because it had three more of his films in the can. Mitchum's posture in jailhouse photos, swabbing down a cell-block, got him over. The public would love him like the black sheep of the family. In stir, Mitchum got an odd benediction: a visit from megamogul Howard Hughes. RKO's new owner took a shine to the fallen star. Hughes told him not to worry about his career, he'd always take care of him. Outside, reporters asked Mitchum what he'd thought of jail. "Just like Palm Springs — without the riff-raff," he cracked.

We'll revisit Mitchum, and give him his full due. For now, consider this exchange from *Out of the Past*: "Don't you see," Jane Greer tells Mitch after dispatching Kirk Douglas, "You'll only have me to make deals with now."

"Then build my gallows high, baby." Only Mitchum could toss off such a delirious and stilted line and make it as fluid as hard bop.

BY THE LATE FORTIES, the glorified gumshoe was weary to the bone. In Chandler's last two major novels, *The Little Sister* and *The Long Goodbye*, Marlowe was more likely to be bellyaching over a chilled gimlet than chasing down a hot lead. Chandler nosed around in the legit literary landscape he'd always wanted to explore, but he put the brakes to the velocity of his earlier work. The writing was magnificent in stretches, disjointed in spots. Chandler, like Marlowe, was struggling to keep it up.

Virginia Huston and Robert Mitchum in *Out of the Past*.

Hastening him to pasture was the success of Marlowe's evil twin and successor, Mike Hammer. As Chandler struggled to work without a net — forced to sift for original storylines once his lode of short stories was fully mined — author Mickey Spillane started churning out a series of detective novels that pushed Hard Boiled around the bend, toward Psychotic. The dilemma of the chivalrous hero acting honorably in a corrupt world was disassembled by Spillane: his Hammer was a righteous killing machine. If Mike felt you'd done him — or his country — wrong, he'd stomp a mudhole in your chest and walk it dry.

Young, Brooklyn-born Spillane wrote comic books, served in the Air Corps in WWII, and pumped out his first potboiler in 19 days. They came at a brisk clip after that, each successive fat advance making him the highest-paid author in the world.

The title of the first Hammer novel, *I, the Jury*, cut straight to the heart of the Spillane phenomenon. It was published in 1947, as the anti-commie crowd began fueling patriotic hysteria. Hammer rode the wave of reactionary fervor. It gave him free rein to pummel anyone who didn't conform to old-fashioned, conservative, berserk, misogynist, apple-pie values. A far cry from the apolitical knight errants of Hammett and Chandler, Hammer wallowed in half-baked ideology. "So I was a sucker for fighting a war," he bellows in *One Lonely Night*. "I was a sap for liking my country. I was a jerk for not thinking them [the Reds] a superior breed of lice!" Spillane was blocking out the cartoon outlines of a brand of sanitized fascism that would go mainstream with Barry Goldwater's Republican rallying cry: "Extremism in the defense of liberty is no vice."

Marlowe was a misfit; Hammer was a misanthrope. He hated everybody. As Spade slickly pitted his antagonists against each other, while Marlowe wearily prescribed himself another shot of wry, Hammer just waded in and busted heads. The violence is pure pornography. This dick rendered all kinds of perverse sexual thrills. To quote *My Gun Is Quick*: "I rolled on top of him and took that head like a sodden rag and smashed and smashed and smashed and there was no satisfying, solid thump, but a

sickening squashing sound that splashed all over me." The country went nuts over this elopement of sex and violence.

Dash and Ray had been doppelgangers of their detectives. So, it seemed was Mickey: a mercenary thug at the typewriter, pounding out prose the way Hammer pounded out Commie teeth. He sported a jarhead's flattop. His promo stills showed him smacking dames around. It was all a put-on, to be sure, but how could an audience hungry for this sex and blood smorgasbord be in on the joke? In sales, Spillane beat the pulp out of both Hammett and Chandler, selling by some estimates as many as 60,000,000 books by 1953. Teenage boys bought the latest 25-cent Signet edition thrill ride and tore out the pages as they went, lightening the load in their back pocket. Pages featuring rough sex were, of course, saved for later. Spillane was the czar of cheap, instant gratification.

The movies couldn't keep up. Producer Victor Saville tried to make a splash with a 3-D version of *I, The Jury* (UA, 1953), starring Biff Elliot and Peggie Castle. Hype of Hammer's misogyny was shameless. PR flacks quoted Elliot as saying that "Women readers go for Mike Hammer because they like the way he handles his girls. He'd as soon hit them as kiss them, and somehow that sort of treatment appeals to the latent atavism in women."

But the fireworks never ignited onscreen. There was simply no way Hollywood's production code would allow America's theater screens to be splashed with the bodily fluids Spillane enthusiasts craved.

It wasn't until 1955 that a memorable movie would be fashioned around America's favorite unglued gumshoe. *Kiss Me Deadly* (UA, 1955) held some surprises for diehard Hammer fans. Adapted by writer A. I. Bezzerides (*Thieves' Highway, On Dangerous Ground*) and director Robert Aldrich, the film simultaneously exploited and lampooned Spillane's casual sadism and breakneck momentum. As Hammer, Ralph Meeker shattered the fictional detective's code of honor as cavalierly as he snaps apart one informant's cherished recording of Caruso's *Pagliacci*. This Hammer is the most arrogant, vain, lazy dick ever.

Mr. Hammer's wild ride begins when he almost runs down a barefoot woman (Cloris Leachman) bolting in terror down a lonely highway. She's on the lam from the nuthouse, and begs Hammer to shepherd her to safety. He's ticked she almost wrecked his sporty MG, but gives her a ride anyway. Mystery men waylay them, and the woman is tortured to death in a roadside shack. Hammer, unconscious, is crammed in the car with her body. Then they're both sent over a cliff.

Once recovered, Hammer begrudgingly pursues the mystery of the dead woman. He'd rather be squeezing big fees from husbands and wives in ugly divorce cases, using his loyal aide Velda (Maxine Cooper) to set up philandering husbands while he handles the wives himself. Mike and his moll aren't truth-seekers; they're deceitful manipulators like all the other scumballs. But the dodge keeps Hammer outfitted with all the latest perks of free-thinking American manhood: fast cars, vintage booze, electronic gizmos. He's the kind of wild and crazy guy who dreams of strongarming an invite to the Playboy Mansion.

Hammer's not exactly a textbook investigator. He meanders around, indiscriminately intimidating people. His efforts spin threads of a plot, but he's too thick-skulled to stitch any of them together. The undercover operators tire of his bulldog tenacity and take several cracks at killing him. This makes Hammer madder, but no wiser. After they execute his mechanic — the essential person in his life — it becomes a vendetta. The convoluted trail leads to a locker at the Hollywood Athletic Club. Hammer scopes a strapped-up strongbox. Its seething contents burn his wrists.

Turns out it's a batch of raw nuclear material swiped from the Los Alamos Nuclear Test Site. That really makes Mike's head hurt.

None of this fall-out was sheltered in the novel. Spillane's original climaxes, like most, with a jolting juxtaposition of lust and death. Sexpot Lily Carver emerges as the villain, and as she pumps a couple of .45 slugs into Hammer she tantalizingly doffs her robe to reveal that *There was no skin, just a disgusting mass of twisted, puckered flesh from her knees to her neck making a picture of gruesome freakishness that made you want to shut your eyes against it.* Hammer lights up a Lucky to soothe his nerves, then zaps Lily with his Zippo, igniting her. Did we forget to mention that she'd "brought the sharpness of an alcohol bath in with her, so that it wet her robe..."?

Bezzerides coaxes this crazy climax to apocalyptic heights. Lily (Gaby Rogers), an unscarred, pixieish Pandora, can't resist a peek inside the strongbox that everyone's died to get their hands on. Hissing like a harbinger of Hell, the incendiary contents swallow her whole. Hammer tries to pull the kidnapped Velda to safety as Lily flares up like the Human Torch. Then everything blows sky-high. THE END zooms out of the firestorm. Many viewers interpreted it literally, nuclear annihilation being the core of the Cold War paranoia that defined the mid-Fifties.

For years, critics have troweled endless symbolism onto *Kiss Me Deadly*, finding hidden meaning in character names, checkerboard floor tiles, veiled allusions to Greek myths, even in Nick the mechanic's *Va-Va-Voom* tagline. That's a lot of extra baggage for Hammer to stuff into

In Aldrich's version of *Kiss Me Deadly*, Hammer and Velda (Maxine Cooper) scramble from the exploding beach house and into the uncertain sanctuary of the surf. The studio's inexplicable decision to lop off these shots enhanced the film's nihilism, helping make it a later critical favorite.

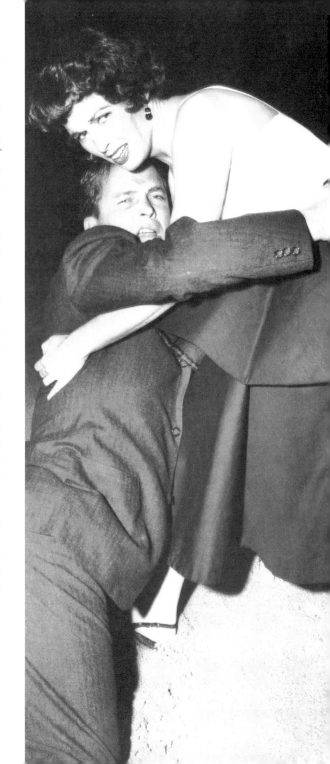

the boot of his tiny roadster. No such acclaim attached itself to Aldrich's *Attack!*, a better film made the following year, and a darker vision of the human battlefield. But through the magic of critical hindsight, this swaggering, brass-knuckled lark has been hoisted into the pantheon of "meaningful" movies. What it really deserves is a place on any double bill with *Dr. Strangelove*: a pair of mordant black comedies about dangerous demagogues in places high and low.

FEDORAS WERE OUT BY THE EARLY SIXTIES; the fresh hero sported a crop of thick hair, à la Jack Kennedy. Even the President was a fan of the new macho icon, Ian Fleming's James Bond. Once America became obsessed with the space race, and the Cold War's flashy technologies, the rumpled shamus was trampled in the stampede of Matt Helms, Derek Flints, men from U. N. C. L. E. — suave playboys out to save their cool Op-Art world from tractor beams and death rays. It wasn't until 1974 that an old-style detective returned to Dark City, following in the gummed shoes of Sam Spade and Philip Marlowe.

Chinatown (Paramount) finally made good on the cinematic promise in the work of Dashiell Hammett and, especially, Raymond Chandler. But it was no mere homage. It insidiously extended their bleak vision. Woven into its sinuous plot is a bitter rumination on how human progress works, how the rapaciousness that drives a father to corrupt his daughter is also what erects majestic cities in the desert.

Screenwriter Robert Towne had spent two years trying to fashion a narrative that interbred a detective story about cloistered family secrets with a sprawling fact-based history of the Owens Valley water scam that was central to the development of Los Angeles. His inspiration was pure noir. An L.A. vice cop who'd worked Chinatown told the writer, "You don't know who's a crook and who isn't a crook. So in Chinatown they say, 'Just don't do a goddamned thing.'"

The resulting 180-page script was ambitious and unwieldy, but producer Robert Evans sensed a hit beneath the surface of the tangled narrative. He was eager to deliver another huge success like *The Godfather*, without having to share credit with a bunch of co-producers. Evans's smartest move was hiring director Roman Polanski, whose personal familiarity with lurking evil would bring black depths to a project most participants considered a pleasant dip in the Hollywood nostalgia pool. Polanski and Towne collaborated for a combative two months, emerging with a shooting script that charted a brilliant course toward an uncertain destination – the two men couldn't agree on the ending. Filming commenced nonetheless.

The production of *Chinatown* was alchemy. Running feuds and temper tantrums tested each participant's mettle, but everyone produced gold. Cinematographer John Alonzo and production designer Richard Sylbert perfectly conjured the spoiled hope of Chandler's L.A., avoiding the curse of florid retro nostalgia. Polanski's supple direction evoked the first-person spirit of Chandler's writing without resorting to showy gimmickry.

Jake Gittes (Jack Nicholson) tries to shake some sense out of the mystery of Evelyn Mulwray (Faye Dunaway) in *Chinatown*.

J. J. Gittes (Jack Nicholson) is a fastidious little P. I. who manages to keep his natty suits cleaned and pressed while rummaging through his clients' dirty laundry. A former cop, he gloats about escaping the beat, and basks in the reflective glow of glittery Hollywood, where he never runs out of divorce cases. But then he's played as a pawn in a plot to discredit Hollis Mulwray, an official in the Department of Water and Power who's blocking a massive dam project crucial to the city's growth. Gittes thinks he's handling just another simple, sordid case of adultery. But as he wades deeper into the lives of Mulwray and his mysterious wife, Evelyn (Faye Dunaway), he uncovers a flood of conspiracies, personal and political. At the mouth of the polluted stream lies civic powerbroker Noah Cross (John Huston, whose presence fuses the noir circuit). Gittes realizes that solving the case means laying bare the ugly truth about one of the city's most powerful and respected founding fathers. The amoral Cross has raped more than just a bunch of Okie orange growers; for decades he's committed crimes of both power and passion.

"Most people never have to face the fact," says Cross, "that at the right time, in the right place, a man is capable of just about *anything*." (Engrave that in a plaque outside the Dark City Hall of Justice.) Gittes struggles to untangle the web of corruption Cross has woven across the arid basin, gamely trying to prove that a couple of little flies can somehow survive in a world of heartless predators.

Nicholson's performance is crafty and deep. He displays subtle allusions to noir avatars: a bit of Bogart's sass-mouth delivery and flourish with a cigarette, traces of Mitchum's flirtatious insolence, a lot of Alan Ladd's over-compensating sartorial splendor — references that help paint a melancholy portrait of a guy propping up his low-rent reality with crutches of wish-fulfillment.

Like the Hollywood hero he wants to be, Gittes falls for Evelyn, the dangerous, damaged femme fatale, and risks all in an attempt to save her. In Towne's original script, Evelyn exacts her revenge, shooting her incestuous father to death in a symbolic rainstorm that ends L.A.'s drought. She and Gittes cling to each other in a rousing, old-fashioned fade-out. Evans and Towne could hear the audience's appreciative applause for such a richly evocative piece of pure entertainment. A throwback to the classics. But this was to be Roman Polanksi's film. Few filmmakers are as darkly cynical as Polanski. Fewer still have earned the attitude as painfully.

Roman Polanski teaches Gittes what happens to nosy fellas. "Next time I cut off the whole thing and feed it to my goldfish. Understand?"

The ending was one of the last things filmed, and Polanski wrote the finale the night before it was shot. All the main characters converge on a Chinatown street. Gittes believes he can pull off a masterful parlay: sneak Evelyn and her daughter Katherine off to Ensenada, while handing over the murderous Noah Cross to the cops. But everything goes horribly wrong. The police arrest Gittes instead. The distraught Evelyn tries to flee. A trigger-happy flatfoot squeezes off a lucky shot. Dark City holds its collective breath as the horn on that luxurious Packard convertible starts wailing. A crowd gathers around the car. Evelyn slumps from the driver's seat, shot through the head. Katherine screams uncontrollably, unable to look away from her dead mother. Cross wraps a massive paw across her eyes; she's now in the clutches of the monster who spawned her. Gittes stares slack-jawed, engulfed by futility.

Towne hated Polanski's ending. He called it "The tunnel at the end of the light." Polanski responded: "I thought it was a serious movie, not an adventure story for the kids." Polanski was right. The final version of this great film belongs to a man who survived a childhood of punishment by Nazis in a Warsaw ghetto, and used artistic ambition and talent to work his way from Poland to the sunny splendor of Hollywood – only to have his beloved wife and friends randomly slaughtered by the Manson family. It's Polanski's scarred vision that transforms *Chinatown* from a beautifully crafted, diverting piece of detective fiction into the ultimate film noir.

Vixenville

Don't bother looking for a church in this part of town. The air's too hot and heavy for hymns. Not that you can't find houses of worship. Check out the windows, flickering in the night like offertory candles. Within the rooms are supplicatory men, on their knees, praying for a different kind of salvation. They bring to the altars gifts of fragrances and lace, hoping they'll be judged worthy. Most will end up crucified, for believing that holiness comes wrapped in seamed silk, redemption stretched sheer around a shapely calf.

Welcome to the spiritual center of our lovely community. Home to hundreds of luminescent, enigmatic goddesses. A while back some concerned citizens tried to quarantine this section of the city, claiming that what went on here was a degrading, immoral spectacle. Tales emanating from these parts, they charged, were insulting to the fairer sex, making all females seem manipulative, cold-hearted, and evil. Not all, exactly. Just the interesting ones.

These nay-sayers believe that just because women are created as nurturers, responsible for the propagation and care of the species, they aren't capable of the same violent behavior as men. Tell it to the victims of Livia, Augustus Caesar's scheming wife. She bumped off scores of friends and countrymen tightening her hold over ancient Rome, the original Dark City. Most power-mad women are smart enough not to bloody their own hands. That's what men are for.

"Women encourage killers," says scientist and philosopher Howard Bloom, in *The Lucifer Principle*. "They do it by falling in love with warriors and heroes. Men know it and respond with enthusiasm. The Crusaders marched off to war with ladies' favors in their helmets…. The heroes sliced up adults and baked infants on spits, all the while thinking of how the damsels back home would admire their bravery."

In every species in the animal kingdom, Bloom argues, females develop a craving for a certain kind of guy, and all the males compete to live up to that feminine ideal. "And what have human females gone for in nearly every society and time? 'Courage' and 'bravery.' In short, violence."

In a civilized society women want a man who provides security. But who's talking about a civilized society? The Second World War had just left millions of young soldiers shaken by the extremity of human savagery.

A face to die for:
noir glamour-puss
Lizabeth Scott.

They'd seen grunts in the trench with them, who'd said their prayers every night, take a round flush in the face. Back home they peered in the windows of restaurants they couldn't afford, to see councilmen and criminals ordering off the same menu. These men needed something to believe in, something more immediately attainable than the everlasting Kingdom of Heaven. They found it, or so they thought, in the glorious peaks and valleys of Vixenville.

This is no place to raise a family – although you'll find plenty of fathers across town from Hate Street, blowing the kids' college tuition on diamond earrings and champagne cocktails, searching for the Holy Grail. Some of the women here started out as gawky kids in Hoboken, but they've learned that a little rouge and a lot of attitude can make a deity of a simple dame. And what they're offering these men isn't strait-laced, soldier-for-the-church sex. It's a chance at transcendence.

"In the beginning was desire, which was the primal germ of the mind." That's how the story of creation is told by one Veda. Not Mildred Pierce's provocative daughter, but one of the sacred Hindu scriptures, dating back to the second millennium, B. C. What guys were pursuing through these penthouses and ginmills was apparently akin to tantric sex, as Nigel Davies describes it in *The Rampant God: Eros Throughout the World*: "The sex act, no longer a mere means of procreation, is a beacon pointing the way to salvation; according to this comforting doctrine, heaven was the reward, not for abstinence, but for indulgence. Only by copulation can a man attain true knowledge of the One, the Brahma."

To many, that's a lot of bull. But to Hindus sex has always been sacred, one root of spiritual belief. "Her lap is a sacrificial altar; her skin a soma press; the two lips of the vulva are the fire in the middle," says a later Hindi scripture, an Upanishad, from around 500 B. C.

A lot of men felt the same way around Dark City, 1946.

The erotic heart of film noir: The sensuous Stella (Linda Darnell), by simply opening a door, can drive men to murder in *Fallen Angel* (20th, 1945). Darnell herself was the perfect example of a young woman, pushed by her mother, who was chosen by the priests of her tribe to serve as exalted movie star. She married, at 21, the man who shot her screen test. The union eventually fell apart, and Darnell struggled, at times staggered, to maintain her image as a two-dimensional goddess. She was infertile, and unable to sustain any long-term relationships. She pondered suicide. Before she turned 40, her reign as a deity was over. After watching one of her old films while visiting friends in Chicago, Darnell fell asleep while smoking. A fire raged through the house, burning her to death. She was 43. "My problems were not those of my real self," she once said, "but a sort of synthetic, unreal self known as Linda Darnell."

The troubles start when these fervent beliefs collide headlong with a culture of deep-seated, puritanical thought. In the tales that have become legend in Vixenville, men and women break out of the molds cast for them in the rigid spiritual and social structures of the ruling patriarchy. Sexuality, positive and negative, surges — as if from severed, snaking electrical cables. The powerful blue arc fuses recklessly. The sparks rain. Somebody has to get burned.

The desperate man finds out that his savior is just a cunning little chippie trying to carve out sanctuary using the only tools she has. The woman snaps when she realizes she isn't cut out for this savior business. Bad things happen. As any holy man will tell you, being the object of so much spiritual neediness can leave you high and dry.

Stella (Linda Darnell), a gorgeous hash slinger who worked in a crummy café in a little town off the highway, knew all about that. A series of men thought of her as a *Fallen Angel* (20th, 1945). One of them, a transient grifter named Eric Stanton (Dana Andrews), concocted a cruel plot to win her love. Since Stella was only interested in men who could pay her way out of this jerkwater, Stanton courted the monied but mundane June Mills (Alice Faye). After he'd tapped into her family fortune, he planned to drop June and run away with Stella. But Stella ended up murdered. There was no shortage of suspects: they worshipped daily at her formica altar, sipping coffee and dreaming of how they might sample the delights within that snug uniform. Stella was just one of many women in Dark City sacrificed on the slab of a man's thwarted desire.

But women weren't always the victims. Although the times dictated fables in which the renegade double-X chromosome must be vanquished before the fade-out, film noir allowed women to savor for themselves the pungent, acrid nectar of unleashed power and violence. "A dame with a rod is like a guy with a knitting needle," cracks Jack Fisher (Steve Brodie) in *Out of the Past*. Of course, that's before Fisher gets an extra orifice blown open compliments of Kathie Moffett (Jane Greer), one of Vixenville's empresses. There's no greater kick in this town than when a woman finally wraps her delicate fingers around the trigger of a .38 Linga and blasts away every bit of genetic encoding and cultural repression in a roaring fusillade of little lead forget-me-nots.

The last passage from the labyrinth is always guarded by a woman. Sometimes it's the spirituality of Beatrice, other times it's the sorcery of Circe. Here, it's the dangerous duplicity of Elsa Bannister (Rita Hayworth), in *The Lady From Shanghai*, Orson Welles's delirious, home-movie pipedream of his marriage to, and murder of, the Forties' greatest sex symbol.

IN AN OPULENT FOURTH-FLOOR APARTMENT, at a swank East Side address, lives Laura Hunt. She's at the heart of the most famous murder story ever told in this neighborhood. *Laura* (20th, 1944) isn't a schemer or a calculating bitch, just a beautiful, naive innocent whose only crime was her determination to live by her own free will. But her "authentic magnetism" inspires a devotion in others that leads to obsession and murder.

When Laura (Gene Tierney) is found dead in the entryway of her apartment, her face obliterated by a shotgun blast, Detective Mark McPherson (Dana Andrews) is assigned the case. He encounters upper-crust suspects a world apart from the usual street rabble. There's fey columnist Waldo Lydecker (Clifton Webb), who runs Wilde: "In my case self-absorption is completely justified. I have never found any other subject quite so worthy of my attention." There's also Southern playboy Shelby Carpenter (Vincent Price), and jealous society woman Ann Treadwell (Judith Anderson). Even Laura's servant, Bessie (Dorothy Adams), seems unnaturally devoted to the young beauty.

McPherson's in no hurry to solve the crime. In fact, the various probes conjure in him a bewitching vision of this dead enchantress. He secretly makes arrangements to buy the portrait of Laura that hangs above her mantle. "You better watch out, McPherson, or you'll end up in a psychiatric ward," chides Lydecker. "I don't think they've ever had a patient who fell in love with a corpse."

But when Laura walks back into her apartment — still alive and none the worse for wear — McPherson is spurred to action. Not only does he have to uncover the identity of the faceless corpse, he has to compete for Laura's affections in a league where he's way out of his depth. In a battle of wits with Waldo, McPherson's unarmed.

When it seems Laura is about to reunite with the shady Shelby, McPherson makes her the prime suspect in the case – so he can possess her at his whim. His fixation turns infatuation to interrogation. The victim, it turns out, was Diane Redfern, a model having a fling with footloose Shelby. It was Waldo — who credited himself for the Pygmalion-like creation of the delectable Laura — who mistakenly shotgunned the unfortunate Diane in a jealous, and nearsighted, rage. He attempts to kill Laura again, this time as the front end of a murder-suicide, but McPherson's men gun him down. "Goodbye, Laura... my love," he wheezes out with appropriate theatrical flourish.

The very much alive Laura Hunt (Gene Tierney) ends up competing with her own dreamy image in the mind of Mark McPherson (Dana Andrews) the detective assigned to investigate her "death."

Although it's little more than a succession of dialogue scenes, *Laura* mesmerizes audiences, due in no small measure to a quick-witted script and the strange erotic tension pulsing beneath the film's high-gloss surfaces. Sexual drives may be strong, but the orientations are ambiguous. Waldo appears decidedly gay, and even Shelby's manner seems lavender-tinged. Lydecker's love of Laura is non-sexual, but there's a spark of something physical in the way he sizes up McPherson. Most of the film's messages were couched in telling sidelong glances. The interplay between the droll columnist and the taciturn cop is legendary. "Have you ever been in love, detective?" Lydecker asks. "A dame in Washington Heights once got a fox fur out of me," offers McPherson.

Producer-director Otto Preminger must have gotten a good laugh out of his film's eventual status as a classic. Darryl Zanuck, head of 20th Century-Fox, despised Preminger, and swore that, though under contract, he'd never direct at 20th. Zanuck at last allowed Otto to produce, on a short leash, this B-plus quickie, adapted from a lugubrious Vera Caspary novel. Three writers labored over the script, which everyone but Otto hated. Zanuck hired Rouben Mamoulian to direct, and fought Preminger's desire to cast relative unknowns Dana Andrews and Clifton Webb. (Zanuck wanted John Hodiak and Laird Cregar, with Jennifer Jones as Laura.)

Early rushes stank, so Zanuck buried the hatchet (in Mamoulian), passing the directorial reins to Otto. Aided by brilliant cinematographer Joseph LaShelle, who'd win an Oscar for his work, Preminger painstakingly crafted what he was sure would be his breakthrough film. An advance screening was held for Zanuck and his corps of yes-men. They all hated it. Too confusing, they said. Zanuck demanded that a new ending be filmed, to his specs. Preminger, not yet the tyrant he'd become, consented. Weeks later, another studio preview. All assembled panned it anew – except a visitor in the back row. Walter Winchell, the most powerful newspaper columnist and radio broadcaster in the nation, raved to Zanuck. "Darryl, that was big time — big time — great, great, great! But are you going to change the ending? What's happening at the end? I don't understand." Zanuck let Preminger restore his finale. Another classic had managed to steal away from the Dream Factory. The film's 88 minutes of elegant moodiness still beguile viewers.

Laura cast a spell on its players, as well. Clifton Webb would for the rest of his career play some variation of Waldo Lydecker, most famously the cantankerous *Mr. Belvedere* of the 1950s film series. Dana Andrews's acting style would become so tightly wound that only a steady infusion of Scotch could loosen his screws. By the time he filmed *While the City Sleeps*, in 1956, he was regularly gassed onscreen. But it was Gene Tierney who would be most haunted by Laura's theme.

A Brooklyn debutante who came west to fashion a career from her extraordinary face, Tierney lived a life that, short of the shotgun blast, was as compelling as Laura's. She was romantically pursued by two of America's leading men, Howard Hughes and John F. Kennedy (but then, who wasn't?). Aly Khan, son of Pakistani spiritual leader Aga Khan, would eventually prefer Tierney's beauty to that of his wife, Rita Hayworth. Men were more captivated by what Tierney's ravishing looks did for them, than by genuine love.

Love is strange: Detective Mark McPherson (Dana Andrews) dreams of loving a dead woman, fetishizing her portrait. High-brow columnist Waldo Lydecker (Clifton Webb) isn't too snooty to receive the handsome cop while bathing. With *Laura*, Otto Preminger fashioned a popular entertainment rich in subtle deviance.

Tierney shocked her family by eloping with continental couturier Oleg Cassini – Waldo Lydecker's real-world twin. The ferret-faced Cassini was of White Russian heritage, and wielded a rapier wit worthy of Waldo. When Louella Parsons disdainfully suggested that his only source of attraction to women must have been his rakish moustache, Cassini fired back: "Okay Louella, you win. I'll shave off mine, if you'll shave off yours."

Like Waldo, Oleg treated Tierney as his great creation, applying a lacquer of worldly sophistication and dressing her in Hollywood's most magnificent fashions. Unlike that of Waldo and Laura, the relationship was not platonic. In 1943, the couple had a child, born drastically premature. Weighing only two and a half pounds, the baby, Daria, needed eleven blood transfusions, but miraculously survived.

The complications were due to Tierney's contraction of rubella early in the pregnancy. Daria turned out to be brain damaged; in a decision that would forever prey on her conscience, Tierney had her daughter institutionalized for the rest of her life.

A year after Daria's birth, a woman introduced herelf to Tierney at a party, claiming they had met before, when Tierney was doing her bit for the war effort by gladhanding with the troops. "Did you happen to catch the German measles after that night?" the woman asked, smiling. "The whole camp was down with the German measles. I broke quarantine to come to the Canteen and meet the stars. Everyone told me I shouldn't go, but I just had to go. You were my favorite."

IN THE WAKE OF *LAURA*, at the height of her popularity, Gene Tierney would score her critical triumph, playing the most deranged femme fatale ever. In *Leave Her to Heaven* (20th, 1945), based on a soapy bestseller by Ben Ames Williams, she was Ellen Berent, a Technicolor princess with

"You're not making very much progress, Danny." Ellen Berent (Gene Tierney) orchestrates the demise of any rival for her husband's affection, including the drowning of his brother (Darryl Hickman), in *Leave Her to Heaven. Opposite:* Ellen later aborts her unborn child by falling down the stairs to induce a miscarriage.

pathological jealousy lurking behind her luminous green eyes. Ellen is the flower of her wealthy clan. But she's never been quite right since her beloved father died, and in their concern for protecting her fragile beauty, the family is blind to the damage hidden inside her. "There's nothing wrong with Ellen," says her mother. "She just loves too much."

Ellen captivates and weds a novelist, Richard Harland (Cornel Wilde), who shrugs off his resemblance to Ellen's late father. It should have been a big hint. Richard squires her to his magnificent woodsy retreat in Maine. She promptly dismisses the caretaker. Ellen doesn't believe in sharing her paradise with anybody. This leads to two of the most notorious — and memorable — scenes in all noir. First, she decides that her husband's crippled younger brother, Danny (Darryl Hickman) is too much of a rival for Richard's attention. When Danny eagerly tries to impress Ellen with how well he's learned to swim, she turns his pubescent vanity against him, enticing him beyond his limits. As he sinks below the lake's surface, struggling for his life, Ellen watches implacably from behind her fashionable sunglasses.

Later, when she fears that the child she's carrying will purloin her husband's affection, she stages an "accidental" tumble down a flight of stairs, killing the unborn baby. When Ellen's husband gets too friendly with her sister, Ruth (Jeanne Crain), she delivers the coup de grace: she poisons herself, arranging it to implicate her two-timing husband and sister as her murderers. There was no precedent for the morbidity of these scenes, somehow made all the more malignant by the overripe lushness of Leon Shamroy's cinematography.

"As much as any part I played," Tierney said in her memoirs, "Ellen has meaning for me as a woman. ... She believed herself to be normal and worked at convincing her friends she was. Most emotionally disturbed people go through such a stage, the equivalent of an alcoholic hiding the bottle." Tierney's real life would outstrip her Oscar-nominated performance. Starting in the mid-Fifties, she suffered a series of mental breakdowns, convinced — among an avalanche of delusions — that every book, everywhere, was filled with cataclysmic Communist ravings. Twice she was escorted, in a very déclassé straitjacket, from her posh Sutton Place apartment and taken to the soft rooms of the Menninger Clinic in Topeka, Kansas. There, Hollywood's greatest beauty was strapped to a gurney and bound in ice-cold wet sheets, an Ike-era attempt at shock therapy. On the outside, she pondered a suicidal leap from her 57th Street window. Only her vanity cut through the haze in her brain. "If I was going to die," she'd write later, "I wanted to be in one piece, a whole person, and look pretty in my coffin."

Tierney's saga ended triumphantly, however. Released from Menninger's in 1959, she took a steady job as a clerk in a Topeka dressmaking shop. Throughout her recovery she was gently courted by, and eventually wed to, Texas oil millionaire Howard Lee, an ex-husband of actress Hedy Lamarr.

Gene Tierney never returned to Dark City.

SEE THAT OLD FELLA OVER THERE, shuffling through the park? He's the saddest character who ever got lost on this side of town. Name's Christopher Cross, and you'd never know it to look at him, but he once was a solid, respectable citizen. Worked as a cashier for as long as anyone could remember, punched in and out at the same time every day. His wife, Adele, was pure misery. Chris always came up short when she compared him to her late, heroic husband, a cop who drowned in a rescue attempt. But Chris could tolerate her indignities; his Sunday hobby, oil painting, was all the distraction he seemed to need.

But then one night, feeling blue after a testimonial dinner at which his 25 years of servitude earned him only a lousy watch, Chris (Edward G. Robinson) strays onto *Scarlet Street* (Universal, 1945). He comes across a man and woman, fighting. With a lucky swat of his umbrella, Chris is able to fend off the attacker. It earns him a drink with the woman, Katherine "Kitty" March (Joan Bennett). From Jump Street she takes him for a gullible boob. He thinks she's an actress, still dressed up from a show, walking home late. She laughs, and deals him a fresh hand: "I'll bet you're an artist!" He decides to play those cards, becoming, for this gorgeous woman only, the man he's always wanted to be. Tumescence makes him oblivious to the dismissive twinkle in Kitty's eyes.

What the poor sap doesn't know is that Kitty's sparring partner was her pimp, Johnny (Dan Duryea). When Johnny learns the daffy geezer has fallen for his punch, he encourages Kitty to nuzzle up to the old guy, then fleece him

Scarlet woman: As the languorous Kitty "Lazy Legs" March in *Scarlet Street*, Joan Bennett displayed as much raw sexuality as Hollywood's Production Code would allow.

for all he's worth. Chris rents Kitty a spacious playpen, where he comes each Sunday to paint, her presence rekindling his ardor for life, love, and art. When he leaves, Johnny shows up at the all-expenses-paid roost, where he debauches "Lazy Legs," the goddess Chris worships.

Prowling for more pocket money, Johnny unloads one of Chris's paintings. It starts a buzz on the street. Ever the operator, Johnny convinces Kitty to sign her name to the canvases, which he sells to a pretentious uptown gallery. Katherine March is lauded as the art world's latest discovery. Even this doesn't faze Chris. He's a happy acolyte, content to serve his priestess. She particularly appreciates his delicate brushwork on her manicured toenails. ("They'll be masterpieces," she purrs, looking down on him.) But soon she's demanding greater offerings, and Chris must embezzle to keep her — and, by extension, Johnny — satisfied.

Chris's fortunes take another tumble when his wife's first husband turns up alive. He tries to blackmail Chris, thinking he'll pay anything to preserve the marriage. Instead, Chris sets him up to reunite with Adele, happily breaking his uxorial bonds. He runs to Kitty with the good news. That's when he discovers her in another man's arms: "Oh, Johnny! Oh, Johnny!" Chris slinks back later, fortified by several fingers of Old Crow, and forgives Kitty her betrayal. Johnny must have forced himself on her, he reasons. Now that he's free, Chris exclaims, they can be married. Kitty buries her head in her pillow, shaking. "I know how you feel, but that's all over now," Chris consoles. "Please don't cry."

Kitty looks up, laughing uproariously. "How can a man be so dumb.... I've been wanting to laugh in your face ever since I met you. You're old and ugly and I'm sick of you!" Chris picks up a discarded icepick and punctures Kitty over and over, through the satin bedcovers.

It's Johnny who's arrested for the murder, tried, and convicted. He insists Chris Cross murdered the renowned painter Katherine March, but who takes the word of a pimp against a respectable citizen? Chris rides the train up to Sing Sing with a pack of journalists to witness the execution. "Nobody gets away with murder," says one of them. "No one escapes punishment."

Chris ends up in a Bowery flop, tortured by voices in his head. Not the judge, pronouncing a death sentence on an innocent man. No, he only hears Kitty, endlessly exulting "Johnny, I love you, Johnny!" He tries to hang himself, to no avail. So he wanders the streets alone. He begs every cop to arrest him and strap him in the electric chair – just make the voice stop. The cops smile, prop him up, and send him on his way.

The few authenticated Katherine March canvases hang in the homes of only the most wealthy and powerful people in Dark City, having skyrocketed in value after her murder.

Scarlet Street, the darkest tale of sexual desire to emerge from Vixenville, was based on *La Chienne — The Bitch* — the 1931 Jean Renoir film adapted from Georges de la Fouchardière's novel. Its immediate antecedent was *The Blue Angel*, in which the slavishly infatuated Emil Jannings humiliates himself for the woman of his desires, Marlene Dietrich. *La Chienne* was originally purchased by Paramount, with the expectation that Ernst Lubitsch would create an Americanized version. By that time, Hollywood had implemented its rigid Production Code, and Lubitsch felt the material would never translate in a watered-down rendition. It remained untouched until Fritz Lang resurrected it as the first project to be made under the independent banner of Diana Productions. The company was formed by Lang, producer Walter Wanger, and actress Joan Bennett (Wanger's wife; the company was named for her daughter). Screenwriter Dudley Nichols was also a boardmember.

Upon its release, *Scarlet Street* reaped more controversy than praise. It was one of the first Hollywood films since the imposition of the Production Code in which a guilty killer went free, while an innocent man was executed. It could have been that by 1945, Hollywood was no longer as eager to insult the intelligence of its customers, figuring they could handle an adult story that concluded, not with the loose ends tidily tied, but with a rope cinched around the audience's neck. Or just chalk it up to Dan Duryea's detestable sleaziness: Everybody wanted him dead. Some markets objected to the number of times Chris stabbed Kitty with the icepick; some prints have seven, some four, others just one.

Most critics considered *Scarlet Street* almost identical to Lang's *The Woman in the Window* (RKO, 1944), released the previous year. Both feature the same three main players, and concern meek individuals smitten by beautiful connivers. In the earlier film, Robinson plays a professor who meets a fabulous femme (Bennett), accepts her offer of a nightcap, and ends up putting the shears to her

Chris (Edward G. Robinson) is in Kitty's thrall, but Kitty belongs to Johnny (Dan Duryea). It's sick, but stable. Until Chris is convinced that he, not Johnny, is the man she needs. *Scarlet Street* went beyond *The Woman in the Window* to show the tragic consequences of its sexually-charged roundelay.

brutish boyfriend when he barges in on them. They dispose of the body, but it's discovered by the police. The noose tightens further when the dead man's bodyguard (Duryea), who knows the truth, blackmails them. Robinson sees no way out, and mixes himself a poison cocktail. But Duryea dies in a gun battle with the cops, and they conveniently pin his boss's murder on him. Bennett calls to tell Robinson they're in the clear. The camera pulls back to reveal him slumped in his chair, apparently dead. But then he bolts up — it's all been a dream. Audiences loved the film; many critics slammed the unreal ending.

Lang felt the two films were thematically distinct. *The Woman in the Window* was a cautionary tale of how a person "must always be on guard." He believed that a "logical" ending to the film, in which a man's life is destroyed by a brief flirtation, would have been too "defeatist." Victimized merely by coincidence, Robinson's punishment would have outweighed his crime. But Chris Cross was different: he willfully pursued his misery, begging to be hurt.

Starting with *Scarlet Street*, Lang claimed that all his films "wanted to show that the average citizen is not very much better than a criminal." We must always be on guard from ourselves, and our deepest desires. Lang's early films displayed a dark fascination with the vagaries of fate. After *Scarlet Street*, that changed. In 1974, accepting a tribute, he declared, "I don't believe in fate anymore. Everyone makes fate for himself. You can accept it, you can reject it and go on. There is no mysterious something, no God who puts fate in you. It is you who must make fate yourself."

"YOU'RE A LITTLE MAN WITH A BRIEFCASE," says beautiful Mona Stevens (Lizabeth Scott). "You go to work every morning and you do as you're told. Today they told you to go to such and such an address and pick up some stolen goods. So here you are. Tonight, when you're sitting around with the boys, you'll say 'You shoulda seen the babe I ran into today. Not bad. But you know me — strictly business when I'm on the job.'"

"Is that the way I impress you?" counters insurance agent John Forbes (Dick Powell). Mona: "That's the way."

Johnny: "How *should* I be?"

"If you were a nice guy, you'd cry a little bit with me, and feel sorry for a girl whose first engagement ring was given to her by a man stupid enough to embezzle, and stupid enough to get caught."

Before you know it, it's three o'clock in the afternoon, and Mona's sobbing into Johnny's gin at a dimly-lit cocktail lounge. Any other day, Forbes would be found dutifully filing claim reports. But today, his by-the-book life has encountered a major *Pitfall* (UA, 1948). He's supposed to confiscate for Olympic Mutual Insurance all the gifts showered upon Mona by her lover, Bill Smiley. Just like Chris Cross, Smiley swiped company funds to pay for his costly tokens of devotion. But Smiley got pinched, and must stew for a year, wondering if Mona will wait for him.

To her credit, Mona fesses up about the motorboat Smiley gave her. She even takes Johnny for a ride. The dizzying skips over the waves, the sea spray, the closeness of this saucy gamine — Forbes's buttoned-down facade of fidelity starts to dissolve. Mona doesn't have to beg to have the boat left off his report. Johnny wants some more. He wants to tempt his fate.

Forbes has a problem bigger than his guilty conscience. Mack MacDonald (Raymond Burr), the freelance P. I. he hired to find Mona, is also obsessed with her. MacDonald's a trifle unstable. Shadowing Mona has stoked his psychosis. When he spies Forbes leaving her house after office hours, he goes over the edge. He tries to sandbag Forbes, threatening to reveal his deletion of the boat from the recovery report. That fails, so he treats Forbes to a savage beating.

Once Mona learns Johnny is married, she drops the femme fatale act: "Aren't you a little relieved to get out of it this easily? This is a set-up. This is the kind of girl you always dreamed about, and I'm going to let you off without an angle. I could be nasty, but I'm not going to be." Forbes takes the hint. Although he lives only a hedge or two from Hate Street, he doesn't want to move there.

MacDonald now sees a clear field. He hounds Mona, driving her nuts. She cracks and asks Forbes for help. To regain his pride, Forbes gives MacDonald a payback pummeling, returning to the wife and kid a stronger, happier man. But MacDonald plots revenge. He visits Bill Smiley in jail, who's only a month away from parole, and tells him Forbes is moving in on Mona. Jealousy festers. When Smiley's released, MacDonald goes so far as to drive him to Forbes's house and slap a pistol in his paw. Warned by Mona, Forbes is ready. He kills Smiley when he tries to break in. The police, seeing no connection between the two men, treat Smiley as a plugged prowler.

Forbes can't tell the truth about the dead man; it would give him a motive for the killing. Having orchestrated the demise of both his rivals, Mack pounces on Mona. "People are born to have certain things," he smugly tells her, as he forces her to pack up for a Reno wedding. "Smiley didn't have the nerve, Forbes didn't have the chance – so it's me you end up with." He caresses her stilettos as he lays them in a suitcase. "The only reason I did all this is because I really love you." Mona breaks off the elopement with two love notes from a snub-nosed .38 – another undocumented gift from the late Bill Smiley.

Unable to lie any longer, Forbes confesses the truth. The ending jerks no tears. Forbes's masters — the law and his wife — muscle his libido into place and send him back to his cubicle. "If a man has always been a good husband, except for twenty-four hours," says his wife, Sue (Jane Wyatt), "How long should he be expected to pay?" Forbes isn't saddled with Chris Cross's living-death sentence, just a few months of chastened melancholy.

Mona, on the other hand, gets the rawest deal. She's arrested for the murder of MacDonald, and the last Forbes sees of her, she's being swallowed into the maw of the injustice system. He can't even muster a "Tough luck, kid." This was how Hollywood movies typically dealt with the other woman. Although they carried all the emotional power, they were never shown the last-ditch escape route reserved for the leading man. While John Forbes stewed over his indiscretion, Mona Stevens had to cope with the fixation of a horny married man, the return of a vengeful ex-con, and the obsessions of a psychotic stalker.

Although *Pitfall* is a terrific movie, revealing how boredom and ennui, when pitted against middle-class values, can create lustful fires – Mona's backstory is even more compelling. Karl Kamb's script, based on the novel by Jay Dratler *(Laura, The Dark Corner, Call Northside 777)*, is noteworthy for its realistic depiction of this femme fatale. That makes it all the more disappointing when she's virtually banished from the plot once she blows away MacDonald.

LIZABETH SCOTT, ONE OF THE STALWART DAMES of Dark City, was no stranger to Vixenville herself. She even worshipped at the same temples of the flesh. Born in Scranton, Pennsylvania, with the decidely un-vixenish name of Emma Matzo, she was discovered by producer Hal Wallis in 1942, understudying Tallulah Bankhead in an all-star stage version of *The Skin of Our Teeth*. History didn't record the extent of the lessons Lizabeth absorbed from the legendarily omnisexual Tallulah.

The PR boys know the play in Dark City — put the gat in a pretty gal's hand.
Lizabeth Scott in a beguiling publicity pose for *Pitfall.*

Scott made her Dark City debut as Van Heflin's romantic interest in *The Strange Love of Martha Ivers* (1946). She's stilted and awkward in a thankless role, but for a neophyte, just holding her own against Heflin and Barbara Stanwyck — not to mention Kirk Douglas — was quite enough to ask.

Soon she was a fixture in Vixenville: *I Walk Alone*, *Dead Reckoning*, *Too Late for Tears*, *The Racket*, *Stolen Face*, *Two of a Kind*, the astoundingly bizarre *Desert Fury*, and *Dark City*.

Even more than from her sultry eyes, Liz's sex appeal emanated from her husky, bedroom voice. It sounded soaked in gin and burnished by endless cigarettes, hung over from long nights of laughing or crying too hard. It could talk you into things never dreamed of. If you had to have a voice whispering in your ear, hers was the one.

Offscreen, Liz reserved the pillow talk for other women. Today, she'd be the toast of Hollywood. In 1952, *Confidential* magazine effectively flattened her career by charging that she was "prone to indecent, illegal and highly offensive acts in her private and public life." Even this was part of witchhunt hysteria, which overflowed from political crusade into a campaign for conformity. "You can hardly separate homosexuals from subversives," said Cornhusker Republican senator Kenneth Wherry.

Liz hired high-caliber attorney Jerry Giesler to sue *Confidential*, but her petition was dismissed on a technicality. (The magazine couldn't be sued in California, because it wasn't actually published there, and had no representatives in residence.) By the Sixties she was living in seclusion, returning only once to Dark City, in Michael Hodges's witty spoof *Pulp* (1972).

Although no one mistook Scott for a terrific actress, she still has a legion of fans who recognize her as one of Dark City's most luminous stars.

ONCE, MEN MANUFACTURED SPIRITUAL ICONS from marble and stained glass. Things got trickier in Hollywood, where actual flesh and blood was a necessary intermediate step before man's ardent desires could be embodied in silver nitrate.

Hollywood's holiest goddess was born in Queens, in 1918. Margarita Carmen Dolores Cansino was the shy, quiet daughter of Latin dance partners Eduardo and Volga Cansino. When her father realized she had inherited a passion for dance, he scotched her schooling and added her to the act. She was twelve, but puberty had its way early with her. Her joyous abandon not only entertained crowds, it fired the darkest parts of some imaginations, including her father's. Before going off to drink and gamble, Eduardo would lock Margarita in her room. He said it was for her own protection. She had no protection when she really needed it – after Dad returned, hammered and amorous.

The Cansino family moved to Los Angeles in 1930, with hopes of retiring. Eduardo was grooming his daughter as his stakehorse. At fifteen, she was spotted by studio scouts while performing at the Agua Caliente Jockey Club, a shady retreat north of the Mexican border where gangsters and picture folk swapped dangerous glamor. Winfield Sheehan, a pal of 20th Century–Fox boss Joe Schenck, was the first in a long line of Margarita's "mentors." He shortened her name to Rita, and got her plugged into numerous trifles as the Dancing Latin. Former car dealer Edward Judson, a shifty operator of uncertain means, asked Rita's parents for permission to squire their daughter around town, hinting that he could make her a star. The dubious Cansinos consented, even though Judson was old enough to be Rita's father. Judson drove his prize straight to a roadside chapel in Nevada, where naive and helpless, Rita said the few necessary words.

Enter Harry Cohn. Hollywood's most unrepentently vulgar boss — a portrait of Mussolini hung in his office — Cohn was taking Columbia Pictures from Poverty Row to major status by devouring cash-poor rivals. Judson and Cohn, perceptive masters of hype, knew just how to sell their new girl: whitewash her. Rita's black hair was dyed auburn, and two years of painful electrolysis raised her Latin-level hairline to Anglo heights. Her last name was changed to Hayworth.

The public loved her. Cohn couldn't get over the fact that he'd created such a gorgeous fantasy figure. He felt she belonged to him – the ultimate gangster's moll. He clumsily pursued her the way Raymond Burr stalked Liz Scott in *Pitfall*. He spied on her, harangued her, wiretapped her house. While he badgered one of his producers, Virginia Van Upp, to create a picture that would reap millions off his prized show pony, an unexpected stranger entered the scenario: Orson Welles.

The prodigiously talented enfant terrible was at a crossroads. *Citizen Kane* had made him the most sensational dir"ectorial star since D. W. Griffith, but he'd veered from the inside track with the self-absorbed fiasco of *The Magnificent Ambersons*. He tried to right himself with workmanlike efforts *Journey into Fear* and *The Stranger*. The way to prove he was a Hollywood player, he figured, was to marry a movie star. And, being Orson, he set his sights on the brightest and most beautiful. Without ever having met her, Welles guaranteed in print that he would marry Rita Hayworth. It should have come as no surprise that he backed up his boast. He was, after all, an accomplished magician.

Making movies, Welles once said, was like playing with the world's biggest train set. There was no pithier assessment of Welles's approach to life, work, and love. He and Hayworth lived high for almost two years. But with Welles, nothing

ever lasted. While Rita bulged with their baby, Welles's attention wandered. Rita Hayworth became last year's Christmas present.

Meanwhile, Virginia Van Upp constructed a vehicle for Hayworth that propelled her into the crucible of public consciousness.

Gilda (Columbia, 1946) is more a tango than a movie. The script is a pretext for watching overheated players enact a dance of sexual passion. It's also the kinkiest movie Hollywood had made to that point. Or maybe since.

Johnny Farrell (Glenn Ford), a gambler living off his wiles in Buenos Aires, is spared from a stick-up by the intervention of suave and sinister Ballin Mundson (George Macready). Johnny shows up at Mundson's lavish casino, angling for a job. Even while bowing to Production Code constraints, Mundson and Johnny are clearly bisexual. Mundson "buys" Johnny, and Johnny surprises himself by warming to life as a tuxedoed punk. Then one day Mundson brings home a new acquisition, the wild, ravishing Gilda (Guess Who). Johnny and Gilda once were lovers. They shower sparks all over the scenery, scathing each other with tantalizing, corrosive insinuations.

Halfway in, *Gilda* douses the fireworks and hastily sets about constructing a plot. Things fizzle. Nazi agents skulk around. One is murdered in the club. Mundson fakes his death to evade the police. In honor of his late lover, Johnny marries Gilda, but locks her away – apparently to sap the sexual ardor he can't handle. The fraudulent ending reunites Johnny and Gilda, cooing like teenagers. The vengeful Mundson returns to kill them both, but is stabbed by the washroom attendant.

Not that plot mattered. As Harry Cohn knew, it was all in the way Rita looked, spoke, and moved. Her first appearance, tossing back a mane of fiery hair as she kneels on her bed, made

Rita is *Gilda*

blood pressure rise the world over. Her "Put the Blame on Mame" striptease...well, you know. *Gilda* was a phenomenon. When the first A-bomb was tested on an armada of discarded ships in the Bikini atoll, it was nicknamed Gilda, and adorned with a painting of Hayworth in a negligée. She had become a literal bombshell.

Hayworth's popularity only exacerbated her estrangement from Welles. His dream project, *It's All True*, was a shambles, his career scattered all over the cutting room floor. Cohn, wielding power in a way that would excite Ballin Mundson, offered Welles a shot at redemption — creating another filmic firecracker to keep Hayworth burning in the public's mind. Cohn was determined to own these two, like Mundson owned Johnny and Gilda.

Yet even as he acquiesced, Welles rebelled. He rewrote *If I Die Before I Wake*, a small-scale potboiler by Sherwood King, turning it into an immensely complex, globetrotting affair, retitled *The Lady from Shanghai*. Cohn called Welles's bluff. He gave the erratic genius complete control — letting him write, produce, direct and play the lead — and lavished a two-million-dollar budget on him. Right off the bat, Welles had Hayworth's cherished coppery coiffure bleached platinum and finger waved. The war with Cohn was underway.

Hayworth agreed to be Welles's marionette for one pragmatic reason: a profitable hit might fill his barren coffers, leading to heftier child support payments once the divorce was final.

From associate producer William Castle's diary entry in Mexico: *"November 17...Cloudy and the heat oppressive. First day of shooting on Lady from Shanghai. The dark clouds seemed like an evil omen..."* Prescient. On the first take, the assistant cameraman keeled over dead from a heart attack. Production of the film would become Hollywood legend, something akin to the journey upriver in search of the demented Kurtz in Conrad's *Heart of Darkness*.

The tale concerned a rogue Irish seaman, Michael O'Hara (a blarney-filled Welles), hired by famed lawyer Arthur Bannister (Everett Sloane) to skipper his yacht from East to West coast. O'Hara is a gullible fish, hooked by the lawyer's glamorous wife, Elsa. O'Hara feels there's redemption in her; he can't see that life long ago cored out Elsa. George Grigsby (Glenn Anders), Bannister's partner, offers O'Hara five grand to sign a confession stating that he accidentally killed Grigsby. That way Grigsby can vanish into a new life. The wily Bannister will then exonerate O'Hara. But Grigsby turns up stiff, and O'Hara is cuffed for the murder, confession and all. Bannister, savvy to what's been going on behind his back, provides O'Hara with vaudeville schtick in place of a solid defense. Realizing he's

cooked, O'Hara breaks from custody. Several disjointed scenes later, he learns Elsa is the real culprit. She and her vengeful husband ("I'm aiming at you, lover!") shatter all remaining illusions in the Hall of Mirrors shootout that climaxes the film. O'Hara leaves Elsa bleeding on the funhouse floor, crying "I don't want to die!" as he walks into the sunrise.

It makes some sense in a pared-down retelling. But when Welles delivered the rushes to Columbia, it seemed a sprawling mess. Cohn yanked control from Welles and assigned editor Viola Lawrence to whip it into shape. She gamely fashioned a bumpy 88-minute ride out of what Welles envisioned as a 155-minute epic. When Cohn saw the final cut, he bellowed "I'll give one thousand dollars to anyone who can *explain* this thing to me!" Welles and Hollywood never meshed after he achieved narrative perfection with *Kane* right out of the gate. After 1941, he became obsessed with poetic inspiration. He rarely mustered the patience required for coherence.

As for his soon-to-be-ex-wife, Welles treated her like fallout from the Bikini test. Elsa Bannister was a glowing, radiant menace, too dangerous for any sane man to touch. Like the bomb, she was a siren luring men to self-destruction. It was a chilling, mean-spirited vision, in a film too personal to be dismissed as a tossed-off entertainment. Welles may have had the attention span of a six-year-old, but he never crafted mere diversions. As David Thomson suggests in *Rosebud: The Story of Orson Welles*, it's tempting to consider that Welles conceived of Elsa and Arthur Bannister as doubles of Rita and Harry Cohn. In life, as in the film, Welles left them to each other – once he realized he wasn't the man who'd rescue the helpless beauty from her monstrous pimp.

Harry Cohn was so incensed with the desecration of his biggest star that he shelved *The Lady from Shanghai* for more than year, finally leaking it out on the bottom half of double bills. Welles was finished in Hollywood. Hayworth, sadly, was pretty much done herself. She formed her own production company, and valiantly tried to crack the femme fatale mold, but the public had already hardened her into an icon. Cohn presented her as *Salome* and *Miss Sadie Thompson*, refusing to let her shed the Queen Slut image. Just as Welles abandoned her after his initial excitement wore off, so did her legion of fans – once Marilyn wiggled into town and slipped into the form-fitting role of new sex goddess.

Hayworth married Prince Aly Khan, but the royally spoiled rich kid tossed her aside when his greedy gaze fell on Gene Tierney. Hayworth lived in a mansion, still worked full-time fending off Harry Cohn, and sleepwalked through several films a year. Her ability to cloud men's minds remained intact.

One day a man named James Hill arrived by mistake at her front door. Thinking he was sent from a house-cleaning agency, she ushered him in and set him to work.

"After she showed me how to use [the scrub brush] with a professional circular motion, even getting down on her knees and all to demonstrate," Hill would later recall, "I wanted to tell her what a miracle sort of thing it was to find her doing this, but I didn't dare for fear of frightening her, or what was worse, maybe waking up and discovering it *was* just a dream after all." With *Gilda* coursing through his head, Hill watched Hayworth polish the silver. "She had these artistic hands with long, slender fingers. I found myself wishing I was a piece of that silver, and how nice it would be to have her polish me." This was clearly a Jim Thompson novel masquerading as real life.

Hayworth and the Stranger at the Door would marry. Hill dreamed of being the man who could turn her career around, by capturing the "real" Rita on film. Their boozy, roller-coaster romance ended in a Majorca hotel room where, drunk beyond comprehension, they staged their own noirish denouement. "It was a macabre parlor game," Hill wrote in his memoirs. "Each of us was to write down our complaints about the other. The one who had the greatest grievance would get the first shot. We would put one bullet in the gun, then spin the barrel [sic]...an injustice collector's version of Russian roulette." The Guardia, alerted by a shot, burst in. They found both Hill and Hayworth passed out and a bullet hole in Hayworth's favorite hat. Neither could remember who'd been wearing it, nor who had pulled the trigger.

Pulling back from the precipice, Hayworth left Hill to pursue her only two untattered ambitions: to paint, and to discover the simple pleasures Margarita Cansino had never enjoyed. She managed both successfully for a number of years, before Alzheimer's disease left her stranded in perpetual childhood.

The imperious Rita presides over Ted de Corsia's demise in *The Lady From Shanghai*.

Burt Lancaster's steaming virility was turned into thin gruel by Ava Gardner in *The Killers* (Universal, 1946). Gardner was the real thing: Hollywood's earthiest femme fatale. She married Mickey Rooney, Artie Shaw, and Frank Sinatra. She had affairs with, among *many* others, Clark Gable, Robert Taylor, David Niven, Robert Walker, John Huston, Peter Lawford, Howard Duff, Robert Mitchum, and — of course — Howard Hughes. Mitchum actually called Hughes to ask permission to sleep with Ava. "If you don't," Hughes replied, "they'll think you're a pansy."

SAPS. FOOLS. MARKS. FLUNKIES. DUPES. CHUMPS. Call 'em what you will, the women of Vixenville needed foils, men they could bend to their will. The more handsome, the better. Any tramp could hook a wizened geezer like Chris Cross. It was far more challenging, and satisfying, to bring a thoroughbred to heel.

Take this guy, for example. He's slowly striding through Slim Dundee's nightclub, turning every head. He coolly cases the joint, sniffing the play with dismissive nonchalance. Women can't help what flashes through their minds: their hands roving in his thick wavy hair, across his broad muscled shoulders. Men know what their dates are thinking. Jeez, that guy could have any woman in the place. But don't forget where we are. Virility gets you only so far in Vixenville.

Just ask Burt Lancaster — the guy in Slim's. He'd had his heart broken here before, but he always came back for more. He was ruined by so many women, so often, it was plain there wasn't much spine supporting all that beefcake.

Burt's big screen debut showed one of the most indelible images of vanquished masculinity ever. In the early minutes of *The Killers* (Universal, 1946), a pair of assassins track down former boxer Ole "The Swede" Anderson (Lancaster). He's been warned, but the Swede doesn't run. He just lies back in bed, awaiting his deliverance. The rest of the film explains, through flashbacks, how the Swede became entangled with a bunch of crooks, and had his heart cut out by two-faced Kitty Collins (Ava Gardner). The film was based on a Hemingway short story. The makers of *The Killers* hustled Papa into the back of a black Lincoln and gave him the ol' Dark City okey-doke.

Lancaster had been cast by Mark Hellinger, a Runyon-style newspaperman and short story writer turned producer of brass-knuckled crime thrillers. Hellinger knew Burt Lancaster was the real thing as soon as he laid eyes on him. So did the American public.

Born in East Harlem in 1913, Lancaster was a young man with a mind as developed and limber as his body. Although he'd acted a bit growing up, he disdained it as a profession. Too "sissified." Up until his late twenties, he earned a meager living — but a world of experience — as a circus acrobat. A hand injury forced him to fall back on a series of odd jobs. During military service in Europe he met his future wife, Norma, a USO entertainer. Back in New York, he was meeting his bride at her office when he was spotted by a theatrical producer. One brief audition later he had the lead in *A Sound of Hunting*. It played only three weeks, but Lancaster hooked seven Hollywood offers. He was that obvious.

Starting with *The Killers*, Lancaster appeared in a series of noirs in which the main attraction was the somewhat kinky spectacle of a chiseled Adonis mercilessly flogged, either by brutal authority or treacherous women. It clearly made him a sympathetic favorite with the distaff denizens of Dark City. In *Brute Force* and the even more aggressively titled *Kiss the Blood Off My Hands* (Universal, 1948), Lancaster bared his torso to endure the lash of savage jailers. Women swooned over his "swell build."

But there was more to Burt than beef. From day one on a soundstage he soaked up film technique and business acumen. He quickly became a valued behind-the-camera contributor, as well. By his eighth film, *Kiss the Blood*, he was co-producing. The following year he made *Criss Cross* (Universal, 1949), capping a three-year sojourn in Dark City in which he starred in six noirs (*The Killers, Desert Fury, Brute Force, I Walk Alone, Sorry, Wrong Number, Kiss the Blood Off My Hands*) and an adaptation of Arthur Miller's *All My Sons*.

Criss Cross was the culmination of this fecund cycle. It reunited the brain trust from *The Killers*, with one unfortunate exception: Mark Hellinger, only 44, died of a heart attack just as the deal came together. He'd recently scored his biggest success with *Naked City*, and seemed bound for a long career as Dark City's dominant storyteller.

Hellinger was inspired by Don Tracy's novel about a daring race-

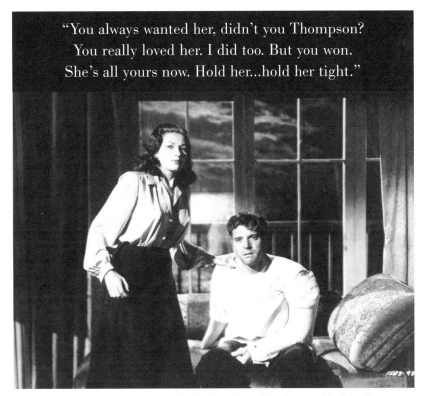

"You always wanted her, didn't you Thompson? You really loved her. I did too. But you won. She's all yours now. Hold her...hold her tight."

Slim says adios to Anna (Yvonne De Carlo) and Steve (Burt Lancaster) in *Criss Cross*.

track robbery, complicated by sexual passions. Daniel Fuchs fashioned the screenplay for pinch-hitting producer Michael Kraike. *Criss Cross* wasn't a home run. But like a ball off the top of the fence, daringly legged into a triple, a slight shortcoming doesn't diminish the excitement.

Steve Thompson (Lancaster) is an armored car guard who still has it bad for ex-wife, Anna (Yvonne De Carlo). He's drawn back to Slim's, a club where their passion burned brightest. He discovers that she's now in thrall to Slim Dundee (Dan Duryea), a slick, flamboyant operator. Anna, in fine femme fatale fettle, ignites a firefight between the two. When Dundee catches him with Anna, Steve blurts out a cover story: he's willing to act as an inside man so Dundee can knock over one of his company's armored cars. Both men stage a cagey mating dance, while setting each other up. Steve plans on swindling Slim, grabbing his cut and running off with Anna. Slim plans to kill Steve in the heat of the heist.

During the robbery, Steve is wounded and his partner killed. He

shoots a pair of Dundee's henchmen. Steve wakes up in the hospital to find out he's a hero. Meanwhile, Anna takes it on the arches with his share. One of Dundee's button men, masquerading as a vigilant hospital visitor, kidnaps Steve. But before the underling delivers him to Dundee, Steve bribes him with a promise of ten grand of the loot.

The guy drives Steve to Anna, who is ensconced at a secret beach house. Steve figures she's holding tight, waiting with the money. Wrong. "Don't you see," she barks, "Don't you know what's going to happen? He's on his way back to Slim – he'll tell Slim where I am right this minute!" As Steve looks on helplessly, Anna packs her bags. "Why'd you have to come here in the first place?" she snaps. Steve responds numbly, "I never wanted the money. I only wanted you." Slim materializes, glowing in a shaft of moonlight. He shoots them both, slipping into the darkness as wailing sirens close in.

One of the lasting pleasures of *Criss Cross* is its stylishness. Robert Siodmak, who also directed *The Killers* and many other terrific film noirs, had a tremendous flair for compositions and camera movements ominous yet graceful. Images that are simultaneously inviting and forbidding are essential to the noir vision, and Siodmak could muster them like nobody's business. From the start — the camera swooping down like a nightbird to catch Lancaster and De Carlo in a secret embrace in the parking lot of Slim's club — he infuses the drama with an urgent dreaminess that gets under your skin like a narcotic.

The acting couldn't have been more stylish, either. In the best noir, actors play with a bold flourish. They understand that memorable moments are way up there – dangerously close to over-the-top. Lancaster had been a trapeze artist, for God's sake. In noir, where he usually played a predator turned prey, he always suggested an imminent eruption beneath his implacable machismo. (When he left the wariness of Dark City behind, Lancaster's fearlessness could result in awe-inspiring vaults to the heights of hamminess.) Co-star Dan Duryea possessed an innate sense of how to colorfully sketch a character — a caricature, really — while nailing the priorities: advance the story, and *entertain* the audience.

A look at Steven Soderbergh's remake of *Criss Cross* provides a telling contrast between then and now. Retitled *The Underneath*, it's well-told and engrossing. But to accommodate the supposedly more sophisticated tastes of contemporary audiences, the film is relentlessly "realistic." It bricklays motivations for every character, to lend the proceedings as much credibility as possible. The actors sell the material with the studied naturalism now required of dramatic film acting. As a result, the film is an involving, but forgettable, 120 minutes.

During its 88 minutes, *Criss Cross* shoots out little slivers of art that will never leave your head. The lanky Duryea, dangling like a jackal in a zoot suit; Lancaster's lovelorn face as he watches De Carlo rhumba around the dance floor; robbers in gas masks firing blindly through a smoke haze. Vivid, dynamic imagery — and vivid, dynamic acting — stick in the mind long after the extraneous details of "naturalism" have evaporated. Modern film noir plays like real life. Classic film noir plays like fevered memory.

Burt Lancaster earned his greatest tribute from Louis Malle, who cast him as the aging two-bit gangster in *Atlantic City*, writer John Guare's brilliant vision of old-style romanticism juked up by modern mores. When Lancaster strolls the Jersey boardwalk and pauses to sigh, "You should have seen the Atlantic back then – now there was an ocean," it was the perfect capper to his Dark City career. Susan Sarandon was a nice retirement present.

We won't see anything like the swank, unforgettable performances of Lancaster and Duryea again. Times, and tastes, have changed too much.

Robert Mitchum: Smoothest threads, softest touch.

LANCASTER'S ONLY EQUAL on the roster of prize chumps was Robert Mitchum. It's fitting that Mitchum started out in westerns. The saunter in his gait and languor of his speech branded him a cowboy, worn out from a day's hard work, hankering for a roll in the hay and a quiet, thoughtful smoke.

It was an image that came easily to him. He'd spent his fatherless youth wandering all over America, working as a deck hand, coal miner, roustabout, whatever got him down the road. "In those days motion itself seemed an adequate philosophy for me," he'd later say. "Moving around like I did, though, I could be just any place, not high maybe but somehow alone and free." His take-it-as-it-comes attitude assumed larger-than-life proportions once he became a leading man.

Not everyone was impressed. "You can't act," Katharine Hepburn informed him on the set of *Undercurrent*, her lone trip into noir territory, "and if you hadn't been good-looking you would never have gotten the picture. I'm tired of playing with people who have nothing to offer." Mitchum loved to recount the moment, with a dead-on impersonation of the haughty Miss Hepburn.

For a guy who couldn't act, Mitchum made some memorable movies in the Forties: *When Strangers Marry* (Monogram, 1944), *The Story of GI Joe* (UA, 1945), which earned him an Oscar nomination, Raoul Walsh's brilliant noir western *Pursued* (WB, 1947), and *Blood on the Moon* (RKO, 1948), another revisionist sagebrush saga.

When Mitchum drifted into Dark City, where the prairie was paved over with asphalt, his eyes always betrayed an awareness that any chance for a good, free life was hopelessly lost. With *Out of the Past* (RKO, 1947) Mitchum became the quintessential noir protagonist: not a hero or a crook, just a guy trying to go his own way, at his own pace. He struck a pose rough as bark, hiding the sap at his core. The moral wreckage was surveyed with a jaundiced gaze, but you sensed that Mitchum had his compassion stashed in his hip pocket, waiting on the off-chance he'd find a woman who was easy to love.

Such dames were rare at RKO, where Howard Hughes took Mitchum in after his infamous dope bust made him persona non grata at other studios. Once in a while he'd find *His Kind of Woman* (1951) – a lusty, laid-back doll like Jane Russell. But Hughes liked pictures about demented women with gorgeous faces and diseased souls who toppled the toughest studs. Maybe Mitchum was supposed to be Hughes's fantasy image of himself.

The zenith — or nadir — of Mitchum's susceptibility to feminine wiles came with *Angel Face* (1953). Frank Nugent and Oscar Millard reduced Chester Erskine's unpublished spider-woman story into a concentrated black roux. Otto Preminger, working quickly with a crafty veteran crew, took only 19 days to concoct a noir gem that is suffocating in its morbid, almost geometric sense of entrapment and futility.

Mitchum plays ambulance driver Frank Jessup, another cowboy out of time. Frank meets 20-year-old heiress Diane Tremayne (played with a touch of narcolepsy by dreamy Jean Simmons) when he is called to the family's hilltop mansion in response to the near-fatal asphyxiation of Diane's stepmother. Accident or attempted murder?

The question vaporizes as soon as Frank lays eyes on Diane, spookily playing the piano while the life-and-death commotion transpires upstairs. Word that her mother will survive brings a tearful overreaction from Diane, and Frank applies some of his limited medical know-how — he slaps her across the face to halt her hysteria. She slaps him right back, hard and unhesitating, her depthless black eyes brimming with an erotic instability.

Start making up a room in hell for these two.

Frank accepts a job as the Tremayne's chauffeur, sampling both the largesse of their affluence and the illicit charms of their daughter. Day-by-day control of his life shifts to the lazy and spoiled Diane, even after he catches on to the twisted set-up of the happy home: Diane and her father are the real lovebirds, and step-Mom must go. And go she does, hurtling backwards over the cliff in the couple's land-yacht convertible. But Daddy goes too, in a twist that fate wedges into Angel Face's devious scheme.

At every turn Frank has the chance to walk back into the good graces of his girlfriend Mary, the hard-working, sensible, mother-in-the-making. But Frank thinks he can have his cake and eat it, too.

He's the prize over whom Mary and Diane battle, and he makes the fatal mistake of thinking that his insouciant sexuality will let him slip the worst punches any woman can throw. Diane is willing to pay a steep price to teach him otherwise.

Jean Simmons leads Mitchum straight to hell in *Angel Face*.

Faith Domergue shows Mitchum *Where Danger Lives.*

Mitchum checks *Out of the Past.*

After being tried as co-defendants for the murder of the Tremaynes — and acquitted — Frank determines, a little too late, that Diane just isn't worth the risk. Jilted by Mary, he decides to flee to Mexico. Is it a final gesture of gallantry, a tender courtesy toward the hopelessly deranged — or a nihilist's self-awareness — that makes Frank accept Diane's offer of a last ride to the bus station? The best epitaph we can offer Frank Jessup is that he looks great popping the cork on a bottle of champagne just before Diane slams the roadster into reverse, launching them off the cliff.

Jean Simmons came hot on the high heels of Faith Domergue, who had previously shown Mitchum *Where Danger Lives* (1950). Domergue was a Howard Hughes "project," which meant that she spent almost a decade as a well-kept prisoner in his Hollywood harem. The mogul played with fantasies of molding Faith into another Jane Russell, whom he'd hyped to sex bomb status in *The Outlaw* (1941).

In *Where Danger Lives*, Domergue is Margo Lannington, a full-figured fruitcake wed to wealthy San Franciscan Frederick Lannington (Claude Rains). She seduces Dr. Jeff Cameron (Mitchum), convincing him that Rains is her father. After learning he's been duped, Dr. Jeff accidentally knocks Lannington out in a brief scuffle. While he seeks first aid, Margo finishes off her outmoded husband, then talks her new beau into taking it on the lam. She jerks Jeff's chain and he follows, concussed but obedient. He finally turns on his master in a sleaze pit near the Mexican border. Margo administers the doctor a hot lead injection, and tries to make the border alone. Staggering after her in the street, he fingers her for the law; she gets riddled. You'd think he'd have wised up after that.

But remember, this is the same guy who didn't learn anything when Kathie Moffett (Jane Greer) came from *Out of the Past* to snuff him in 1947. When a beautiful woman looked deeply into Mitchum's sleepy eyes and told him to pack his bags for the ride of his life, it was definitely check-out time at the Prize Chump Hotel.

By the mid-Fifties, Mitch had had enough. Vengeance flared up from the embers of his passive vulnerability. He'd show the liars and double-crossers how bad it could really get. As psychotic evangelist Harry Powell in *Night of the Hunter* (1955) he tortured women and children without remorse. And as sadistic rapist Max Cady in *Cape Fear* (1962), the cowboy drifted all the way into darkness, brandishing his lazy carnality as a weapon — sly smile still in place, conscience gone completely.

Mitchum enjoyed a noir revival in the Seventies, starring in *The Friends of Eddie Coyle* (Paramount, 1973), one of his best films, and *The Yakuza* (WB, 1975), an intriguing hybrid of gangster, western and samurai genres.

It was, however, far too late for him to effectively portray Philip Marlowe in remakes of *Farewell, My Lovely* (Avco Embassy, 1975) and the disastrous British version of *The Big Sleep* (ITC, 1978).

Mitchum effortlessly kept his career moving along deep into the 1990s, making him Dark City's master of longevity. Shows how far a little insolence can take you in this town, even when you make a habit of succumbing to temptation.

Lupino as Lily Stevens in *Roadhouse*.

BEFORE WE ANKLE OUT OF VIXENVILLE, there's one last individual you have to meet. You hear a lot about folks being one-of-a-kind. In Ida Lupino's case, it wasn't just blowing smoke. Unless you didn't take her seriously — then she'd blow it right in your face.

Born in London, Ida was in the show as soon as she could walk. Her father, Stanley Lupino, was the most venerable comedian on the British boards. The family's theatrical roots reached back to the 17th century, so there was little question of Ida's calling. At fourteen she was already projecting womanly confidence in several British films. Hollywood director Allan Dwan "discovered" her and invited her to the film capital. Producers herded her into the overflowing starlet stable, hiding her distinctiveness beneath a Jean Harlow bleach job. Ida bristled, and wasn't afraid to warn movie magazines, "I cannot tolerate fools, won't have anything to do with them. I only want to associate with brilliant people." Columbia's Harry Cohn, the town's most brilliant fool, told Ida, "You are not beautiful, but you've got a funny little pan," then inked her to a two-picture deal.

Scarcely twenty, Ida became a popular Hollywood figure: the sweet-faced ingenue who dispensed straight talk with a tart tongue. In early 1936, she gained notoriety as the star witness at the media-saturated probe into the death of Thelma Todd. The actress had been found dead in her garage after a party in her honor at the Trocadero, thrown by Ida and her family. Later that year Ida developed a "blind devotion" to actor Louis Hayward, even though she told interviewers that "I never expect anything to last...neither success nor love...I can't be hurt." Hayward and Lupino became one of the town's most high-profile married couples, presiding over a sprawling communal household filled with family, friends, music, dance, and the arts.

Her breakthrough came in William Wellman's 1939 release *The Light That Failed*, in which the funny little pan served up a startling menu of emotion. Then the one-time student of the Royal Academy of Dramatic Arts was whisked into the rugged man's world of producer Mark Hellinger. He cast Ida as the nail-tough broad between

George Raft and Humphrey Bogart in *They Drive by Night* (WB, 1939). Ida promptly stole the show. Although possessed of an almost porcelain delicacy, Ida had a wide streak of raucous humor, a hair-trigger temper, and a no-bullshit demeanor that made her a favorite of the tough guys. She could hold her hooch and crack wise with any of them.

She also carried her own water, bearing the rigors of shooting *High Sierra* (WB, 1940), Hellinger's rough and romantic gangster saga. Initially wary of each other, she and co-star Humphrey Bogart became compadres (while Bogey's jealous wife Mayo, lurking off-set, tried to scare her with threatening looks and gestures). Ida's popularity earned her top billing over Bogart. She followed *High Sierra* with the socially-conscious, proto-noir *Out of the Fog* (1940). She and co-star John Garfield reunited later that year to make *The Sea Wolf,* cementing a life-long friendship that would prove to be, for him, tragically short.

Like most women in film noir, Lupino had to prove herself in a man's world by showing that she could take a beating, mentally and physically. Humphrey Bogart, as "Mad Dog" Roy Earle, sizes up Lupino's salt in *High Sierra.*

She then astounded everyone by playing, at a luminous twenty-three, the role of a severe middle-aged murderess in *Ladies in Retirement* (Columbia, 1941). It should have propelled her onto the "A" list. But having shed the ingenue stigma, she now found herself typecast as a villainess.

She rejected so many scripts that Warner Brothers put her on suspension. Mark Hellinger, also disgruntled with Warner's ways, had moved over to 20th Century-Fox, and he took Ida with him. They made *Moontide,* a heaping helping of greasy hashhouse melodrama co-starring Jean Gabin. To prepare for their roles, Gabin and Lupino waded through the fetid underbelly of Los Angeles. Ida never forgot what she saw there.

The Hard Way (WB, 1942) followed, a mean-spirited movie produced by Jerry Wald as a sort of warm-up for his *Mildred Pierce.* Both depicted the scary single-minded drive of obsessed stage mothers. Lupino hated making the picture; she felt burned out by the histrionics, and frequently suffered spells that interrupted shooting. Not that it mattered: the film was a success, and she pulled rave notices.

Then her life came apart. As of 1943, husband Hayward was a Marine captain, supervising a photography corps in the South Pacific. Responsibility for making a visual record of the infamous amphibious assault on the Tarawa atoll nearly destroyed him. During a sleepless four day frenzy of artillery shelling, sniper fire, and hand-to-hand combat, Hayward documented the slaughter of more than six thousand men, Americans and Japanese, battling for control of this strategic landing strip. He came home shellshocked; incapable of "normal" life. Movies meant nothing to him any longer. Ida helplessly watched the love of her life descend into numbed depression. They were eventually divorced. Ida gamely joked that she was now Hollywood's leading "bachelor girl," but in truth she was devastated.

She bravely struggled through making *The Man I Love* (WB, 1947). Her character, torch-singer Petey Brown, embodied resilient feminine spirit; a talented, smart-mouthed gal with a tender spot just waiting to be pierced. She returns from the lonely road life to discover that her family has become a catalogue of wartime crises: too many babies, not enough money, an angry shellshocked vet, a nephew straying into crime, a floozie neighbor cheating on her husband, and so on. Ida whirls among them, a sexy sage belting ballads and tossing off wise cracks. ("Well, well...the people you run into when you're not carrying a gun.") She's the Lone Ranger in gold lamé.

Single-handedly, she straightens everything out — except herself. To save her no-good nephew from a murder rap, she submits to the attentions of slick operator Nicky Toresca (Robert Alda). Her true love, alcoholic pianist Sam Thomas (Bruce Bennett), sails out of her life on a freighter. This overheated bouillabaisse is salvaged by two indelible moments. When the distraught Johnny (Don McGuire) threatens to kill Toresca, Ida steps in, knocks the gun loose, and slaps him silly. Moments later, after kissing Sam goodbye for the last time, she strides up the wharf with tears streaming down her face. She then gives up a tight little grin: Yeah, life's cruel, it says, but I'm here to play out the string. *The Man I Love* simultaneously tugged at and toughened women's heart-strings. It was a huge hit, the peak of Ida's career as a glamorous Movie Star.

She tired of acting and decided to give free rein to her creative impulses, seeking out fresh scripts to produce – and crafting her own. At 29, she formed an independent production company with Ben Bogeaus. She favored stories about "poor, bewildered people. That's what we all are." Ida met Italian director Roberto Rossellini at a party. He complained to her that, "In Hollywood movies, the star is going crazy, or drinks too much, or he wants to kill his wife. When are you going to make pictures about ordinary people, in ordinary situations?" The director's acclaimed neo-realist masterwork was, remember, *Open City*. Apparently he'd never been to *Dark City*. Regardless, his observations were an inspiration to Ida. She'd soon embark on a second career (discussed in detail later) as the industry's only active distaff director.

In the meantime, affluent agent Charles Feldman tried to win Ida's affection by purchasing and tailoring a property for her, a novel entitled *The Dark Love*. It would be renamed *Road House* (20th, 1947), and become one of the biggest hits of the year. Playing a whiskey-voiced chanteuse, Ida proved she could do anything: for the first time, it was her own voice in a film's musical numbers. "One for My Baby," written by Johnny Mercer and Harold Arlen, and performed by Ida Lupino, went to the top of the Hit Parade.

In this film, Ida was the subject of two of the sharpest cracks ever uttered in this burg. Her first night on the job a regular patron gives her the once-over and says "She reminds me of the first woman who ever slapped my face."

After she's shot Jefty (Richard Widmark), the screw-loose rich boy who can't accept losing her to his old buddy Pete (Cornel Wilde), he looks up at her, smiling as he dies, and says, "I told you she was different."

Jefty knew. He was nuts, but he knew.

**Lupino, with Robert Alda in *The Man I Love*.
The gown was so tight Ida passed out on the set;
it had to be cut off so she could be resuscitated.**

The Stranger on the Third Floor

W hat did I do? Where did things go wrong? Was it stopping for that drink last night? Answering the phone in the hotel lobby? I shouldn't have picked up that wallet. But I did – now I can kiss off everything I thought was important. Forget the raise – hell, forget the job. Likewise the fur for Cathy, and the trip out west. None of it matters. The future may not stretch another ten minutes. Why did this happen? Out of all these people on all these streets and in all these buildings — why am *I* the one being punished? Tell me, God — if you care at all — *WHY ME?*

Blind Alley

Once upon a time, movies were all about order. No matter how the train ran off the rails in real life, a quarter could buy you a double dose of reassurance at the Rialto. But on September 1, 1940, doubt snaked into cinemas across the land. RKO released a 64-minute programmer called *The Stranger on the Third Floor.*

Fledgling newspaperman Mike Ward (John McGuire) earns a front-page byline when he happens to witness the grisly murder of a shopkeeper. He fingers jittery cabbie Joe Briggs (Elisha Cook, Jr.) as the culprit. His courtroom testimony not only helps rid the city of a crazed killer, it makes him a "star reporter," and the envy of all his pressroom pals. His fiancée, Jane (Margaret Tallichet) is the only one unimpressed. She can't stomach the dispatch with which Briggs — all the while crying his innocence — is convicted. While Mike dreams of how his twelve-dollar raise will help rent a ritzier place uptown,

Jane wonders if Mike is strapping the wrong man into the hot seat.

Mike himself begins to waver. "What if he isn't guilty," he asks a seasoned crony. "What if they fry an innocent man?" His colleague, a Dark City native, responds, "So what? There's too many people in the world as it is."

Back in his gloomy tenement, Mike spots a strange man entering a neighbor's apartment. His newfound angst fuels paranoia: Mike lurks in the shadowy stairwell, suspecting some dreadful deed. When the stranger skulks out, Mike gives chase. The odd fellow, hustling like a hermit crab, escapes into the night. Mike convinces himself that his neighbor, elderly Albert Meng (Charles Halton), has been murdered. When he falls asleep, guilt roils in Mike's unconscious: he dreams that he is arrested for Meng's murder. Witnesses attest to his hatred of the victim. Motive is established. Circumstantial evidence

Peter Lorre

mounts. Mike is strapped, screaming, into the electric chair.

Bolting from his nightmare, Mike barges into Meng's apartment and discovers him dead.

Like the shopkeeper, Meng's throat's been cut ear-to-ear. Mike is now certain the stranger killed them both. He hotfoots to the cops, hoping to prevent Briggs's execution. But the bulls like Mike as Meng's killer. The nightmare turns real. Only Jane buys Mike's account of the weird little stranger. While Mike sits in stir, she prowls the streets, searching for the shifty homunculus. When Jane happens across him, she sizes him up as a pathetic loon. He befriends Jane, but when he realizes that she intends to hand him over to the cops, he cracks. As he chases her through the streets, he's run down by a truck. Dying, he's pumped about the two killings. He confesses, but he's so nutty he'd have said anything.

The ending turns on the lights and cleans things up, but by then *The Stranger on the Third Floor* has broadcast more fear and paranoia than it can pack away with a tidy wrap-up. Never count on order, it says, not in a city where chaos stalks the streets and stairways and random mayhem is the only constant. The biggest blow to normalcy in the film is the obsolescence of the old moral compass. Truth is relative, Frank Partos's script suggests. Who you are isn't as important as how other people perceive you. One wrong move and your fate could be in their hands. In a building packed with suspicious sight-seers, only one has to put the finger on you. "Lock this guy up — we've got a reliable witness."

The vagaries of fate are a venerable subject. But this was the first time an American-made film handled the theme with the hallucinatory delirium typical of the German expressionist school of filmmaking, which favored audacious artifice over quotidian naturalism. McGuire's guilty conscience is made palpable through dramatic lighting, exaggerated art design, and surreal directorial flourishes that twist and stretch RKO's prosaic theatrical facades into an unsettling melding of objective and subjective reality. This match-up of theme and style made *The Stranger on the Third Floor* the first Hollywood film to affect the look later known as noir.

In truth, the film was more historical footnote than trendsetter. *Citizen Kane*, released the following year by RKO, used many of the same techniques, more subtly and influentially, in the service of a far grander story. No one would mistake *Stranger*'s director, Boris Ingster, for Orson Welles. Yet both films can stake a claim to changing the grammar of film storytelling. A major part of the visionary success of *Kane* can be traced to art director Van Nest Polglase, fresh from the vividly realized designs of *The Stranger on the Third Floor*. And in his lighting of night-shrouded streets, ominous corridors, and shadow-stabbed rooms, director of photography Nicholas Musuraca established many visual motifs that would become film noir's daily bread.

Welles would forever alter mainstream film language; Ingster, Polglase, and Musuraca would have a similar impact on the world of "B" movies — they showed how fresh, shorthand storytelling techniques and a bold imagery could enliven the lowest-budget production. (The idiomatic look of noir was, in truth, often the result of economic, rather than purely artistic, considerations.)

The other special ingredient in *The Stranger on the Third Floor* was Laszlo Loewenstein, a diminutive Hungarian with the stage name Peter Lorre.

As the bent, reptilian Stranger, Lorre epitomized unnerving weirdness skittering loose in the big city. "The squat, wild-eyed spirit of ruined Europe," as David Thomson precisely put it. Indeed, Lorre's un-American visage was iconic: there was strange foreign matter now coursing through the back lot's bloodstream. Lorre was the thespian incarnation of the Germanic-inspired darkness about to suffuse American movies.

Lorre had already made an indelible impression in Fritz Lang's *M* (1931). As the Düsseldorf child murderer, he showed the anguish and inevitable derangement of a small man trampled at the bottom of the pecking order – beneath even the most corrupt criminals who are understandably delighted to discover a lower rung on the social ladder. Displaying a soul so tortured it's lost in lunacy, Lorre became the first actor to put a sad, scary — and human — face on crime. This was essential to the development of noir, and *M* deserves to be recognized among the genre's earliest progenitors. As the *New Republic* film critic noted when *M* had its American premiere:

"It is a picture which I do not believe could under any circumstances have been made in Hollywood – indeed, any American director who suggested such a thing would probably find his own sanity suspected. Nevertheless, Hollywood will make better pictures after seeing this one."

While never approaching the heights, or plumbing the depths, of *M*, *The Stranger on the Third Floor* starkly, if timidly, expressed the grimmest theme in film noir: the cruelty of fate. If Dark City's random pitfalls don't get you, a guilty conscience will. It doesn't matter if you're innocent. Around here Justice truly is blind, but not because she's impartial: Either God's poked her eyes out, or she's earning good dough by looking the other way.

This is Blind Alley, the bleakest part of this merciless town. No maps sold here. You're on your own.

IT'S ALWAYS THE LITTLE GUY who takes it in the shorts. Innocents just trying to scrape by: bank tellers, teachers, truckers, letter carriers. The juiceless citizens of Dark City. They don't *know* anybody, and they wouldn't know how to buy them if they did. You never see an alderman, bank president, newspaper publisher, or rich society dame careering for their lives through Blind Alley. The corrupt powerhounds don't wait around for fate. They take matters into their own hands, doling out revenge and retribution round the clock. As the city's "elite" showed less and less concern for the wheel of fortune, the once-omnipotent specter of Fate — former keeper of the civic order and sentinel over men's darker thoughts — got a chip on its shoulder. It started kicking around the smallest dogs.

Consider *Quicksand* (UA, 1950). It might just as well have been called *Andy Hardy Goes to Hell*, since the film starred America's post-pubescent Boy Next Door, Mickey Rooney. Danny Brady (Rooney) works in Dark City as a hot-rod-loving grease monkey. Caught flat broke after lining up a date with dishy waitress Vera (Jeanne Cagney), Danny lifts a double sawbuck from the garage till. He plans to cover it the next day with twenty a pal owes him. The following morning, the bookkeeper shows up ahead of schedule. To restock the register, and save his job, Danny buys a fancy watch for only a dollar down, then turns around and hocks it for thirty. Next thing he knows, a cop is down on him. The jeweler thinks Danny plans to skip on the bill. A grand theft charge is looming now, if he doesn't pay off the watch in 24 hours.

Danny rolls a guy at an amusement park

who's loaded with gin and fifties. Except everybody on the boardwalk knows the victim, ancient gashound Shorty — including Nick (Peter Lorre!), a morose arcade operator carrying a torch for Danny's trampy gal (she's been up and down the promenade a few times). Nick figures Danny as the amateur who mugged Shorty, and he forces the kid to steal him a new car off the lot. Danny sinks further when his boss, mean old Mr. Mackey (Art Smith) calls

Danny Brady (Mickey Rooney) tussles with arcade operator Nick (Peter Lorre) in Irving Pichel's *Quicksand*. Needless to say, it was a short fight. The film drew its atmosphere from Long Beach's famed waterfront amusement park, The Pike. The following year, Rooney would make another crime picture, *The Strip* (MGM), in which an innocent guy is entangled with mobsters on the Sunset Strip.

him on the theft. The car must be returned, or Danny will be stuck for the three-grand price tag. Vera encourages Danny to rob Nick's arcade – and she ends up cadging half the dough to buy a fur coat! Old man Mackey takes the payoff from Danny – but still calls the cops. Danny goes berserk and strangles him. He takes it on the lam, running for his life.

Quicksand, directed by Irving Pichel from an original screenplay by Robert Smith, is an archetypal Blind Alley thriller, revolving around the pursuit of money, and its perilous pitfalls. Although fate plays a part in his downfall, it's the naked greed, flashed by everyone Danny encounters, that pushes him under. He's a naive chump, learning the hard way that everyone is far more corrupt than he ever could have imagined.

These "twist of fate" scenarios were low-rent "B" morality plays, fright shows in which basically good people are shown the horrors that await if they succumb to the temptation of easy money. If they really had a moral, it wasn't much more sophisticated than the message of highway disaster films like *Red Asphalt* or *Signal 30*, screened in high schools from the dawn of driver training: If you value your life, don't get in the car with the bad boys.

Side Street (MGM, 1949) is the best of these rollercoaster rides. Farley Granger, the quintessential sweet-faced innocent, plays Joe Norson, a vet struggling to support his pregnant wife Ellen (Cathy O'Donnell) as a part-time letter carrier. His dream of opening a service station is dissipating. (Nice guys always wanted to open a humble filling station.) Desperate, Joe steals a folder that he believes contains $200, from an unlocked office on his route. When he discovers it holds $30,000, his low-rent dreams blow up in his face.

The dough came from the office of crooked shyster Victor Backett (Edmond Ryan), who runs a shakedown racket with psycho parolee Georgie Garsell (James Craig). They've blackmailed an uptown burgher with some in flagrante photos, and then murdered the girl (Adele Jergens) they used to set him up. When her cadaver surfaces in the river, the cops

From *Side Street* : When Joe Norson (Farley Granger) tries to come clean about stealing thirty grand, he's stunned to hear Victor Backett (Edmond Ryan) profess ignorance of the whole thing. *Opposite:* Anthony Mann meters out the tension as psycho Georgie (James Craig) takes Joe for the climactic ride.

(Paul Kelly and Charles McGraw) pursue the rats and mice through a maze of coincidence and mistaken identity. Joe leaves the gift-wrapped money with his local barkeep, Nick (Ed Max), telling him it's a nightgown for the wife. While Ellen goes into labor, Joe, stricken with conscience, wanders dazedly, waiting for the hammer to fall. Unable to bear the guilt any longer (he doesn't want his newborn son to have a thief for a father), he marches back to Backett's office, spills his guts, and pleads for leniency. Backett betrays no knowledge of the missing money; he's convinced that Joe is working for the cops, whose murder probe has gotten uncomfortably close.

Honesty is fine, but in Dark City, it's better to leave yourself a back-up.

When Joe returns to the bar to reclaim the money, he discovers that old pal Nick has lifted it, substituting a real nightgown as a parting joke. Joe has to race crazy Georgie to locate Nick. He loses. Joe finds Nick strangled in his apartment, and loiters just long enough to be ID'd as the prime suspect. Joe goes into hiding, swallowed up by Dark City. The cops try to strong-arm Ellen into making Joe turn himself in. Instead, with the same impulsiveness that drove her husband to steal the money, she screams into the tapped phone, "Run, Joe! Run!"

Joe follows the trail to Georgie's former flame, sodden songstress Harriet Sinton (Jean Hagen). She betrays Joe, walking him right into the killer's hands. For her trouble, she gets throttled by her old beau. George cold-cocks Joe, stuffing him and the dead thrush into a taxi driven by his doltish sidekick, Larry Giff (Harry Bellaver). The cops come up hot on their tail, and a thrilling chase ensues at dawn through the desolate downtown canyons.

Side Street, written by noir maestro Sydney Boehm and shot by MGM's premier cinematographer, Joe Ruttenberg, was the grandest production yet from director Anthony Mann. Born Emil Anton Bundsmann in San Diego, Mann was hired by David O. Selznick in 1939 as an all-purpose underling. Within a couple of years, having rechristened

113

Mann's world: *Raw Deal* (Eagle-Lion, 1948) managed to pack every noir theme and bit of visual iconography into one 80-minute movie. Marsha Hunt (top, left) plays the good girl who competes with moll Claire Trevor for homme fatale Dennis O'Keefe. It looks like no contest – until Hunt proves her love by blasting O'Keefe's nemesis, John Ireland.

himself, Mann was helming imaginative "B" pictures for Republic. His visual style was so strong he could turn a silly little lark like *Strange Impersonation* (1946) into a moodily engrossing diversion. His breakout came with a small-scale thriller, *Desperate* (1947), which he co-wrote. It exhibited a full-throttle but even-handed command of the medium. (Mann also benefitted from the collaboration of cinematographer George Diskant, one of the great light painters. With Ruttenberg, Diskant, and John Alton behind the camera on his noirs, Mann's films never failed to be visually compelling.)

In *Desperate*, freshly-hitched trucker Steve Randall (Steve Brodie, a noir stalwart), drives down a blind alley one night when he agrees to a spur of the moment hauling job. It's a heist, staged by the evil Walt Radak (Raymond Burr), an old friend of Steve's turned bad. The piece-of-cake job blows up, a cop gets shot, and when Randall cuts out, Walt's brother is nailed as a cop-killer. Randall and his bride (Audrey Long) beat it to the sticks, pursued by both the law and Walt's gang. Another sorry example of an honest Joe whose life is nearly ruined by his pursuit of some easy cash.

In both *Side Street* and *Desperate* (as well as the equally enjoyable *Railroaded*, *Raw Deal*, and *Border Incident*), Mann's storytelling is as swift and seamless as a seasoned shakedown. He chose to confront the self-evidence of "B" material directly, giving it unexpected urgency through a visceral, and at times brutal, style. He had an unsurpassed feel for stories in which vile human nature put the screws to people seeking calm, rational lives. He could invest a scene of domestic bliss with patient sweetness, then jolt the audience with an episode of startling violence. Unlike Robert Siodmak, who stood at a dignified remove from the travails of his characters, Mann dragged viewers headfirst into a maelstrom that, for the times, was unrivaled in its intensity.

By 1950, Dark City proved too civilized for Mann's tastes. He turned his noirish sights on the frontier, directing a series of westerns during the 1950s that were a gritty antidote to the sticky sentimentality of John Ford's epic oaters. His ersatz return to noir, *Serenade* (1956), was off-key. Mario Lanza was hopelessly miscast as Cain's tortured opera singer. What's torturing him remains a mystery, since the strange sexuality of the novel was completely purged by the Production Code.

LOOPHOLE (ALLIED ARTISTS, 1954) ALSO OFFERS UP STOLEN MONEY ruining a man's life, although this poor sap is in no way responsible for his downfall. Mike Donovan (Barry Sullivan) is a bank clerk victimized by a clever "inside job" that lifts fifty grand from his teller's cage. Another teller at a crosstown bank, wise to the dodge, poses as one of a group of federal inspectors. He slips the loot in his briefcase, easy as you please, while feigning a routine reconciliation. Donovan is so stunned by the loss he's afraid to report it at the Friday total-up. By the time Monday rolls around, Donovan's the lone suspect.

The bank's bonding company has six months to retrieve the money before it has to reimburse. The bondsmen assign investigator Gus Slavin (Charles McGraw) to dog the suspect. Slavin mercilessly shadows Donovan's every move, spreading the word he's a thief, costing him jobs – and nearly his sanity. There's no relief as Donovan gets squeezed between the real crook's callous thievery and Slavin's ferocious need to exact punishment. It's worth noting that *Loophole*, made at the tail end of the McCarthy witchhunts, replaced the fear of outlaws, typical of Blind Alley films, with the fear of authority run amok. McGraw displays the scary, thick-headed righteousness of the arrogant establishment torpedo, be it an insurance investigator, commie-hunting FBI agent, or renegade L. A. cop. There's no difference between this "law-abiding" McGraw and the ruthless gunsel he played in *T-Men:* either way, he's mean and cruel for the hell of it, relishing the license he's been given to torture.

Money isn't the only thing that leads Dark City naifs down blind alleys. As we've seen in Vixenville, plenty can go wrong when the unprepared go trolling for the pleasures of the flesh. In *The Accused* (Paramount, 1949), Wilma Tuttle (Loretta Young) is a spinsterish psychology professor who's studied all the dark corridors of the human mind, and elected to retreat to the sanctuary of her lonely apartment. That lasts until she's lured out by the randy blandishments of a precocious student, Bill Perry (Douglas Dick). He's got the book on the prim teacher: he knows that in between the tight bun and the square-toed sensible shoes there's a woman longing for sexual release. He's right, but the cock-sure kid is too insistent. He takes Wilma for a moonlit swim, then forces himself on her. She defends the fortress with a tire iron, putting a crease in Bill's skull. She uses "reverse resuscitation" to blow salt water into his lungs and dumps him in the ocean, to make it look like he slipped on the rocks and drowned.

Murder apparently does wonders for Wilma's pheromones. She's romantically pursued not only by Bill Perry's legal guardian and mouthpiece, Warren Ford (Robert Cummings), but by Lt. Ted Dorgan (Wendell Corey), the cop investigating Perry's death. As Wilma desperately attempts to camouflage her guilt, the two men battle over her. Ford learns the truth and tries to protect her; Dorgan suspects the truth and tries to break her. He takes a little too much pleasure in relentlessly exposing what lies beneath her frigid facade. Dorgan, a bitter, jaundiced lawman with no love life, won't turn Wilma loose. He wants her down in the muck with him, guilty as everybody else. He finally gets his wish, when Wilma cracks on the witness stand. But Ford's impassioned plea of self-defense wins leniency, and Wilma.

The Accused, adapted from the novel *Be Still, My Love* by June Truesdell, was tricky subject matter for a 1949 film. Although Ketti Frings gets screenwriting credit, no fewer than five other writers had a hand in softening and sanitizing a story of rape, in which men fall in love with a woman they suspect is a murderess. The film is notable for backing a woman up against the alley wall, a rarity for the genre. While it was common for women to be the engineers of a man's demise, it was considered bad form to hang them with the same noose that was always ensnaring the men of Dark City.

The Accused: Cocky psych student Bill Perry (Douglas Dick) comes on a little too strong with professor Wilma Tuttle (Loretta Young), who's about to set him straight with a tire iron.

Above: Out for a night on the town, Wilma is horrified when a boxing match sparks memories of the murder she has tried to wipe from her memory.

By comparison, consider the case of Frank Bigelow, another citizen who can't feature why life doesn't dish him some fleshier pleasures. In *D.O.A.* (UA, 1950), this sad sack is saddled with a destiny no Dark City dame would be made to suffer. One of our town's wildest stories begins when Frank (Edmond O'Brien) marches into the homicide department of an L.A. police precinct to report a murder — *his own*. The cops have been expecting him; Frank has left a trail of carnage during the preceding 48 hours. The doomed man reels out his testimony for the record:

It starts innocently enough. Bigelow, a penny-ante beancounter in the one-horse town of Banning, wants a breather from his fiancée Paula, who's eager to clamp the matrimonial bridle on him. Frank's not sure he's ready to sacrifice the carefree bachelor life — certainly not before he's actually lived it. So he bolts to San Francisco to sow belated wild oats. Paula gamely lets him go, confident Frank will come home all the wiser.

Buddying up with a gaggle of pub-crawling conventioneers, Frank casts his net at The Fisherman, a steamy juke 'n' jive joint near the downtown Ferry Building. As he's trying to reel in a likely blonde at the bar, a mystery man in overcoat and slouch fedora enters. He stays just long enough to swap Frank's bourbon for a luminous toxic cocktail, neat. Frank returns to his hotel feeling a little queasy; the lush life isn't quite as carefree as he thought it would be. Waiting for him is a beautiful bouquet from Paula, and a loving note. Frank tears up the blonde's phone number and hits the sheets, alone and content.

Come morning, Frank's all topsy-turvy inside. A quick visit to an M.D. delivers startling news: he's been poisoned. Down the street a second opinion confirms the worst. This doctor even produces a beaker of glowing liquid that one must assume is Frank's radiant urine. Frank demands fast, effective remedies. The doc, displaying a blunt bedside manner, says, "I don't think you understand, Bigelow. You've been murdered."

The victim, in his own doomsday panic, races through the streets of San Francisco. For several moments, *D.O.A.* leans toward heavy allegory: the radioactive man, running out of time, inventories the mundane daily activities that could be atomically annihilated in an eye-blink. Bigelow stares into the sun, bright as a bomb blast, and contemplates armageddon as he knows it: "A day, two, maybe a week at the most."

But with Edmond O'Brien in the driver's seat, there's little chance of *D.O.A.* veering off into anything deeply meaningful. Instead, it becomes a breakneck, almost berserk, spin on the classic detective yarn, as Bigelow tries to hunt down his killer before he dies.

A PICTURE AS EXCITINGLY DIFFERENT AS ITS TITLE!

in all the annals of police history there has never been a story like this: OF A MAN WHO HAD 48 HOURS TO FIND HIS OWN MURDERER!

HARRY M. POPKIN presents "D.O.A." starring EDMOND O'BRIEN and PAMELA BRITTON with LUTHER ADLER · Beverly Campbell · Neville Brand · Lynn Baggett · William Ching · Henry Hart · Laurette Luez

The trail leads back to L.A., where Bigelow scrambles through a plot as densely twisted as *The Big Sleep*. It revolves around trade in the ominous mineral iridium, and the nefarious characters who have bought it, sold it, and stolen it from each other. And just like when Marlowe goes snooping, people start dropping dead. Bigelow, determined not to drop until he's reasoned out his death, is a more frantic inquisitor than Marlowe: "Why'd Eugene Phillips kill himself? Who's George Reynolds? Where do I find this Raymond Rakubian? Who are you? Majak! Who's Majak? What's Halliday got to do with this? You mean he's having an affair with Mrs. Phillips?!"

Bigelow even endures a patented private eye excursion, the "last ride" with a bloodthirsty goon (Neville Brand): "You know how you're gonna get it, Bigelow? I'm gonna give it to you in the belly – you don't like it in the belly." The ritual allows Bigelow to escape, and culminates in a wild shootout in a drug store.

As he searches for his fatal piece of the iridium puzzle, Bigelow recognizes his true love for Paula, but spares her the gruesome details of his imminent demise. It turns out that Bigelow's notarized bill of sale was evidence that could have foiled a plot to make importer Eugene Phillips' murder look like suicide (or something like that). Distraught at being trapped in a blind alley with no outlet, Bigelow clutches Paula and moans, "All I did was notarize one little paper — one paper out of hundreds!"

Frank stows his rage long enough to "successfully" conclude his own murder investigation. In the atmospheric Bradbury Building, he tracks down the man who slipped him the lethal cocktail, and reciprocates with several shots, straight up.

After giving his statement, Bigelow keels over. "Better call the morgue," says a hardened homicide cop. "What'll we tell 'em?" comes the off-screen prompt. "Tell 'em — Dead On Arrival."

The bulk of the cases filed from Blind Alley aren't whodunits, but Houdinis — as in "How are they going to get out of this one?" As such, they have great built-in entertainment value. In truth, most Blind Alley noirs are the nasty equivalent of the old banana peel gag. It's entertaining as hell to watch somebody else take the big fall. In films of this type the victims, bent and bruised, dust themselves off and walk away at the fadeout.

D. O. A.'s most memorable quality, in contrast, is its downbeat finish. Lots of critics dig deep to show how Bigelow is ultimately punished by higher powers for ranking casual encounters over marriage vows. Lighten up. *D. O. A.* is about the closest any film noir ever got to being a Warner Bros. cartoon. Realizing that the convoluted plot is little more than a succession of gab-happy interrogation scenes, director Rudolph Maté gave O'Brien free rein to push the proceedings to a fever pitch. O'Brien responded with a performance more animated than Daffy Duck. He frantically lunges in and out of rooms; you can almost see the animated motion lines poof from the doorframes. He skitters and slides down hallways, outrunning his feet in the best Chuck Jones tradition. O'Brien is so overheated he can't stand still for a moment, lest he drown in a pool of sweat.

This isn't a complaint. When directed to play it straight, as he was in *The Killers* and *White Heat*, O'Brien acted the ideal Everyman, trying to make sense of the blackest corners of Dark City. But whenever material threatened to go stiff, O'Brien could be counted on to shake and stir the batter. Faster than any actor, he could go from Average Joe to disheveled dervish, flapping his prodigious pompadour around like an overgrown cock's comb. His noir résumé is lengthy: *The Web* (1947), *A Double Life* (1947), *An Act of Murder* (1948), *711 Ocean Drive* (1950), *Between Midnight and Dawn* (1950), *Backfire* (1950), *Two of a Kind* (1951), *The Hitch-Hiker* (1953), *Shield for Murder* (1954), and *A Cry in the Night* (1956). In all of them O'Brien was never less than entertaining. Sometimes outrageously so.

Fatally poisoned Frank Bigelow (Edmond O'Brien) ducks the villainous Majak (Luther Adler) and his henchmen in *D. O. A.*

To most viewers — and creators — these dramas of twisted coincidence were no more than whirlwind diversions. For overly sensitive souls, they were the modern equivalents of consigning Christians to the lion's den. Life or death as spectacular entertainment. Thumbs up or down, if one man could be called the bard of this blind alley, it was Cornell Woolrich.

The preeminent scribe of noir suspense, Woolrich sampled success in the Twenties, when two early novels gained him notoriety and quick paydays. Easy Street turned into rough road during the Depression. Woolrich retooled his craft, and vision, as a "penny-a-worder," pumping out an array of stories for pulp magazines.

Sales of his work to the movies, radio, and television would eventually make him the most financially rewarded "pulp" author ever. It was all meaningless to Woolrich, who lived like a pauper and packed his own short dog, in a brown paper sack, to the few literary fetes he'd attend. "All I was trying to do was cheat death," is how he once described his writing career. No amount of cash can buy you that safe passage.

Woolrich spent his youth in Mexico, being dragged here and there by his father after his parents divorced. The old man, Genaro, bounced around south of the border, administrating construction projects with his son — a gangly, carrot-topped wraith — in tow. The insecure kid had to come off as macho. He bribed a local bully into withstanding harmless beatings within sight of Señor Woolrich. Only when his father took him to a French touring company's Mexico City performance of *Madama Butterfly* did Cornell feel a stirring of direction in his life — a desire to tell (and perhaps escape into) dramatic stories. But dreamy ambition would always squirm beneath Damocles' sword. In his never-published autobiography *Blues of a Lifetime*, Woolrich recalls how one night "when I was eleven and, huddling over my own knees, looked up at the low-hanging stars of the Valley of Anahuac, and I knew I would surely die finally, or something worse...I had that trapped feeling, like some sort of poor insect that you've put inside a downturned glass, and it tries to climb up the sides, and it can't, and it can't, and it can't."

Woolrich's biographer, Francis Nevins, calls the facts of Woolrich's life as elusive as smoke. The writer was an almost pathological liar, Nevins notes, rewriting facts for the sake of a better story. The true Woolrich may be the one he left on the page. A man who made a living by assembling his cancerous neuroses into breathless, urgent communiques from the loneliest outskirts of Dark City.

For most of his life, that outpost was an apartment in the Hotel Marseilles, Broadway at 103rd, in Manhattan, which he shared with his mother, Claire. From his upper-floor room, he'd survey the roofs and alleys and fire escapes of Dark City, imagining the myriad terrors that could befall the souls streaming through those clogged arteries. Every time he heard a siren, he must have started pounding the typewriter — that's how prolific he was.

He wrote slavishly, but uneasily, like a man under a death sentence. Taken individually, his tales are often masterful excursions into nail-biting suspense. As a life's work, they offer an unrelentingly bleak world view. Each story is a brick in a massive wall of malevolence Woolrich spent his life building. Nevins's epitaph: "He had the most wretched life of any American writer since Poe."

It didn't start out so bad. Cornell prospered, perhaps prematurely, during the Twenties, when a Jazz Age novel called *Children of the Ritz* brought comparisons with F. Scott Fitzgerald and a trip to Hollywood to assist with the First-National screen adaptation. While in Los Angeles, the moody and mercurial writer met, and impulsively married, Gloria Blackton, daughter of J. Stuart Blackton, founder of Vitagraph Studio, and one of the industry's pioneers.

According to Ms. Blackton's half-sister, Marian, Woolrich professed a "reverence" for his wife that precluded consummation of the marriage. Three months after they exchanged vows, Woolrich suddenly disappeared.

Gloria soon came across a diary in which Woolrich had penned graphic accounts of homoerotic encounters on the L. A. docks. Maybe that explains the sailor suit she once discovered in a valise he usually kept locked and stowed. Even more shocking to the rejected young wife was Woolrich's mocking revelation that he had married Gloria only as a joke.

Woolrich returned to Manhattan and his mother, with whom he'd live until her death in 1957. He became a morose recluse, a man who'd snugly fit any serial killer profile. Fortunately, Woolrich confined his mayhem to a Remington portable typewriter, on which he mastered the art of injecting pathos and despair into stories of exhilarating excitement.

His specialty was laying a razor-edged latticework of coincidence over the dreary lives of beleaguered Americans (in Woolrich's novels, the Great Depression never seemed to end). Those frantically looking for a break took fate's boot heel square in the kisser. People raced the clock, and unbeatable odds, to avert disasters, murders, and executions. Sweat-soaked nightmares were reenacted during waking hours, driving the dreamer inexorably mad. The love of someone's life — one's only scant ray of hope — might be an evil impostor. Or might one day vanish without a trace, as if they never existed. When these dazed souls turn to the law for help, they usually encounter cops like the one in Woolrich's "Dead on Her Feet" — a sick flatfoot who forces the innocent boyfriend of a dancehall murder victim to tango with the corpse until he goes insane.

In the Forties, Woolrich was Johnny-on-the-Spot: the perfect writer to provide source material for the confluence of stylish European existentialism and gritty urban crime drama that was seeping onto the shooting schedules of all the picture factories. Studios snapped up Woolrich's novels and short stories.

Street of Chance (Paramount, 1942), based on *The Black Curtain*, was the first film to capture the mordant Woolrich spirit. It starred Burgess Meredith as an amnesiac who struggles to recapture the three years missing from his life. The follow-up novel, *Black Alibi*, was purchased by RKO and transformed by Val Lewton and Jacques Tourneur into a spellbinding film: *The Leopard Man* (1943), in which something — man or beast? — stalks the city, killing at random. (In many ways, it's a precursor to the ubiquitous "slasher" movies of a later era.)

In 1944, the pivotal year for film noir *(Double Indemnity, Murder, My Sweet,* and *Laura* were also released), Universal issued *Phantom Lady*, adapted from the first novel Woolrich had written under his pseudonym, William Irish. It was a classic Blind Alley thriller. A husband angrily ditches his wife and spends an evening on the town with a woman he picks up in a bar. He returns home to find his wife murdered, and cops ready with the cuffs. His companion that evening, all that stands between the dupe and his unjust doom, has apparently vanished into thin air. A loyal co-worker races against time to uncover the needle in a haystack, her only clue an extravagant hat worn by the mystery woman.

Phantom Lady was also a breakthrough film for its director, Robert Siodmak, who chose to sacrifice some of Woolrich's screw-tightening tension in favor of a waltz into the darkness of the author's urban nightmare. In addition to the inky wash of menace he delicately brushes over desolate locations, Siodmak amplified the sounds of urban dread: the

In *Phantom Lady,* Franchot Tone mesmerized hapless Elisha Cook, Jr. before dispatching him. Born in San Francisco in 1906, the Big Quake never ended for Cook. Prior to this film he trembled through *The Stranger on the Third Floor, The Maltese Falcon,* and *I Wake Up Screaming* (20th, 1942). Dark City's favorite fall guy, Cook would be savagely slapped, brutally beaten and mercilessly murdered dozens more times in a career that seemed like one long death scene.

screeching of elevated trains, the echoing of tentative footsteps on wet pavement, and, most famously, the scary abandon of an after-hours jazz club.

In 1946, three Woolrich-inspired films were released. *Deadline at Dawn* (RKO) was an intriguing attempt by several left-wing luminaries of New York's Group Theater to elevate the moist pulpiness of the novel into something loftier. Producer Adrian Scott, fresh from the success of *Murder, My Sweet*, hired

A 1941 Woolrich novella, "And So to Death," served as the basis for several "B" films. In *Fear in the Night (above, Paramount, 1947)* DeForest Kelley (right) plays a man who dreams of committing murder in a mirrored octagonal room and finds pieces of the dream relentlessly reappearing after he awakens. Writer-director Maxwell Shane would remake the film in 1956, under Woolrich's alternate title, *Nightmare* (UA). The same basic story was used in *Fall Guy* (Monogram, 1947), one of many Poverty Row quickies adapted from Woolrich stories.

compatriots Clifford Odets and Harold Clurman to adapt the tale of a man who has from midnight until sunrise to find the real perpetrator of a murder for which he'll be charged. The splintered frenzy of Woolrich's novel was a poor match for artists as mannered as Odets and Clurman; they seemed to lose interest somewhere around 3 A.M. Only the reliable atmospherics of Nicholas Musuraca and Susan Hayward's turn as a prickly taxi dancer enliven Odets's stilted adaptation.

It was common for screenwriters grappling with the complexities of Woolrich's narratives to abandon everything but the sensational premise. When it came to the "Houdini" set-up, no one could match Woolrich, especially in his short stories. But the novels often had scattershot structures, which led down frustrating cul-de-sacs. Screenwriters, paid to keep the traffic flowing, often blockaded these outlets, funneling everything onto one main avenue. What mattered most in a thriller was speed, how well you held the turns, and what interesting sights you glimpsed as they rushed past. Develop all the characters you want within the cab, just keep the damn hack moving. Odets and Clurman drove about 30 mph, and ensured that all the passengers routinely checked in with annoying pronouncements about the Meaning of Life. Shut up and drive already.

The Chase (UA), was a much wilder ride. Screenwriter Philip Yordan threw out the map (*The Black Path of Fear*) in the middle of the trip, and seemed happy to arbitrarily change destinations thereafter. Director Arthur Ripley didn't even bother with the brakes. As a result, *The Chase* is as spellbinding as a car wreck. Downtrodden vet Chuck Scott (Robert Cummings) gets a chauffeur's job with Miami gangster Eddie Roman (Steve Cochran) after returning the guy's wallet untouched. While Eddie and his aide de camp Gino (Peter Lorre) spend most of their time trading elliptical non sequiturs, Chuck falls in

Black Angel (Universal, 1946) was a stylish variation on the Woolrich novel. Boozy songwriter Marty Blair (Dan Duryea) visits ex-wife Mavis Marlowe (Constance Dowling) to give her a ruby brooch as an anniversary present. Mavis is later found murdered, with the brooch missing. Kirk Bennett (John Phillips) is convicted of the crime, and Marty teams up with Bennett's wife Catherine (June Vincent) to uncover the real killer before Kirk is executed. Although the film veers dramatically from the novel's storyline, the resolution is pure Woolrich: in the eleventh hour, Marty realizes that *he* committed the murder in a drunken rage. This time it's not fate, but whiskey, over which a desperate man has no control. This was the last film directed by Roy William Neill, best known for the long-running Sherlock Holmes series, starring Basil Rathbone. Englishman Neill planned on taking his Hollywood spoils and retiring to his boyhood home of Maidenhead-on-Thames. After eagerly anticipating the day of his return for fifteen years, Neill died of a heart attack upon entering the house. Cornell Woolrich hated the film version of *Black Angel*, but might well have appreciated its cruel real-life epilogue.

love with Roman's French wife, Lorna (Michelle Morgan), whom Eddie keeps a virtual captive. She talks Chuck into arranging their escape, via freighter, to Havana.

Once Chuck and Lorna flee Miami, things move at a sluggish and sexy pace, as if everything is happening on heavy, shifting sand. When the enraptured lovers embrace in a bustling Havana nightclub and Chuck breathes "I love you" into Lorna's rapt face, it plays like a death sentence. Seconds later, Lorna slumps to the floor, dead, a knife with a jade monkey handle jutting from her back.

The Woolrich fever is perfectly captured: The police hound Chuck;

menacing witnesses pop up to lie about his actions that night; the exoticism of Cuba is frightening in itself. There's the palpable feeling that the world — or Chuck's head — has come loose from its moorings. The audience feels the same way when Gino reappears and *kills* Chuck, just as he's about to solve Lorna's murder.

But hold on, we're only halfway in. Chuck wakes up in his chauffeur's uniform, back in Miami. It's all been a fever dream, induced by a recurring dose of malaria Chuck contracted in the Pacific. If things weren't confusing enough, Chuck suffers amnesia, an unexpected offshoot of his disease. Eddie and Gino bow out in a train wreck, and Chuck and Lorna do escape to Havana — to be greeted by characters from Chuck's dream.

Critics of *The Chase* call it a hopeless mess. But Philip Yordan is too good a writer to grope so blindly for "unexpected" twists. As in two other films he scripted, *The Big Combo* and *Johnny Guitar*, Yordan showed a knack for firing up classic scenes while simultaneously lampooning genre standards, be they gangsters, westerns, or psychologically loopy thrillers. *The Chase* perfectly evokes Woolrich's world of doomed romance and terrifying helplessness. It also mocks the implausible set-ups and lapses of logic required to sustain that special brand of mental illness.

The most successful of the Woolrich adaptations was *The Window* (RKO, 1949), based on the short story "The Boy Cried Murder." Woolrich's lean yarn is a Dark City remake of Aesop's fable about the little shepherd with the outsized imagination. Tommy Woodry (Bobby Driscoll) eases the misery of impoverished tenement life by telling tall tales to his family and friends. When he takes his pillow onto the fire escape one night, to beat the stifling heat, he witnesses a murder in the apartment above. No one believes him. He persists, so his fed-up mom teaches him a lesson — she embarrasses him by marching him up to the Kellersons' apartment and forcing him to confess his fibs. Woolrich's paranoia is all the more wrenching when it's entangled with a child's vulnerability — Tommy's own mother (Barbara Hale) leads him to the slaughter!

No character seemed as close to the real Cornell Woolrich as Tommy Woodry, a boy trying to overcome his fear of the darkness, in the world and himself. Claire Woolrich was 83, and had struggled for more than a year with the residual effects of a massive heart attack, when she died in 1957. In line with Cornell's suspicious view of life, he believed that the nurse who cared for his mother in her final days had killed her when he went for a walk. Woolrich, true to form, felt inconsolably guilty for having left her side.

Woolrich then spent ten lonely years as a dead man walking. He scared off admirers with his penchant for marathon stints of ill-tempered imbibing. The once-prodigious wellspring of fiction evaporated; he tapped out a few meager efforts a year, at best. One of them, "A Story to Be Whispered," published in 1963, offered a disturbing window into Woolrich's self-loathing. A man picks up a floozy in Prohibition-era San Francisco and accepts an invite back to her dingy room. Poised for his sexual release, he suddenly beats his lover to death. The surprise ending: "...It wasn't as though I had killed another man. Or even (God forbid) as if I had killed a woman. Or yet (banish the thought) killed a little child. All I had killed was a queer."

As the days dwindled, Woolrich's life and fiction merged. He was convinced another resident of the Sheraton-Russell Hotel was covertly persecuting him, searching his room, trying to assume control of his life. Then a chafing shoe caused an infection. Left untreated, it turned gangrenous. Now a virtual prisoner in his rented room, Woolrich watched his leg rot. He might have found this appropriate, for it was a foot infection that had incapacitated Woolrich decades earlier, leading him to write his first short story.

His leg was eventually amputated and Woolrich proudly told people that this "miracle" led him to return to the Catholic church, which he'd abandoned as a boy. Could several months of prayer have staved off the terror Woolrich had spent a lifetime anticipating?

Cornell Woolrich was found passed out in his hotel room on September 19, 1968. He died six days later, without regaining consciousness.

ONE OF THE FEW WHO could have commiserated with Woolrich in his final days was his artistic and spiritual brother, Alfred Hitchcock. Maybe they would have found comfort in swapping scary stories, like mama's boys away at camp for the first time. More likely, they would have mercilessly picked at each other's human frailties, deriding in the other the weaknesses they struggled to hide in themselves.

Like Woolrich, Hitchcock was a populist, a maker of escapist potboilers, who always had a chip on his shoulder about not being accepted as a profound artist. Even though he became the most recognized movie maker of all time, it was long after his best work was behind him that critics began appreciating the artistry Hitchcock brought to films that had been praised, but dismissed, as mere exciting entertainments. Like Woolrich, his specialty was the Blind Alley thriller. But unlike the wordy recluse, who rarely let his characters skip town, Hitchcock had a well-stamped passport: his expansive, colorful imagination was never trapped within the boundaries of Dark City. It roamed the corners of the globe. He was able to find the same fear and guilt lurking everywhere.

These two strange sensibilities meshed most famously in *Rear Window* (Paramount, 1954), Hitchcock's gripping adaptation of Woolrich's 1942 short story "It Had to Be Murder." Its premise captures the essence of both men: physically "incapacitated" voyeurs who view the world from a distance — but one that is never safe enough. Broken-legged photographer L. B. Jeffries (Jimmy Stewart) enjoys observing the miniature passion plays enacted within the window frames of neighboring apartments, until he spies a gruesome uxoricide. The killer (Raymond Burr) knows Jeffries is a witness, and steadily pulls the spectator into the game.

It's the same story as *The Window*, but unlike that Dark City fable, *Rear Window* exists wholly in Hitchcock's manufactured studio world. Its calculated artifice is a perfect example of the engrossing, unchallenging thriller.

A classic Alfred Hitchcock love scene: Bruno Anthony (Robert Walker) strangles Miriam Haines (Laura Elliott) outside the Tunnel of Love in *Strangers on a Train,* one of Hitchcock's finest suspense thrillers. Bruno is a twisted rich boy who, during a chance meeting with tennis pro Guy Haines (Farley Granger) proposes a "criss cross" of mutual benefit: he'll kill Guy's clinging wife, if Guy will snuff out Bruno's hated old man. Guy's guilty of only one "crime" (besides cheating on his wife) — dismissing Bruno as a fruitcake. After killing Miriam, Bruno threatens to frame Guy for the murder unless he upholds his end of the "deal."

Hitchcock, at his devilish best, makes the audience root for Bruno, merely by contrasting the intensity of his "mission" with Guy's smarmy aloofness. The script was adapted by Raymond Chandler from the novel by Patricia Highsmith, although Czenzi Ormonde's rewrite constituted the final shooting script. Chandler and Hitchcock, schoolboys of similar temperament, detested each other. The surly writer referred to the director as "that fat bastard."

"All things had opposites close by," wrote Highsmith, "every decision a reason against it, every animal an animal that destroys it."

Most of Hitchcock's excursions down Blind Alley were vacation trips, pumped up with a few hair's-breadth brushes with disaster. But sometimes the journeys were laden with guilt. When he was able to adroitly combine the two, as in *Shadow of a Doubt* (Universal, 1943) and *Strangers on a Train* (WB, 1951), Hitch produced masterpieces. Both those films feature villains forcing irrational darkness into the lives of stable — if vaguely culpable — plain folk.

Shadow of a Doubt's Uncle Charlie (Joseph Cotten) is in many ways Hitchcock's alter ego – the charming dinner guest who unnerves a complacent family with straight talk about man's innate evil. Charlie's devoted niece (Teresa Wright) discovers that her idol is a peripatetic psychopath. Although she slips his assassination attempts, she'll never shake the shame of finding him so desirable. Transference of guilt is also the theme of *Strangers on a Train*, in which dangerously demented Bruno Anthony (Robert Walker) acts out Guy Haines's (Farley Granger) secret desire to get rid of his wife. Hitchcock relished stories in which morally confused innocents were tortured by morally bankrupt predators.

"He considered all life unmanageable," declared Hitchcock biographer Donald Spoto. "The paradox of Alfred Hitchcock was that his delight in his craft could never be liberated from a terrible and terrifying heritage of desire and its concomitant guilt."

Sounds like an already nervous boy educated by Jesuits. The Catholic church instilled in Hitchcock all the terrors that awaited the tempted, but gave him no earthly weapons with which to defend himself. What peace is there for anyone who believes that dark imaginings will result in real punishment? As screenwriter Arthur Laurents noted, "It was obvious to anyone who worked with him that he had a strong sense of sin, and that whether he was a regular churchgoer or not, his Victorian Catholic background still affected him deeply. He might have been indirect in dealing with sexual things in his films, but he had a strong instinct for them. He thought everyone was doing something physical and nasty behind every closed door — except himself."

The runaway success of *Strangers on a Train* curiously left Hitchcock creatively off-track and unsure of his next destination. With the stabilizing influence of his wife Alma (like Mrs. Raymond Chandler, she was as much a mother as a spouse), Hitchcock opted to finally undertake a pet project he'd had on the back burner for years, an adaptation of the 1902 play *Nos Deux Consciences* by Paul Bourde. The result, *I Confess* (WB, 1953) is one of Hitchcock's most darkly brooding films, and one that directly confronts the mystery of faith at the heart of his Catholic indoctrination. It concerns a priest who is forbidden by the sanctity of the confessional to reveal the identity of a murderer. Father Michael Logan (Montgomery Clift) chooses to adhere to his spiritual principles even when *he* is tried for the murder. Guilt has a field day in the film, especially considering that the murder victim was blackmailing a woman with whom Logan had an illicit love affair years earlier. As in *Strangers*, an innocent man is tormented by guilt over a crime that he may have wanted to happen, but did not commit.

Montgomery Clift was an intriguing choice to don the cleric's collar in *I Confess*. A neurotic, bisexual alcoholic, Clift was adept at projecting a brittle vulnerability. Hitchcock, notoriously impatient with actors, endured Clift's halting Method techniques, and his dependence on personal dialogue coach Mira Rostiva. He took cruel revenge by hosting a post-production party, preferring a steady stream of booze and relishing Clift's descent into incoherence. He capped the evening by daring Clift to drain a full flagon of brandy. The actor did as directed, and keeled face first into unconsciousness, to the horror of guests.

I Confess was Hitchcock's most personal film in a career that by then had spanned 25 years. It raised to metaphysical heights Hitchcock's perennial theme of a lone person facing down an unjust fate. It clearly pitted a system of fallible human justice against the conceit of God's divine plan. It's the conundrum lurking at the heart of every Blind Alley thriller: is there hope of cosmic balance, or is chaos the only true god? The palpable dread that this question inspired in Hitchcock twitched beneath even his most diverting escapades.

Hitchcock's films, like most Blind Alley stories, are about fate —

The Wrong Man was based on the true story of Emanuel Balestrero, a bass player at New York's Stork Club, who in 1953 was arrested for a string of hold-ups around his Queens neighborhood. So many witnesses positively identified Balestrero at his trial that it prompted one juror to blurt out "Do we have to listen to any more of this?" A mistrial was immediately declared. During the defendant's excruciating wait for a new trial, the real culprit was serendipitously arrested for another petty robbery, clearing Balestrero.

and by extension, they ponder the existence of God. These stories revolve around the lost and impoverished — in short, the Chosen.

These are timeless tales. Take the Jews, for example, dominated by the original Dark City powerbrokers, the Romans. Pontius and the boys showed how savagely challenges to the status quo are dealt with, nailing the Jews' most influential storyteller. But the disciples knew the value of a good story, and their collected works made for the greatest story ever told. The battle between those wielding earthly might, and those claiming the kingdom of heaven has always been the catalyst of theological belief — in a word, faith. In Dark City, it's a given that the Romans' descendants will always be in charge, because around here muscle counts for more than heavenly dispensation. So for the powerless, belief in the invisible god becomes the most vital survival tool.

Hitchcock would grapple with this theme in *The Wrong Man* (WB, 1956). The day trip into Dark City represented another personal departure for the director. He eschewed the controlled environment of the studio for the grim starkness of location shoots, to more effectively convey the real-life terror of Christopher Emanuel Balestrero, who's accused unjustly and ushered unceremoniously into Kafka's worst nightmare. The story combined several Hitchcock obsessions: fear of the police, transference of guilt, and the mystery of divine intervention.

The director always maintained that the seminal event in his youth (and art) occurred when he was locked in a jail cell — his father's way of shocking him onto the straight and narrow. Hitchcock's production designer, Robert Boyle, thought that chestnut was apocryphal: "Hitch told it so often, and it was convenient for the press, that he probably came to believe it himself." Another bond with Woolrich.

Whether drawing on experience or not, Hitchcock created in *The Wrong Man* a sinking sense of despair as the innocent Balestrero (Henry Fonda) is sucked inexorably into the bowels of the ravenous, but indifferent, justice system. Fonda plays Manny as the ultimate victim. He barely raises his voice to protest his treatment, and when he does the sound of it embarrasses him. Manny doesn't rail, he doesn't fight. He just goes gentle into that not-so-good night.

Emotionally, the film couldn't be further from the colorful, cavalier (and often cruel) spectacles that marked Hitchcock's fertile mid-1950s style. But neither was it the dispassionate venture into cinema verité Hitchcock initially intended. The direction and cinematography are brilliantly calculated noir, nothing like the flat, documentary images Hitchcock claimed he was after. *The Wrong Man* has a full ration of stylistic and technical flourishes; but it is a film that, for once, the director stripped of all romantic pretense.

Hitch paints an uncharacteristically sympathetic portrait of Manny's wife, Rose (Vera Miles), who succumbs to the mounting pressure and adopts the thousand yard stare endemic to Hitchcock's vanquished innocents. "It's all my fault," she says, assuming responsibility for her husband's travails. "I haven't been a good wife to you." As the walls close in, she finally cracks. "It doesn't matter what you do, or how innocent you are," she declares. "They've got it all fixed so that it goes against you. We're going to lock the doors and stay in the house. We're going to lock them out and keep them out." Although Manny is eventually cleared of his "crime," Rose serves out the sentence in a sanitarium.

The muted climax of the story comes when Manny's mother, a devout Roman Catholic, tells him his only recourse is to pray for a miracle. "I don't need a miracle," he sighs, "what I need is some luck." But Manny, who's muttered rosaries throughout his trial, stares at a picture of Christ and gives prayer one last shot. Hitchcock superimposes a street over his face, and slowly another man — almost his twin — walks up to the camera, his face a perfect fit beneath Manny's. The man then tries another stick-up, but he's collared and ID'd for the crimes hanging over Manny.

Miracle or luck?

Hitchcock regretted the way he handled that scene, claiming it destroyed the "authentic" documentary nature of the film. In hindsight, Hitchcock always seemed uncomfortable with the films in which he didn't hide his insecurities behind a pranksterish facade. He'd quickly confess to "miscalculations" when the public didn't warm to *I Confess* and *The Wrong Man*, the two films where he clearly exposed a fearful confusion over how true believers can be abandoned — or rediscovered — by their God.

The darkness inside Alfred Hitchcock has provided grist for scores of critical interpretations and biographies. Like Woolrich, he was fortunate to have an outlet for his insistent fears and desires. Unfortunately, he was heir to all the terrors of the Catholic church, and none of the balm its rituals of faith are supposed to provide. "I was born a Catholic," Hitchcock told an interviewer late in his life; "I went to Catholic school, and now I have a conscience with lots of trials over beliefs."

When he was dying, going about the pretense of daily work at the studio, he told his aides, "Don't let any priests on the lot. They're all after me. They all hate me." Hitchcock turned tremulous as he neared the finish. There were many maudlin, teary scenes, in which he regressed further into his childhood fears. According to Spoto, he declared not long before his death: "One never knows the ending. One has to die to know exactly what happens after death, although Catholics have their hopes."

As Kafka's friendly cops said in *The Wrong Man:* "Just remember, Manny — an innocent man has nothing to fear."

Although she's suitably dowdy in *The Wrong Man*, Vera Miles was Hitchcock's choice to replace departed Grace Kelly as the director's idealized woman. His obsession with molding blonde goddesses whom he could then manipulate tilted toward the pathological. Hitchcock spent as much time in private "story conferences" with Miles as he did on the set. Her sudden elopement with actor Gordon Scott doused the director's awkward ardor. Hitchcock had great plans to make Vera Miles a star by grooming her for the lead role in the forthcoming *Vertigo,* his dizzying foray into sexual fetishism. Miles's pregnancy interrupted those plans, and Kim Novak became the new object of his obsession.

Robert Ryan, Robert Mitchum, and
Robert Young in *Crossfire*.

The radiator sizzles like rain off the hot barrel of the howitzer. The flashing neon makes him twitch; muscle memory of the muzzle's flash. The ceiling fan spins like the prop blades on the stripped-down bomber that brought him back. He'd tried to burst the gurney's straps and sprint onboard — couldn't wait to get home. But then there was the ward: the daily stench of disinfectant and festering dreams. And big blank gaps in his thoughts, filled up with the faces of the doggies left behind, dead on some cratered road in France.

The Psych Ward

Far from the typical tourist spots of Dark City is the Veterans' Hospital, packed with men who fought their best, but left pieces of themselves in places they never considered visiting. The cold gray building sits at the GI intersection of Guilt and Indignity, in a neighborhood the average citizen rarely sees. Screenwriters, on the other hand, made frequent visits. For them, discharged and disoriented dogfaces offered a new, urgent spin on the same sense of bewilderment and betrayal that the Great Depression had inspired in earlier crime dramas.

Even before the war officially ended, some producers had begun looking past the imminent victory galas to the traumas vets lugged back to the homefront. *The Best Years of Our Lives* and *Pride of the Marines* dealt with disabled vets in heroic fashion — the stoic GI does his patriotic duty by gamely shaking off tragedy, adjusting to his misfortune, and choosing not to ask inconvenient questions of his country. Everyone felt better about armless and sightless soldiers after a trip to the movies.

The nation's concern for vets was codified by the enactment of the GI Bill, which provided funding to soldiers for education and vocational training. The federal largesse of the Bill assuaged America about the fortunes of its brave returning soldiers. But in the musty wards of the Dark City VA hospital, you'd find plenty of old-timers with a different kind of story to tell.

One of their favorites is a real-life crime saga that outdoes anything from Sinister Heights. Back in 1921, President Warren G. Harding (the unofficial Mayor Emeritus of Dark City) appointed a personal friend, Charles Forbes, to run the fledgling Veterans Bureau, as the VA was originally called. Forbes, a Marine Corps deserter, might have seemed an odd choice. But if he had no stomach for combat, Forbes had what it took to brown-nose Washington's power elite.

Once installed in his post, Forbes raised pork-barrel chicanery to a fine, if nefarious, art. He grabbed control of the sale of all surplus supplies from the army's quartermaster general, and wangled jurisdiction over all new hospital

THE DREAM FACTORY could pump out wartime propaganda as jingoistic as the Axis. Whether it was star-studded combat films or espionage thrillers, Americans were presented as can-do cowboys filled with a roughhouse determination that would always outlast the enemy. After displaying fighting fortitude on studio sets, stars dutifully toured military bases to boost the troops' morale. When he wasn't headlining efforts like *Dangerously They Live*, John Garfield founded the famed Hollywood Canteen, where troops could rub shoulders with the stars. Despite its lurid ad campaign, *None Shall Escape* was an earnest exploration of Nazi war crimes against the Russian people, written by Lester Cole and directed by André de Toth. *Behind the Rising Sun* was fire-breathing propaganda, starring Tom Neal and Robert Ryan, and directed by RKO stalwart Edward Dmytryk. Only a few years after concocting these vital examples of patriotic fervor, Garfield, Cole and Dmytryk would all be hounded out of Hollywood by the House Un-American Activities Committee, purportedly for slipping insidious pro-Communist messages into their films.

Hollywood, like Dark City, has always been a "what have you done for me lately?" town.

construction. He got Harding to grant him oversight of military warehouses in Maryland, through which he fraudulently resold pristine goods as "damaged" supplies, pocketing millions.

"Forbes's quarter-billion dollars in accumulated graft, corruption, and inefficiency was to become a landmark by which a succession of VA administrators could be measured," wrote Robert Klein in his history of the VA, *Wounded Men, Broken Promises.* When Harding learned the immensity of Forbes's criminal impunity, he tried to strangle his appointee in the Red Room of the White House. Forbes survived, was sentenced to a two-year stretch in Leavenworth, and was slapped with a $100,000 fine — less than a tenth of one percent of what he stole from American taxpayers.

Forbes's successor, Brig. Gen. Frank T. Hines, was a tight-fisted Republican opponent of the New Deal who assiduously shoveled funds back into federal coffers, rather than squander them on beefed-up veterans' benefits. On Hines's short leash the VA became a bureaucratic boondoggle incapable of meeting the needs of the nation's discharged servicemen. An eight-month Congressional probe proved that the government knew there was a serious problem, but the only

Homefront hoodlum Vince Alexander (Sonny Tufts) and his boys work over returning Silver Star winner Eddie Rice (John Payne) in *The Crooked Way.*

solution forthcoming was the appointment of popular Omar Bradley, the "GI's General," to take over the agency. Bradley forged alliances with many of the nation's top medical schools, but even this was insufficient to deal with the wave of needy veterans.

Hollywood picked up some of the slack, albeit in melodramatic fashion. Within a year of the Hiroshima blast that brought an apocalyptic finish to Pacific combat, movies for the first time touched on the disillusionment of America's combat vets. The least mawkish of these films were noirs. When dislocated GIs were dropped into the framework of a crime drama, pithy analogies crept in about the hypocrisy of a civilized society that demands "the ultimate sacrifice" from its young

men, then forgets their names once the enemy is vanquished. The most terse assessment of the dilemma was offered by John Payne in *Kansas City Confidential,* as he's grilled about his suspected role in an armored car robbery. "He won a Bronze Star and a Purple Heart," notes one interrogator. "Try buying a cup of coffee with them," snaps the embittered vet.

When Johnny came marching home to Dark City, he wasn't welcomed by a ticker tape parade or offered a decent job. He was greeted by a grifter with an easy money scam. Or sometimes, he woke up in the psych ward, suffering from a head wound, crucial patches of his memory missing.

The Crooked Way (UA, 1949) was a prime example. Decorated infantryman Eddie Rice (John Payne) is turned loose from a VA hospital with several bucks in his pocket and not much in his head. When he hits L.A.'s Union Station, he's promptly braced by the bulls, who know him as Eddie Ricardi, a local hood. Eddie's ex-wife Nina (Ellen Drew) shows up, now the main squeeze of gangster Vince Alexander (Sonny Tufts), once Eddie's partner. Vince thinks Eddie enlisted to skip on a job gone sour, for which Vince took the rap.

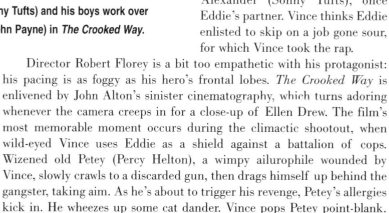

Director Robert Florey is a bit too empathetic with his protagonist: his pacing is as foggy as his hero's frontal lobes. *The Crooked Way* is enlivened by John Alton's sinister cinematography, which turns adoring whenever the camera creeps in for a close-up of Ellen Drew. The film's most memorable moment occurs during the climactic shootout, when wild-eyed Vince uses Eddie as a shield against a battalion of cops. Wizened old Petey (Percy Helton), a wimpy ailurophile wounded by Vince, slowly crawls to a discarded gun, then drags himself up behind the gangster, taking aim. As he's about to trigger his revenge, Petey's allergies kick in. He wheezes up some cat dander. Vince pops Petey point-blank. It's a stroke of originality in an otherwise paint-by-numbers picture.

In *The Clay Pigeon* (RKO, 1949), seaman first class Jim Fletcher (Bill Williams), a quintessential gob, wakes up in a VA hospital with a dose of amnesia. He's stunned to find himself facing a court-martial for treason and murder. In finest noir fashion, the muddy-minded swab doesn't wait to be assigned a judge advocate — he beats it out of the ward to track down the missing pieces of his memory. Within hours he's the target of a manhunt involving the police, naval intelligence, and a gang of southland chiselers. He heads to the home of his closest Navy pal, Mark Gregory, only to learn from the guy's widow, Martha (Barbara Hale), that Gregory is the one he's accused of murdering. Fletcher kidnaps Martha and hauls her along on his search for answers.

Before an economical 63 minutes have elapsed, Fletcher has broken up a counterfeiting ring operated by corrupt Japanese and U.S. soldiers — and gotten hitched to Martha. The matrimonial bond seems to blossom through some sado-masochistic ministrations: "Don't make me tie you up again," Fletcher threatens at one point through a big 'Aw shucks' grin. "You just try it," Martha vamps back, slyly soliciting the rope burns.

The Clay Pigeon, like most noirs that had their sights set on homecoming vets, exploited the soldier's disability for dramatic effect. Battle-induced infirmities — even the ubiquitous amnesia — proved irresistible to scenarists seeking "plausible" motivations to prop up improbable plot twists.

The Crooked Way and *The Clay Pigeon* were pallid knock-offs of Joseph L. Mankiewicz's *Somewhere in the Night* (20th, 1946), one of the first and best of the "amnesiac veteran" movies. In it, John Hodiak plays ex-marine George Taylor, who heads back to L.A. with only two clues to his identity: a nasty letter from an angry woman, and another signed by "Larry Cravat." The hazy vet pursues Cravat through a demimonde of

nightclubs, police stations, and dingy dives, confronting a fully-loaded menagerie of noir's most colorful bit players. In the end he learns that all along he's just been chasing himself (a twist that would be exhumed years later, with devilish overtones, in *Angel Heart*).

As these scenarios suggest, the vexed veteran was the perfect protagonist for films that combined the "Why me?" suspense of Blind Alley thrillers with the hardboiled hegiras indigenous to Shamus Flats. The symbolism of a lost and lonely recruit searching for his identity was too tempting for writers to resist, even after the novelty wore out its welcome.

A far less vulnerable serviceman returned in *Dead Reckoning* (Columbia,'47). Flinty paratrooper Rip Murdock (Humphrey Bogart) investigates the disappearance of jump-mate Johnny Drake, who rabbits just before he's due to receive the Medal of Honor. Rip's search leads to Gulf City, a humid Floridian sister to Dark City, where he encounters local gangster Martinelli (Morris Carnovsky), husky-voiced songbird Coral Chandler (Lizabeth Scott), and the charred body of his war buddy cooling in a morgue drawer. The classically hard-boiled recipe is subtly spiced by the contempt Bogart dishes to crooks who've gotten rich at home while he's risked his life overseas.

The smarmy Martinelli goes out of his way to insult Murdock by boasting that his casino proffers only the best "pre-war" wines and patés. No ration stamps for the well-connected. The gangster's private arsenal is assembled from contraband military ordnance. Rip turns the hunt for Johnny's killer into a re-con mission, making it clear that even though he's on U.S. soil, this vet is still operating behind enemy lines. There's a satisfying symbolism to the climax, when Rip uses an incendiary grenade to flambée Martinelli and his minions.

Dead Reckoning served up a full ration of hard-boiled noir. It assembled all the requisite ingredients — seasoned hero on a dark quest, oily gangster with pretensions to refinement, flavorful femme fatale, sultry nocturnal environs, vinegary voice-over narration — and coated them with the sentimental righteousness of the loyal and solitary warrior. But director John Cromwell couldn't quite raise a souffle from the dense, leaden script, for which no fewer than five writers, including trusty Steve Fisher and Allen Rivkin, earned Purple Hearts.

By '47, Bogart had patented his tough guy persona. Martinelli and his henchmen were no match for the resourcefulness of this battle-hardened soldier. Liz Scott jerks his strings pretty good; in Dark City women represent a more formidable adversary than puffed-up mobsters. In the end, Bogey kisses her off like all the other Vixenville dames who spent the Forties trying to bring him down. It would be a few years before Bogart tempered his screen image with an edgy humanity, culminating in his vivid portrayal of the paranoid Capt. Queeg in *The Caine Mutiny*.

The High Wall (MGM, 1947) showed the flip side of the rough-and-ready fighting man embodied by Bogart. Steve Kenet (Robert Taylor), an army pilot, is put in an overcrowded veterans' asylum after he's found unconscious in an overturned car, his dead wife Helen (Dorothy Patrick) beside him. Evidence of strangulation points to Kenet as Helen's killer. A head wound sustained in combat has left Kenet the victim of periodic blackouts, and he swears to have no recollection of the deadly incident. The authorities believe Kenet is using his brain injury to back a "temporary insanity" defense. Dr. Ann Lorrison (Audrey Totter) persuades the troubled vet that a second operation, to remove a hematoma from his brain, will alleviate his mental distress and free up his memory. Kenet's in a trick bag. He wants to overcome his disability so he can care for his young son — but he's afraid his restored memory will reveal him as the murderer.

Giving Kenet an injection of sodium pen-tothal — recommended by eight out of ten Dark City shrinks — Dr. Lorrison dredges up the buried details of the fateful night. Kenet had discovered Helen in the apartment of her boss, Willard Whitcombe (Herbert Marshall), a publisher of religious tracts. Spotting Helen's overnight bag on Whitcombe's bed, he lunged for her throat, but blacked out.

Convinced Kenet is innocent, Dr. Lorrison helps him reconstruct the night of the killing, and the convoluted story climaxes with her jabbing the needle of truth into Whitcombe to extract a confession.

Dr. Lorrison is a film noir rarity — a compassionate psychiatrist. Typically, head doctors in these films were burbling fonts of Freudian psychobabble. Their role model was Dr. Murchison (Leo G. Carroll) in Hitchcock's *Spellbound* (Selznick, 1945), a condescending European-educated egghead, whose insidious newfangled techniques scramble old-fashioned common sense – and who won't stop at murder to protect his exalted station in the academic pantheon. In Dark City, psychiatrists are as corrupt as gangsters, misusing their "power over the mind" to dominate the hapless and disturbed.

The High Wall was just one of numerous film noirs that shifted danger and treachery from the city's streets and alleys to the penumbral labyrinth of the unconscious. Fear of someone gaining access to — and control of — the deepest parts of the psyche resulted in numerous disparaging portrayals of psychiatrists, from Val Lewton horror shows like *Cat People* and *The Seventh Victim*, to many Woolrich-inspired thrillers, to private eye

stories in which the quack doctor exploits helpless clients.

Rarely-seen, *The High Wall* has eluded critical evaluation over the years, even though it contains seminal noir elements. The flashback-within-flashback structure was challenging for an MGM "A" picture of this period (and may have contributed to the public's lukewarm response). Kenet's anguish was vividly limned

Steve Kenet (Robert Taylor) is a brain-damaged vet charged with murdering his wife in *The High Wall*.

by director Curtis Bernhardt, another German emigré who excelled at conveying tortured states of mind through sinuous, expressionistic visuals. When Kenet attacks Helen, and later reenacts the incident with Dr. Lorrison, the camera looms over the women's terrified faces in a startling display of subjective camerawork. (Paul Vogel's cinematography imparts a glistening menace to the proceedings.)

"Remember, any accusation you make against me will be ridiculed. The ravings of a pitiful lunatic.... There's no possible way you can prove I killed your wife."

— Herbert Marshall to Robert Taylor in *The High Wall*

As a specimen of shellshocked noir, *The High Wall* was unique in a number of ways. The asylum scenes offered a rare, compassionate glimpse of the military generally deemed off-limits. Ample screen time was devoted to the mental casualties of war; there were references to patients housed within VA walls since World War I. When Kenet barks that he wants to see Dr. Lorrison immediately, he's told: "There are twenty-five hundred patients in this hospital and twelve doctors. We'll get to you when we can." A shard of hard truth woven into the film's baroque design.

Screenwriter Lester Cole, who shared credit on *The High Wall* with noir specialist Sydney Boehm, was one of those who would be formally accused of slipping subversive messages into his scripts. Only weeks after *The High Wall* wrapped, Cole was cited for contempt of Congress when he appeared as an "unfriendly witness" before the HUAC in Washington, D.C. As one of the Hollywood Ten, Cole was jailed for refusing to provide the names of known or suspected Communists in the movie industry.

Cole was an industry stalwart who'd been a screenwriter since the early 1930s. He was a member of the Communist Party of the United States of America, and an early campaigner for the unionization of Tinseltown scribes. None of these affiliations had the stigma then that they'd assume after 1947, when the Cold War plunged open political discourse into the deep freeze. In fact, at the time of his appearance before HUAC, Cole was a well-paid favorite of Louis B. Mayer, who was about to bestow lofty writer-producer status on him at MGM. Given the witchhunt hysteria, Cole instead found himself, like other artists committed to "progressive" work, blacklisted out of a job.

The highest-profile "friendly" witness to testify before HUAC, in October, 1947, was Robert Taylor, who seemed to have still been suffering the effects of Steve Kenet's amnesia: "If I were even suspicious of a person being a Communist with whom I was scheduled to work," he declared under oath, "I am afraid it would have to be him or me, because life is a little too short to be around people who annoy me as much as these fellow travelers and Communists do." Cole's work on *The High Wall* must have mightily impressed Taylor for the actor to shelve such deeply-held ideological pretensions.

Taylor had sparked an uproar several months earlier, when HUAC's scouting party first went hunting for Hollywood stool pigeons. He maintained that President Roosevelt himself had postponed Taylor's naval duty so that he'd be able to film *Song of Russia* (MGM, 1944), a goofy musical that became a touchstone of political debate. Power-hungry Republicans sought to discredit Democrats by tarring the late President as a Commie sympathizer. (The right wing was still smarting from Roosevelt's taxation-based New Deal, which helped pull the country out of the Depression. To them, federally-sponsored work programs were socialism by any name.) Linking the late commander-in-chief to a piece of "pro-Soviet" propaganda like *Song of Russia* seemed like a revelatory bombshell to political animals in a feeding frenzy. But Taylor shrank from the furor he released, and recanted his story.

The imbroglio over *Song of Russia* was, in hindsight, low comedy. The film, written by future blacklistees Richard Collins and Paul Jarrico, was insipid romantic claptrap about an American conductor in Russia who falls in love with one of the busty proletariat. It was pure Hollywood nonsense, set to the strains of Tchaikovsky. Arguments flared over the veracity of the film's depiction of Soviet life. At the nadir came the absurd spectacle of libertarian lioness Ayn Rand pontificating as to the fraudulent smiles on the faces of the Russian people. "Don't they smile?" asked Pennsylvania Republican John McDowell. "Not quite that way, no," came Rand's earnest reply.

Imagine that: the subversion of America commencing among the daffy dance numbers of an MGM musical.

As anti-Communist fervor gained momentum, treatment of war-related themes became one of the litmus tests for determining an artist's patriotism – or suspicious pacifism. Films that focused on problems of readjustment, or that simply refused to celebrate victory blindly when the world was in obvious disarray, tended to be written by liberals like Dalton Trumbo, Albert Maltz, Carl Foreman, or John Howard Lawson – many of whom had long-standing ties to the film colony's left wing.

Their loyalties would be challenged by the Motion Picture Alliance for the Preservation of American Ideals, which under the leadership of hawks such as Sam Wood, Leo McCarey, Gary Cooper, Robert Montgomery, John Wayne, and Ronald Reagan, sought to root out the "red menace" among screenwriters and make movie screens safe for loyal, God-fearing Americans. The reactionary pogrom worked. Hundreds of artists, Communists and free-thinkers, were blacklisted either outright or covertly.

It would be more than 30 years before mainstream Hollywood would use the reality of the disabled veteran's plight as grist for a dramatic story. In the meantime, noir crime dramas proved to be the only films willing to suggest — in tone, if not factual detail — that disorientation and mental instability were real problems for combat-scarred soldiers.

Although *The High Wall* offered the dramatic premise of a wounded vet accused of murder, there was never any doubt that Steve Kenet would be found innocent – and not only because he was played by heartthrob Robert Taylor. While vets made great vulnerable protagonists, it was an unwritten rule that they never be found guilty of any crime. That was too insensitive an angle for any scriptwriter to attempt, as Raymond Chandler found out in 1945, when he concocted his own Psych Ward mystery drama, *The Blue Dahlia*.

The film's creation is Tinseltown legend, burnished by an application of apocrypha. In 1945, Paramount desperately sought another hit from its biggest star, Alan Ladd, before his re-induction to the Navy. (Ladd had already served a hitch in 1943, primarily in a morale-boosting capacity.) Producer John Houseman learned that Chandler was halfway into a new novel, and he convinced studio execs to offer the popular plot-spinner a hefty sum to turn the manuscript into an original screenplay. Chandler accepted, and a cast and crew were quickly assembled, with stars Ladd and his favorite leading lady, Veronica Lake, at the center.

The script revolved around the troubles of two returned vets, Johnny Morrison (Ladd) and Buzz Wanchek (William Bendix). Johnny marches home to discover that his wife Helen (Doris Dowling) has become a squirrelly tramp, who tries to hide the fact that her drunken driving killed their young son (she claims it was an illness). Buzz, fresh out of the Dark City VA hospital, is outfitted with a steel plate in his head that causes ill-timed tantrums and memory lapses. Things get complicated when Helen is bumped off in her bungalow. Johnny is suspected, and he spends the rest of the film tracking down the real killer, with the aid of vampish stray Joyce Harwood (Lake) and his loyal sidekick, Buzz.

Chandler's twist was that Buzz was the unwitting culprit. His plate started humming when Helen made disparaging cracks about Johnny, but then he blacked out — shades of Woolrich's *Black Angel*. To Chandler's credit, Buzz was at the front of the woozy line of amnesiac vets that trooped through Dark City. Chandler envisioned a poignant wrap-up to his yarn, as Johnny realizes his addled pal is guilty, and he must decide whether to send him up.

Helming the production was George Marshall, an old-school journeyman who never let freshness or originality interrupt a shooting schedule. His marching orders were to churn 'em out, so Marshall started filming before Chandler even finished the script. Day by day, Marshall gained on Chandler, cranking scenes into the can before new ones could be written. Halfway in, word came from the Department of the Navy that Chandler's projected ending wouldn't pass muster: Buzz couldn't be the killer — bad for the Navy's image.

Chandler was so incensed he threatened to drop the project. Ladd's re-enlistment deadline loomed. A $5,000 completion bonus was dangled before the author. He took umbrage, and got crankier. Houseman was at a loss. Finally, Chandler proposed a disingenuous solution: he must be allowed to work at home, with two secretaries at his disposal, a doctor on call, a pair of Cadillacs to ferry script pages to the set, an open line to Paramount — and the studio's understanding that he could only perform under such pressure while mooned to the nuts. Paramount assented. As Marshall knocked off shot after shot, so did Chandler. Chauffeurs funneled individual pages to the set, thrashed out by the author in a prodigious bourbon bender.

The film wrapped ahead of schedule, and Chandler was feted like a gallant, wounded vet. His solution to the murder, however, was a clunker: the house detective did it, although his motive didn't seem to extend beyond some convenient lurking at the windows and behind curtains — exactly the kind of lame denouement Chandler detested in other writers.

Ladd's real life was far more intriguing. According to his biographer, Beverly Linet, the actor never did reenlist — he hung around his ranch in Hidden Valley while his wife, agent Sue Carol, negotiated a new deal with Paramount. And Ladd's friendship with Bendix, forged when the pair made a film version of Dashiell Hammett's *The Glass Key* (Paramount, 1942), didn't survive the war. The two had been so tight they lived across the street from each other. But when Ladd returned from stateside naval duty in 1943, grousing about its various indignities, Bendix ribbed him: "Quit griping, Laddie, you know you're living the plush life down there in San Diego." Ladd let it pass, but his wife upbraided Bendix: "You're a fine one to talk," she volleyed, "considering you're not rushing off to join up." Bendix, a 4-F asthmatic, huffed out. He and Ladd never bothered to cross the street and patch things up. Just another tragic Hollywood war story.

NEVER TRUST A GUY YOU MEET IN A BOWLING ALLEY. That's advice Howard Tyler (Frank Lovejoy) should have gotten when he did his basic at Fort Roberts. Howard never got shipped over, so he didn't even have a war record to parlay into a steady peacetime paycheck. Howard had moved his wife and kids to Santa Sierra, California, looking for a fresh start. "How'd I know a million other guys would have the same idea," he snaps at his cloying wife Judy (Kathleen Ryan), before stomping out to search for more non-existent work. When he falls by the lanes for a quick beer to buzz the edge off his misery, he meets another vet, Jerry Slocum (Lloyd Bridges).

"What outfit were you with?" asks the rakish Slocum, as he combs back his gleaming locks. "No outfit, really," mumbles Howard. "I never got over. Took my basic at Fort Roberts."

"So did I," beams Slocum. "What a lousy joint — I couldn't wait to get over."

"So you got over. Pretty rugged, huh?"

"That's the rumor I heard in Paris," Slocum smiles. "Ah — *Paree*. You know what I could get for one lousy pack of cigar-ettes? Boy, the mark-up was terrific."

"I wish a guy could get a buck that easy these days."

"Got a car? Maybe I can put you onto something."

So begins *Try and Get Me!*, a largely unseen, unheralded picture that's one of the most disturbing film noirs. Howard spends a few hours basking in Slocum's uptown swagger, sizing up the monogrammed silk shirts, expensive cologne, fancy cufflinks. "Those are platinum, you know, not silver," Slocum points out. Before Howard can drift, Slocum lays out his cards: he needs a wheelman for a series of highway filling station stick-ups. Howard wavers, but finally caves under Slocum's insistence that it's only a few nights' work, in and out, no funny business.

Howard believes he's only detouring into petty crime as a first step toward finally giving Judy all the middle-class creature comforts she craves. But Jerry's nocturnal knockovers put them on the highway to hell. He abruptly ups the ante from robbery to kidnapping. They snatch Donald Miller, scion of a wealthy Santa Sierra family, visions of a big green windfall pushing them on. But as soon as Slocum eyes the rich college boy, his vengeful hatred starts bubbling. "Where'd you get the suit?" he asks the kid, fingering the material. "New York," Miller answers. Slocum sneers jealously: "You guys sure treat yourselves right, don't you?"

In a fit of psychotic pique, Slocum kills the hostage, burying the body in a desolate quarry. Jerry forces Howard to go through with the plot, dragging him along on a double date to another town, from where he'll mail the ransom note. Howard's shaky mental state is further rattled by his spooky date, Hazel (Katherine Locke, in a strange, unnerving performance). He lurches through a lubricious night on the town, convinced the whole world is watching him, laughing at him, accusing him. When he passes out on Hazel's couch, the lonesome spinster starts making love to him. She finds Donald Miller's tie clasp in the cuff of Howard's pants, and he goes wild and tries to strangle her. He collapses in grief, and Hazel runs to the police. Howard is trapped like a cowering dog in a shed behind his clapboard house. "What did my Daddy do?" his son keeps yelping as the cops close in.

Newspaper columnist Gil Stanton (Richard Carlson), at the urging of his publisher (Art Smith), writes a series of articles playing up the brutality of the killing, fueling public outrage. The sheriff asks him to back off, aware that the town is too small for the heat of the flames being fanned. Slocum gets nabbed, but Howard's attempt to pin the killing on him is futile. The media, and the vengeful townsfolk, see no distinction between a genuine sociopath and a poor, misguided sap.

In the film's terrifying climax, a crowd of respectable citizens and students, whipped up by Stanton's editorials, storm the jail. Trapped in his cell, Howard Tyler sees death coming for him in the form of fresh-faced college boys in a frenzy of bloodlust. Slocum greets his seemingly pre-destined fate with giddy cries of "Try and get me!"

Lloyd Bridges and Frank Lovejoy in *Try and Get Me!*, a true story adapted to reflect the disillusionment of World War II veterans. Neither man was ever better than in this 1950 film noir.

One of the most emotionally-charged and bleakest of all noirs, *Try and Get Me!* was adapted by Jo Pagano from his novel *The Condemned*. Its factual basis was the 1933 lynching in San Jose, California of Jack Holmes and Harold Thurmond, who had kidnapped and killed affluent college student Brooke Hart. *San Jose News* publisher G. Logan Payne instigated citizens' unrest with editorials declaring that "If mob violence could ever be justified it would be in a case like this.... There was never a more fiendish crime committed anywhere in the United States...." Ten thousand people filled San Jose's town square to cheer the administration of vigilante justice.

Director Cyril Endfield made hardly a false move in rendering the shocking story. The insertion of a humanistic European professor who lectures Stanton — and the audience — on how society's lack of compassion breeds criminals, is one of the few ham-handed gestures in an otherwise dextrous film. For most of its swift 90 minutes, *Try and Get Me!* (originally entitled *The Sound of Fury*) is every bit the equal of Fritz Lang's similarly themed *Fury* (MGM, 1936),

also inspired by the San Jose lynchings. The finale, with Bridges pacing his cell like a riled beast, vowing revenge on his cohort as the crowd seethes below, is vividly shot by Guy Roe with an early, highly effective use of hand-held camera. The vigilantes' assault is as scary and riveting as anything produced in Hollywood up to that time. As the beaten prisoners are passed across the sea of vengeance, Endfield cuts to Howard Tyler's son waking up in his bed, shaking. Gil Stanton sits quietly in his office, wincing at the roars from the crowd as it metes out its own brand of justice.

Producer Robert Stillman knew he had something special in *Try and Get Me!*, and he proudly attached his name to the film's haunting final image. But the distributor, United Artists, buried the film soon after its release. Another casuality of the anti-Communist crusade. Endfield, a one-time drama teacher and magician, started popping up among The Names, and he soon returned to England (not before releasing another effective noir, *The Underworld Story* [UA] also in 1950). Studio honchos no doubt feared that *Try and Get Me!*, by suggesting that materialist values can foster crime, could be considered un-American. Not to mention that the film was taking a stand against mob mentality as Cold War vigilantism reached its boiling point.

The fear and confusion that was then rampant in the studios was exemplified by UA's wildly misleading advertising for the film, after they re-released it with the new title: "Try and get me! And they tried...6000 people...Including the blonde with the ice cold nerves and the deep, warm curves!!! [That would be Adele Jergens, who's in the film for 10 minutes]... And now you can join... Every excitement-packed step of the way ... From the first angry cry...To the roar that explodes the climax!"

A sincere plea against mob violence sold as a rip-snorting crowd-pleaser. Those were strange days.

FRANK ENLEY IS NO HARD LUCK HOWARD TYLER. He's worked his war-hero status into a thriving contractor's business, married a beautiful woman, and has the middle-class program so knocked he has time to enjoy lazy fishing trips in the mountains. He's left the service with no visible scars, no mental damage. But then Joe Parkson, his one-time bombardier buddy, drops into his life, and the buried horrors emerge into the light.

Act of Violence (MGM, 1949) bristles with anger and guilt, the first post-war noir to take a challenging look at the ethics of men in combat *(Stalag 17* was several years away). Enley (Van Heflin) is stalked by the apparently deranged Parkson (Robert Ryan), who seems perversely bent on destroying his former friend's tranquil life. The viewer at first empathizes with Frank Enley, a solid citizen who's helping promote growth and prosperity. But Parkson's tenacity splinters Enley's psyche, and the truth about his record in the war leaks out.

Captured by Nazis, Enley had ratted out his unit, revealing their escape plan. All his comrades — except Parkson — were killed. He told himself he only squealed to save the lives of his mates. Now Parkson wants revenge. "But Frank, they won't listen to Parkson," his wife, Edith (Janet Leigh), assures him. "They'll listen to you." Edith understands that her husband's tormentor is the kind of brooding, ill-tempered vet the common folk ignore. Her husband, by contrast, is a pillar of the community. He's a charismatic man with the gift of gab, who has recast the truth to make himself seem heroic.

"Do I have to spell it out for you?" snaps Enley. "The Nazis even paid me a price. They gave me food and I ate it. I hadn't done it just to save their lives.... They were dead and I was eating and maybe that's all I did it for – to save one man. Me."

Enley is driven from the sanctuary of his suburban home into the underbelly of Dark City, where he's cast adrift among gamblers, thugs, procurers, and whores. He finds refuge with a played-out hooker, Pat (Mary Astor) whose pimp, Johnny (Barry Kroeger), offers to kill Parkson for a hefty fee. Enley draws Parkson into a nocturnal cat-and-mouse game, luring him into Johnny's trap. At the last second, tortured by Parkson's righteous anger, Enley takes the bullet, trying to atone via a final act of sacrifice.

Robert Richards's screenplay was adapted from an unpublished story by Collier Young, an ambitious assistant to Columbia studio boss Harry Cohn. Young would soon embark on a career as an independent producer with his bride-to-be, Ida Lupino. The film was originally going to be a small indie production starring popular radio personality Howard Duff (who would, coincidentally, succeed Young as Ida Lupino's husband). Then Mark Hellinger picked it up, with the notion of pairing Gregory Peck with Humphrey Bogart. Finally filmed at MGM, *Act of Violence* got the studio's patented polish, benefitting from Robert Surtees's photography, which effectively contrasted the brightness of budding suburbia with the murkiness of the underworld into which Frank sinks.

This was Fred Zinnemann's lone excursion into Dark City. A dispassionate but serious-minded director, Zinnemann was obviously influenced by such recent releases as *The Killers* and *Crossfire*, since none of his subsequent films displayed any of the moody flourishes he adopted here. Fred wasn't a natural on this turf; the pervasiveness of noir pushed him into it, the visuals as much as the themes.

Zinnemann's casting of Robert Ryan as Joe Parkson was also part of a trend. Ryan had recently won notice — and an Oscar nomination — for his role in *Crossfire* (RKO, 1947). Like *Act of Violence*, *Crossfire* was conceived as a "message" picture camouflaged as a crime drama. The driving force behind it was Adrian Scott, whose status at RKO was top-drawer in the wake of two hits, *Murder, My Sweet* and *Cornered* (1945). Scott was committed to producing movies that "mattered," although his fear of possible repercussions played hell with his nervous stomach. *Cornered*, for example, was a thriller steeped in anti-fascist sentiment, but the final cut, perhaps wisely, left most of writer John Wexley's dogma on the cutting room floor.

With *Crossfire*, Scott wanted to fashion another piece reviling the fascists. It's a relatively simple murder mystery, set in an odd liberty limbo, with GIs hanging around Washington, D.C. on terminal leave, awaiting discharge. A civilian (Sam Levene) is beaten to death, and a soldier's ID, belonging to Jeff Mitchell (George Cooper), turns up in his room. Finlay (Robert Young), a local homicide detective, hunts Mitchell down, with the help of two other dogfaces, Keeley (Robert Mitchum) and Montgomery (Robert Ryan). Monty's unrepentant redneck bigotry makes him suspect, as the victim was a Jew. A young grunt, the main butt of Monty's cruel jabs, is used to set him up, and the hateful Montgomery is revealed as the real killer.

By 1946, many Jews in the film industry had been galvanized by the facts emerging about Hitler's death camps, and the campaign for a homeland in Palestine. Semitic issues were considered, for the first time, as possible subjects in mainstream movies. Ironically, most of the Jewish studio moguls — Mayer, Goldwyn, Cohn,

Warner, Selznick — had spent years assiduously trying to cloak their ethnicity, fearing it would hurt their films in the largely gentile mass market. Mayer even had a portrait of Cardinal Spellman on his desk, right next to one of J. Edgar Hoover, to ensure he simultaneously mollified the Catholic church and America's most powerful anti-Semite.

When Jack Warner offered Julius Garfinkel a contract, he demanded his name be changed to James Garfield. The actor protested: "You wouldn't name a goddamn actor 'Abraham Lincoln,' would you?" No, came the response: "Abe is a name most people think is Jewish, and we wouldn't want people to get the wrong idea." "But I *am* Jewish," barked the soon-to-be John Garfield, clinging to the last vestiges of his heritage.

"That bad, huh? What is it? Love trouble or money trouble? I've seen all the troubles in the world and they boil down to just those two. You're broke, or you're lonely. Or both." Van Heflin seeks refuge from his demons with burned-out prostitute Mary Astor in *Act of Violence*.

Steve Brodie is menaced by
Robert Ryan in *Crossfire*.

Sam Goldwyn, explaining why Sinatra got the part Sam Levene played in *Guys and Dolls* on Broadway, said succinctly: "You can't have a Jew play a Jew. It wouldn't work on the screen."

Darryl Zanuck was determined to earn points as the first studio head to mainstream the issue of anti-Semitism, adapting the novel *Gentleman's Agreement*. It told the story of a gentile who learns about bigotry by pretending to be a Jew. Ring Lardner, Jr., after viewing the finished product, disdainfully assessed its moral: "Never be mean to a Jew, because he might turn out to be a Gentile."

Crossfire's creative team of Adrian Scott, writer John Paxton, and director Edward Dmytryk, feared that their film would never be made, but Dore Schary, the newly-installed head of production at RKO, eagerly gave them the green light — he wanted to undercut Zanuck by getting his low-budget thriller into theaters first, copping Zanuck's liberal audience. Scott claimed, disingenuously perhaps, that his story wasn't specifically about anti-Semitism. In a memo to studio bosses, he wrote: "This is a story of personal fascism as opposed to organized fascism. [It] indicates how it is possible for us to have a gestapo, if this country should go fascist. A character like Monty would qualify brilliantly for the leadership of the Belsen concentration camp. Fascism hates weakness in people; minorities. Monty hates fairies, negroes, jews and foreigners. In the book, Monty murders a fairy. He could have murdered a negro, a foreigner, or a jew."

Despite the message being thickly ladled at times, *Crossfire's* dark story was deftly told. And it was *dark*. To those who think the film's more a "message" picture than a true noir, consider that the script contains not one scene that begins EXT. DAY. Robert Young's earnest homilies about brotherhood don't carry half the weight of Robert Mitchum explaining how the war can't be neatly tucked away. "The snakes are loose," he says, like a man who knows how ugly it will get.

Crossfire shocked everyone, including Schary and Scott, scoring a hit at the box office. Whether its success was due to its timely message or its taut storytelling, no one was sure (although surveys prior to the film's release suggested little clamor among the general public for ethnically-charged stories). Even as the picture reaped several humanitarian awards, though, anti-Communist crusaders moved in on Scott and Dmytryk. Both were painted Red and sent to jail, as members of the Hollywood Ten. Scott's longed-for dream of producing significant movies was over. He'd end up writing television scripts, using a "front," during the 1950s.

Dmytryk, along with fellow director Elia Kazan (who'd helmed *Gentleman's Agreement*), became famous examples of blacklistees who bartered their way back into Hollywood by repudiating ties to the communists — and fingering colleagues for federal investigators.

CHALK UP THE LASTING IMPACT OF *CROSSFIRE* TO ROBERT RYAN. While Scott and Dmytryk worried themselves sick about its reception, Ryan showed no fear as he shouldered the film's rancid burden. His sneering ferocity got his career on track — and cast him in an evil mold he'd spend the rest of his professional life trying to break. Ryan was, in truth, the antithesis of the mean, racist, venal characters he excelled at portraying.

Born in Chicago in 1909, of an Irish family in the building trades, Ryan was a shy kid with a precocious fondness for Shakespeare. His father nudged him into the boxing ring in an attempt to knock the bookishness out of him. The gangly kid surprised: he ended up at Dartmouth, where he studied theater and held the university's heavyweight boxing crown four years running. Ryan's first love was writing, not acting, and he diligently punched out prose with the hope of becoming a playwright or journalist. The Depression encouraged him to be practical.

Ryan's peripatetic pursuit of a living wage was S.O.P. among Depression-era men (although it would stagger the stunted initiative of later generations): engine-room janitor on an Africa-bound freighter, ranch hand in Montana, cemetery-plot pitchman, collector for a loan company, miner, prospector – anything that held promise of a payday.

In '38 the winds shifted when Ryan risked a $300 buy-in on a friend's oil well, and it came a-gusher. Ryan took his two-grand grubstake and headed west. The nest egg funded a year in Max Reinhardt's acting school. Even though Paramount scouts said, after viewing a screen test, that he was "not the type for pictures," Ryan persevered. He hit the local boards hard, even singing and dancing. He ended up with a $75-per-week contract — at Paramount.

Ryan also signed a matrimonial deal with actress Jessica Cadwalader, another pupil in Reinhardt's class. She was ambitious and talented, but as was so often the case back then, she made the career sacrifice for her husband. (She'd later become a successful author of young adult fiction.) In the early Forties, awaiting the draft, Ryan fought the Axis on Paramount sound stages, fattening a growing résumé of "B" war films, if not his reputation. He returned to the legit stage in a minor role in the Broadway production of Clifford Odets's *Clash by Night*. It bombed, but an RKO scout caught Ryan's act, and signed him up after his Paramount pact expired.

For the next two years, Ryan sank into more studio foxholes, playing steely soldiers who rarely drew breath at the fade-out. One of these concoctions, a homefront weeper called *Tender Comrade* (1943), was Ryan's first real starring role, and it united him for the third time with director Edward Dmytryk. He played the groom of Ginger Rogers, who enjoys a single night of wedded bliss before being shipped out. He dies in combat, leaving Rogers to cope as a widowed mother. The actress's mother, Lela, who guarded Ginger's career like a junkyard dog, insisted the studio remove the pinkest lines that Dalton Trumbo's script had her daughter spouting. "This is a democracy — that means share and share alike," for example. Lela Rogers was proud to be a Red-sniffing pioneer.

Later that year Ryan signed on with the real military. First role: a Marine Corps drill instructor at Camp Pendleton. Those two years no doubt helped him distill the lathered-up fury he'd bring to future films. Mustering out, Ryan met fellow jarhead Richard Brooks, who'd recently published *The Brick Foxhole*. Ryan said he'd kill for the part of Monty, and Brooks said he'd put in a good word for him if a film version ever hit paydirt. Two years later it did, renamed, and *Crossfire* launched Ryan's career.

Robert Ryan in *On Dangerous Ground*.

Much later, after he'd breathed miserable life into some of the sorriest bastards ever seen on a screen, Ryan professed that he regretted ever making *Crossfire*. He became so identified with tightly-wound characters that no casting director could see him as a heroic leading man. Ryan rued the loss of numerous "A" roles to Gregory Peck. Even when portraying a good-hearted charmer, as in *About Mrs. Leslie* (Paramount, 1954), a thundercloud of ambiguity hung over Ryan. Was he projecting it? Or was it just that viewers couldn't shake from their minds the seething anger they'd seen in Monty Montgomery *(Crossfire)*, Joe Parkson *(Act of Violence)*, Smith Ohlrig *(Caught)*, Stoker Thompson *(The Set-Up)*, Jim Wilson *(On Dangerous Ground)*, Nick Scanlon *(The Racket)*, and Earl Pfeiffer *(Clash by Night)*? A critic for the *New York Times*, reviewing *Act of Violence*, captured Ryan's persona in two words: "infernally taut."

In the climate of the Fifties, studios shied away from contemporary urban dramas. They favored colorful widescreen spectacles free of political pitfalls. Ryan got sent West. He loathed making westerns, but found himself saddling up with monotonous regularity. Ruminating on his career in 1971 in *Films and Filming*, Ryan talked about how he envied urbane Cary Grant, and the fabulous locations — Monte Carlo, Paris, the Riviera — in which the debonair star always seemed to get work. "I'm fated to work in faraway, desolate places…in deserts with a dirty shirt and a two-day growth of beard and bad food. But that's an act of birth. I get all the worst locations because of the way I look. But I *am* an urban character. I was born in the big city. I also have a long, seamy face which adapts itself to westerns — but I don't for one moment consider myself a western actor essentially."

In the prime of his career, Ryan, Jessica, and their three children lived with an anti-Hollywood modesty. The parents took intense interest in the education of their children, going so far as to fund and construct, in 1953, The Oakwood School, a private learning center offering an alternative to crowded public schools and rich-kid country clubs. Ryan called it "watered-down progressive," and it was the first time his political and philosophical tenets brought him grief. Conservative neighbors egged the building and painted crosses on its doors. A committed leftist, Ryan managed to elude persecution during the witchhunt; but by the mid-'50s he was active in the ACLU, a big supporter of the UN, and president of the Southern California branch of the United World Federalists.

Meanwhile, Ryan continued to portray the men he most despised — amoral racists like Reno Smith in *Bad Day at Black Rock* (MGM, 1954). It was an updated Western in which Spencer Tracy played a one-armed vet who rides into a dusty desert town to present a Japanese farmer with his son's posthumous war medal. Surprise: a gang of rabid townsfolk, led by Ryan, has already murdered the old man in a fit of racism disguised as patriotism. You'd think Ryan couldn't get much more evil than this, but somehow he upped the ante in *Odds Against Tomorrow* (UA, 1959 — an exceptional film discussed later) and Peter Ustinov's salty adaptation of Melville's *Billy Budd* (Allied Artists, 1962). *Films in Review* called Ryan's turn as antagonistic master-at-arms John Claggart the "apotheosis of screen villainy."

Although he built a solid career foundation with the diligence of a stone-mason, Ryan felt trapped by the narrow confines of the parts he was offered. During the Fifties he poured his frustrations over ice and drank them down, becoming a functioning alcoholic. He believed his rejection of the Hollywood lifestyle was working against him. Thinking it might help his career, Ryan moved the family into a tony Holmby Hills spread. Daughter Lisa said it "swallowed us up." She recalls many occasions when her father would sit alone in the unlit kitchen, nursing one of many beverages, railing to the acting gods: "Goddamned 'B' pictures! That's all they give me. Goddamned 'B' pictures!"

By the early Sixties Ryan had become one of Tinseltown's highest-profile liberals, "a militant dove," leading the Southern California Committee on Sane Nuclear Policy, and an outspoken fixture at early Vietnam war protests. In '62, Ryan uprooted his clan and moved to New York, both to pursue more stage work, and dodge death threats from the John Birch Society.

After several years of stage work, Ryan again went West, literally and figuratively. Now in his sixties, he found that his leathery countenance was ideally suited to a new generation of gritty westerns, such as *The Professionals* (Columbia, 1966) and *Hour of the Gun* (UA, 1967). As Deke Thornton in Sam Peckinpah's *The Wild Bunch* (WB, 1969), he and William Holden engaged in a Mexican stand-off over which of the two craggy veterans projected a more bone-tired weariness.

Ryan's last act was perhaps his best. In John Frankenheimer's film version of Eugene O'Neill's *The Iceman Cometh* (1973), Ryan gave a searing portrayal of derelict political activist Larry Slade. It was an all-star cast, but Ryan dominated with a performance of life-or-death intensity. Sadly, he wasn't reaching far for inspiration. Jessica, only 57, had died suddenly the previous year, from cancer. Ryan also had developed the disease, and knew his days were numbered.

On July 11, 1973, he succumbed. Pete Hamill offered a lovely tribute: "There should be a poem of farewell for Robert Ryan. [It] should express his quiet presence through so many lonely years when few people were struggling to bring decency to the world.... Life, death, loneliness, loss: these were some of the things we learned from the quiet art of Robert Ryan, who was a good man in a bad time."

Ryan's pacifistic social work has been long forgotten. But his screen image is still frighteningly fresh, offering a scary, and tragic, message about the unbridled hatred lurking in ignorant men.

Ryan is an unhinged handyman who terrorizes Ida Lupino in *Beware, My Lovely* (RKO, 1952).

The Asphalt Jungle. Sam Jaffe, Sterling Hayden, Anthony Caruso, and James Whitmore (standing) plot the heist. *Opposite:* Caruso punches in at work.

Piece of cake. Five minutes. Stay focused. Fire the drill. Deep breath. The bit's going in like butter. Let the rest of this stinking town punch a clock and live on hand-to-mouth paychecks. *Sirens.* No. Not sirens, screams. Somebody else's problem. *C'mon. Dig.* All those losers busting their humps on eight-hour shifts. I'll be laughing at 'em. Four minutes and we're out with a quarter mill. "Speed it up!" *Shut up.* Don't watch me, keep an eye out. *Oh, NO!* Bit broke. *Hand me the spare.* Wait. "Did you hear that?"

Knockover Square

After seven years in stir Doc Reidenschneider (Sam Jaffe) has returned to Dark City. His legend as a criminal mastermind precedes him; Doc knows the law will be on him like white on rice. But the old gent's angling for one last sensational takedown: more than a million bucks' worth of gems from a seemingly impregnable jewelry exchange. The little general, who hides his predilections beneath a genteel Old World veneer, sets to work assembling his crew: a stakehorse, a fence, a hooligan, a driver, and a boxman.

"What boxes have you opened?" he asks Louie Ciavelli (Anthony Caruso), reputed to be the most versatile of safecrackers. "Cannonball, double-door, even a few Firechest, all of them," Ciavelli ticks off. Confident but not arrogant — just the yegg the Doctor ordered.

This commando unit, operating in the umbrae of *The Asphalt Jungle* (MGM, 1950), gave an injection of realism to the post-World War II crime picture. These crooks were humanized, not demonized. Instead of the snarling, power-mad miscreants seen in hundreds of gangster shoot-em-ups, *The Asphalt Jungle* offered an underworld of struggling laborers, alienated loners, even honorable family men — in addition to the garden-variety leeches and double-crossing shysters. These were neo-realist thieves, after bigger scores than bicycles.

Director John Huston had an affinity for veteran novelist W. R. Burnett's Hemingwayesque approach to the crime thriller. (He'd scripted Burnett's *High Sierra*, another rugged and romantic outlaw caper, in 1940. Burnett had also penned one of the seminal 1930s gangster stories, *Little Caesar*). Huston leapt at the chance to film Burnett's *Jungle* when *Quo Vadis*, an Eternal City costume drama Huston was helming, was postponed. Huston was far more comfortable dealing with dynamics of small groups of men under pressure than he was with hordes of robe-draped extras.

The film was also an opportunity for Huston to exact creative revenge. Bad blood still simmered from his involvement in *The Killers*, the first great post-war caper film. Huston had adapted the Hemingway short story for Mark Hellinger, but when those big egos came a-cropper, Huston quit the project. Hellinger gave credit only to Huston's collaborator, Anthony Villier.

Huston's first bold move in adapting *Jungle* was to 86 Burnett's narrative structure, which framed the story from the perspective of the police, who must cope with "...the nightly toll of crime coming in over the commissioner's radio, the voice of the asphalt jungle..." Huston preferred to stick with Doc and his cohorts throughout. Co-scribe Ben Maddow credited Huston with writing the scene that delineated the picture's theme: "When I think of all the awful people you come in contact with, downright criminals, I get scared," says May (Dorothy Tree), the wife of tainted mouthpiece Alonzo D. Emmerich (Louis Calhern), who is the conduit for the purloined jewels.

To which Emmerich retorts: "There's nothing so different about them. Crime is only a left-handed form of human endeavor."

Huston's fresh take on such sinister pursuits stressed the motivations of his felons. They're not hostile hoods looking for a way to wield power, they're disgruntled city dwellers driven to score some breathing room. Louie Ciavelli doesn't crave a penthouse or fancy cars; he wants enough dough to move his family from a cramped tenement into a decent middle-class home. Doc dreams of retiring to Mexico, where he can while away his twilight years ogling pretty girls on the beach. Dix Handley (Sterling Hayden), the hooligan, is a bluegrass boy bushwhacked by the big city. He needs to pay off his gambling debts before he can ever hope to buy back the family horse ranch in Kentucky. "First thing I'm gonna do is take a bath in the creek and wash this city dirt off me," he tells his girl, Doll Conovan (Jean Hagen).

Gone are the flamboyant gangland flourishes common in previous crime movies, including Huston's own *Key Largo* (1949), in which Edward G. Robinson played a Lucky Luciano-type mobster with the broadness audiences had come to expect from larger-than-life perpetrators. In *The Asphalt Jungle*, crime is as routine as an eight-hour swing shift on the packing line. Huston directs the proceedings with business-as-usual detachment, eschewing sensationalism at every turn.

With practiced nonchalance Huston serves up details of the criminal life, leading viewers through a dispassionate tour of the city's bent by-ways. As a guide, Doc Reidenschneider is a font of sagacity: "Experience has taught me to never trust a policeman — just when you think one's all right, he turns legit." Later, he explains the wisdom of his disarmament policy: "I never carry a gun. You carry a gun, you shoot a cop. Bad rap, hard to beat. You don't carry a gun, you give up when they point one at you."

Doc's first visit is with Cobby (Marc Lawrence), a thriving bookmaker who runs a clearinghouse for clandestine activity. Cobby agrees to underwrite the

venture, allowing Doc to hire his crew for flat upfront fees, rather than a percentage of the spoils. Emmerich, the slippery solicitor, comes into the deal as the fence who will move the stolen gems. But he's far from the solvent sophisticate he purports to be. He's blown his savings on his sexy "niece" Angela (Marilyn Monroe), who allows "Uncle Lon" to reclaim some of his faded youth. When Emmerich can't call in a single marker to pay for the jewels, he's forced to concoct a swindle. "It's my whole way of life," he admits sadly. "Every time I turn around, it costs thousands of dollars. I've got to get out. I've got to get out from under."

MGM boss Louis B. Mayer wished Huston had stuck with the hackneyed stereotypes. He hated the picture, calling it "full of nasty, ugly people doing nasty, ugly things. I won't walk across the room to see something like that." Huston took some flak for his sympathetic portrayal of criminals, but critics overall lauded his work, agreeing with W. R. Burnett that it was "without a doubt one of the best films of its genre."

"Why are you staring at me like that, Uncle Lon?" Angela Phinlay (Marilyn Monroe) is a catalyst for robbery in *The Asphalt Jungle.*

In the *Jungle*, unlike most caper films, the robbery is not the climax. It's barely the mid-way point. Emulating his protagonists, Huston handles the heist crisply and efficiently: no rushed moves, no sweaty palms, no pounding heartbeats. Just men at work. Hollywood's Production Code, intended to ensure the public would never empathize with glamorous gangsters, was helpless when it came to caper movies. Audiences clearly identified with the accomplished, nervy thieves, as they tried to pull off a seemingly impossible job. The blurring of moral distinctions was part and parcel of noir. It reached its apex in *The Asphalt Jungle*, and the dozens of heist stories it inspired. A man's character was determined by his professionalism, his steadiness under pressure, more than his adherence to right over wrong.

Not that Doc's gang is going to get away with it. As they're ditching the vault, Dix overpowers a guard — who drops his gun, discharging a shot that catches Louie in the chest. Gus (James Whitmore), the driver, desperately tries to fix Louie up with a doctor without blowing their cover. When Doc meets Emmerich for the square-up, he sniffs a double-cross. Emmerich has an itchy henchman, Bannerman (Brad Dexter) in tow, a bad sign. The old gents spar with savvy politesse as to the terms of the payout. When the impetuous Bannerman pulls a piece and opts for a crude shakedown, Dix earns his cut: he plugs the mouthy kid with a single slug, but he's gutshot in return.

Huston doesn't sprint to the finish. He delicately shadows the deliberate steps of the men as they head toward their fates. Bannerman's death leads to Emmerich, links to the vault job are quickly found, and "Uncle Lon" is arrested before his beloved Angela's eyes. Rather than face the humiliation of having his wife learn about his sexual escapades — and his financial ruin — Emmerich commits suicide. ("How could he be so foolish?" sighs Doc, "He would have gotten two years at the most.") The cops break down Louie's

Kentucky seems a lifetime away as mortally wounded Dix Handley (Sterling Hayden) is propped up by Doll Conovan (Jean Hagen) and a helpful trucker (Fred Graham).

door – interrupting his private, Old World wake. Doc skips town, taking a taxi all the way to Cleveland. But at a roadside diner he squanders critical minutes indulging his passion – savoring the bodies of young girls. With a million dollars' worth of gems sewn into the lining of his overcoat, and the law closing in, Doc blissfully pumps nickels into the jukebox, keeping a nubile bobby-soxer rocking and rolling. Doc misses the turn-off to Easy Street by the length of a few tantalizing shakes and shimmies.

Dix makes a run for it, headed home with hallucinations of a beautiful black colt spurring him on. Doll tries to get him a doctor, but the delirious farm boy shrugs off any help. He knows he's too far gone, and that any dip in the mainstream will land him back in the joint.

All he wants is that patch of Hickory Wood farm where he once was untouched by corruption. He makes it back, staggering into the fields to greet his only unconditional friends, his cherished horses. He crumples before reaching them. The black colt saunters over and licks the salty streaks from Dix's lifeless face.

STERLING HAYDEN WOULD COME TO SHARE DIX HANDLEY'S ferocious desire to escape. By his own admission never much of an actor, by 1950 Hayden was trapped in the life. For him, Hollywood was truly Dark City, a place that drained the soul of the man he was, and stuffed cash into the pockets of the poseur he allowed himself to become.

When John Huston cast him in *Jungle* — opposite such refined craftsmen as Louis Calhern and Sam Jaffe — he was taking a huge, inspired gamble. Hayden's credit list in the 1940s was filled with roles where he was asked to do little more than display, in vivid Technicolor, his flowing blond locks and bronzed physique. By the close of the decade he was branded with a reputation as a surly malcontent. Paramount fired him when he began to freeze before the camera. He needed therapy to sort out his conflicted feelings about being an actor. "Shit!" Hayden railed in his autobiography *Wanderer*, "I went through the war. I jumped out of bombers. I played kick-the-can with E-boats.... Yet whenever I get a close-up in a nice warm studio I curl up and die. Why?" It would be a while before he'd learn the true answer, but when Huston called him in for the role of Dix, Hayden was just happy to find a kindred spirit, a virile man of action. MGM tried to talk Huston out of using the troubled actor, but the director hung tough. He saw in Hayden real life parallels to Dix's predicament: a simple guy pigeon-holed by a résumé that read like a rap sheet, struggling to reclaim his identity.

Born John Hamilton in Montclair, New Jersey, 1916, the strapping lad shucked a middle-class upbringing in his teens, running away to become a mate on a schooner. His dream was to operate a small merchant-shipping company on the coast of Maine. He earned his sea legs dory-trawling for haddock off Newfoundland. At 22 he sailed the brigantine *Florence C. Robinson* to Tahiti. At a fully-muscled six-five, windburned and sun-bleached, John Hamilton looked like a woman's daydream of a potent Poseidon. Movie director Edward Griffith spied an article about the young mariner and arranged an interview. John Hamilton's decision to forego the sea for a movie career (and a name change) would rack his conscience for years to come.

He inked a $150-a-week pact with Paramount, debuted in *Virginia* (1941) opposite Madeleine Carroll, and married the English actress the next year. But before his career could take off he was summoned to military duty, where his skills as a salt were used in nautical espionage work in the Mediterranean, the Atlantic and the North Sea. He'd return from the war with his conscience even more conflicted: While most vets struggled to reassimilate, Hayden demob'd directly into a lucrative arrangement as Paramount's ultimate beefcake attraction. The publicity department was already billing him as "The Most Beautiful Man in the Movies," and issuing bare-torso promo photos. He ended up divorcing Carroll, marrying socialite Betty DeNoon. He was perpetually at odds with the easy life, embarrassed at how much money he made for "doing nothing."

"If you don't believe in taking what you don't earn," Hayden inquired rhetorically in *Wanderer*, "then how can you be reconciled to the astronomical figures [an actor is paid]? I never was. Furthermore, I couldn't stand the work." He excoriated himself for cashing the checks and "posing." "Where did the weakness lie," he asked, "the weakness that forced you to give up ten or twelve of what might have been the most vital years of your life? It lay, did it not, in the fact that you were flawed. You were big and strong on the surface, but something was wrong inside. You were strong enough to rebel — not strong enough to revolt."

This was the coiled angst Huston channelled into *The Asphalt Jungle;* finally Hayden's tortured introversion meshed with a character. He felt comfortable as an actor for the first time. After *Jungle*, Hayden would check into the Dark City Hotel several more times, playing hard-bitten cops and crooks sickened by the cheapness of urban life, longing for their day of liberation. Not a big stretch for the one-time "Beautiful Blond Viking God."

Just as Hayden's career seemed revitalized, another crisis of conscience struck. HUAC suddenly called Hayden's politics into question. Although he'd served with distinction in WWII, Hayden had been a member of the Communist Party. Like many in Hollywood, he couldn't imagine his livelihood — even one he professed to loathe — could be jeopardized because of some half-assed political beliefs.

He toyed with the notion of facing down HUAC by running an ad in the trades declaring that he'd been a Communist, but *so what?* When his therapist, Ernest Philip Cohen, asked why he didn't go ahead with the ads, Hayden erupted: "Because I haven't got the guts, that's why. Maybe because I'm a parlor pink. Because I want to remain employable in this town long enough to finish this fucking analysis.

WA-106 - 3/10/51 - INP SOUNDPHOTO - WASHINGTON, D.C.. MOVIE ACTOR STERLING HAYDEN TALKS WITH HIS WIFE BETTY AFTER TELLING THE HOUSE UNAMERICAN ACTIVITIES COMMITTEE THAT HE JOINED THE COMMUNIST PARTY FOR SIX MONTHS AS A RESULT OF AN "EMOTIONAL IMPACT" OF WARTIME SERVICE WITH MARSHAL TITO'S YUGOSLAV PARTISANS.. HE QUIT THE PARTY-WHEN CONVINCED THAT THE REDS SEEK TO OVERTHROW THE UNITED STATES.. "JOINING THE PARTY WAS THE STUPIDIST, MOST IGNORANT THING I HAVE EVER DONE" STATED HAYDEN WHO BECAME CONVINCED THAT THE COMMUNISTS WERE TOTAL-ITARIAN IN THEIR METHODS... INP PHOTO BY A. MUTO.. SENT/535 EST....

"Because when it comes time for the divorce I'd like to be able to see my children, and the courts downtown are full of judges who would look askance at a divorced man who was an ex-Communist to boot. That's why. How many reasons do you want, sitting there on your throne?"

Hayden spoke to the FBI privately, stressing that he did not want to name names. He'd offer anything about himself, but didn't want to play the implication game. "They know I was a Party member," he fumed to Cohen before leaving for Washington. "They don't want information, they want to put on a show, and I'm the star. They've already agreed to go over the questions with me in advance. It's a rigged show: radio and TV and the papers. I'm damned no matter what I do. Cooperate and I'm a stool pigeon. Shut my mouth and I'm a pariah."

In front of HUAC, Hayden played it contrite. The Dix Handley death-stare wasn't in evidence. But seven other people were: he ultimately did name names, including his ex-mistress, and emerged with his career — if not his mental health — intact. He told Cohen, "I'm thinking of quitting analysis.... I'll say this, too, that if it hadn't been for you I wouldn't have turned into a stoolie for J. Edgar Hoover. I don't think you have the foggiest notion of the contempt I have had for myself since the day I did that thing.... Fuck it! And fuck you, too."

Hayden's kiss-off came far too late. In a twist straight from the Dark City rewrite room, a flood of rumors swirled that therapist Phil Cohen — a former Communist Party member with a long, liberal client list — was funnelling information from his private sessions straight to the Feds.

"I know he was reporting confidences to the FBI," Abraham Polonsky told Victor Navasky in the latter's 1980 book *Naming Names*. "There's no question about that. And he was turning patients into stool pigeons."

Although Hayden would make several more memorable films, the personal cost of maintaining his career proved too high. "Incredible, really — how I got away with it; parlaying nine years at sea into two decades of posturing. Poor wanderer: trapped in the greenbacked cradle of Outer Hollywood; laced in the straitjacket of the big time — big houses big salaries big fuss when

you walk down a street big fuss as you check into hotels — big big big.... What does a man need — really need? A few pounds of food each day, heat and shelter, six feet to lie down in — and some form of working activity that will yield a sense of accomplishment. That's all — in the material sense. And we know it. But we are brainwashed by our economic system until we end up in a tomb beneath a pyramid of time payments, mortgages, preposterous gadgetry, playthings that divert our attention from the sheer idiocy of the charade."

On January 20, 1959, Sterling Hayden executed the escape that Dix Handley dreamed of. Defying court custody orders, he loaded his four children onto his aged schooner *Wanderer*, and sailed out of Sausalito, California, headed for the South Seas. He chucked the $160,000 annual salary, the rest of his film career, the mounting debts, the threat of punitive action by the government. He had no money, no job, no prospects. But he did have the sea, a small crew — inexperienced but eager — and lots of journal pages to fill.

The ship runs free, he exults in those scribblings. *Your ears are bathed with wind and the sun comes pouring down. Face south and fill your soul with the far horizon's rapture. Now pivot clockwise slowly and rest for a time, looking west. What do you see? Nothing. Nothing but the sea and sky. Turn quietly north, with the line of the sea and the low-hung spread of cloud, the shimmer of light and shade, and the spell of loneliness mixed with the call of the sea — the beckoning, bursting, smiling call with a wild promise of worlds unknown and dreams undreamed and a life to live.*

Hayden pulled off one of most incredible capers in Hollywood history: he recreated himself. *Wanderer*, his briny, blood-on-the-page auto-

Sterling Hayden, tired and still looking for a way out of Dark City, in *The Naked Alibi*.

biography, written as he sailed for Tahiti, became a bestseller. He returned to acting on his own terms, creating the memorable mad-bomber Gen. Jack D. Ripper for counter-culture compatriot Stanley Kubrick's *Dr. Strangelove* (Columbia, 1964). In Coppola's *The Godfather* (Paramount, 1972), Altman's *The Long Goodbye* (UA, 1973), Bertolucci's *1900* (1976), Frank Pierson's *King of the Gypsies* (Paramount, 1978), and William Richert's dizzy adaptation of Richard Condon's *Winter Kills* (Avco Embassy, 1979), all remnants of actor's affectation had been scraped from Hayden like barnacles from the hull of a battered but seaworthy brigantine. He only had to float to be stoically majestic. His epic seafaring novel *Voyage* was the product of awesome solitude, the crowning achievement for a man who had left all conventions at dockside and become master of his own leeward life.

HAYDEN DID SPEND SOME TIME ON THE RIGHT SIDE of the law, as in the jaunty 73-minute caper film *Crime Wave* (WB, 1954). Playing Sergeant Sims, he had a field day as the sort of self-righteous bully with a badge Hollywood liberals saw coming after them in their sleep.

Sims has it in for Steve Lacey (Gene Nelson), a paroled thief gone straight, who becomes helplessly entangled with former cohorts who have broken out of San Quentin. Doc Penny (Ted de Corsia) and Ben Hastings (Charles Buchinsky a/k/a Bronson), hole up with Lacey, forcing him to act as the driver for a bank job Doc's got planned. They hold Steve's wife Ellen (Phyllis Kirk) hostage, to encourage his cooperation.

Sims figures that Lacey's still aligned with his old comrades, and he persecutes him without mercy, ranting "Once a crook always a crook," and vowing to send him back to the joint. Could enacting this role have been part of Hayden's post stoolie therapy?

Director André deToth, whose only other noir was the fine *Pitfall*, enlivens this programmer with unexpected vigor. Bert Glennon's camera snakes through the streets of Glendale, capturing actual locations with a heady hybrid of chiaroscuro and crisp natural light. Sims's hostility is nicely mitigated by subtle humor. Screenwriter Crane Wilbur gives him the added frustration of nicotine withdrawal, which prompts the already high-strung cop to gnaw toothpicks in place of his beloved tar-bars. Hayden, who smoked furiously himself, looks quite annoyed at being deprived of the actor's favorite prop. DeToth makes great use of Hayden's dimensions: rooms, furniture, and cars seem too small for his towering, shambling frame — everything gets in his way.

But Hayden's only the surly ringmaster here. The real show is the supporting cast. Surrounding fresh-faced Nelson and Kirk is a post office wall's worth of creeps. Ted de Corsia, who made his onscreen debut in Welles's *Lady from Shanghai*, is one of the great noir character actors. Barrel-chested and beady-eyed, hair glistening with a hard shell lacquer of Wildroot Cream, de Corsia looked like a guy who'd spent his whole life in boxing gyms and bookie joints. That visage was just an accident of birth: the son of a vaudevillean, he was in touring companies as a youth, before becoming a successful radio actor. Credit Welles with spotting de Corsia's nefarious visual potential, and Jules Dassin for swiftly exploiting it. Dassin cast de Corsia in the pivotal role of killer Willie Garza in *The Naked City*, and the actor lent a sweaty, feral tone to the film's overwrought urban poetry. De Corsia lurked in westerns, hovered in crime dramas, and skulked in prison pictures (a Crane Wilbur specialty), inducing a shiver of menace when he'd finally step to the light and make his play. In *Slightly Scarlet*, de Corsia was immortalized in John Alton's burnished light, which chiseled the actor's hawkish features into a sinister rictus. A just dessert for any great heavy is a memorable death scene, and in *Slightly Scarlet* de Corsia goes out grandly: blazing redhead Rhonda Fleming blows a harpoon into his burly chest.

De Corsia's sidekick in *Crime Wave* is the young Charles Bronson, who not only flexes impressively, but growls a few great henchman lines. Leveling his gun at Ellen, he smiles at her husband: "You want I should clip a curl off the cutie?" DeToth loved the primitive contours of Bronson's face, and his atavistic grace. He used him smartly in several pictures, including the 3-D *House of Wax*. The gang also included the amusingly unstable Timothy Carey, who is so brain damaged that midway through sexually intimidating Phyllis Kirk he becomes distracted and forgets what he's doing. *Crime Wave* was one of the first films that would prompt viewers to ask of Carey: "What the hell is *wrong* with this guy?"

THE NEXT TIME SUCH A COLORFUL CREW would be assembled for a caper, Hayden would again be front and center. In 1955, an upstart 27-year-old New York filmmaker named Stanley Kubrick, who didn't believe that Hollywood held the patent on American filmmaking, teamed up with neophyte producer James B. Harris in an attempt to bust into the big leagues of movie production. Their passport, they hoped, would be a minor thriller they'd bought the rights to, Lionel White's *Clean Break*.

From *Crime Wave*. Top: Paroled thief Steve Lacey (Gene Nelson, left) and his wife Ellen (Phyllis Kirk) receive unexpected dinner guests — Steve's former colleagues Ben (Charles Bronson) and Doc (Ted de Corsia), fresh from a prison break.
Bottom: Sure, I've got a warrant. Sergeant Sims (Sterling Hayden) and his men bust into Lacey's apartment in search of the fugitives.

Kubrick was something of a prodigy, working at a young age as a *Look* magazine photographer. But the bookish, reserved Bronx kid was also wired on noir. His first two features, *Fear and Desire* (1953) and *Killer's Kiss* (1955) were the earliest examples of an aesthete plunging into Dark City in an attempt to distill crude poetry from the iconographic terrain. Unlike the high-toned intellectuals who crafted noirs on sound stages for a hefty paycheck, Kubrick had virtually no budget, but was fueled by the notion that he had a better way to formulate the dark visions that had inspired him.

Harris and Kubrick danced with United Artists to secure funding for their low-budget picture. The money came only after Sterling Hayden committed to star. Perhaps he saw it as a logical extension of *The Asphalt Jungle*. In that film, Dix tells Doll, "One of these days I'm gonna make a killing." Five years later, reincarnated as Johnny Clay, a little older and a little wiser, he'd get one more crack at the Main Chance — in *The Killing* (UA, 1956).

Like Doc Reidenschneider, Johnny is fresh out of prison. He's spent five years plotting the perfect heist, a brazen daylight lift of a quarter million from Lansdowne racetrack. He has it figured step-by-step, a walkthrough: into the counting room and out, five minutes, no gunplay. The trick is installing the right guys — losers all, but stand-up losers — at every potential stress point in the plan.

Here Kubrick flashes his Dark City street creds, populating his caper with the choicest ensemble of noir characters ever. Marvin Unger (Jay C. Flippen) underwrites the job because he's infatuated with Johnny, who's too preoccupied to catch the drift when Marvin says, "I think of you as if you were my own son." Fay, Johnny's befuddled sweetheart, is played by Coleen ("I may not be pretty and I may not be smart") Gray, the most utilitarian of Dark City dames. Ted de Corsia is sold-out cop Randy Kennan, who has a pony jones and walks a narrow barroom and bookie joint beat. Kola Kwarian, a friend of Kubrick's from New York chess clubs, plays Maurice Oboukhoff, a wrestler who creates a brawling diversion at the racetrack bar (He should have been matched with his bullet-headed twin, Gregorius [Stanislaus Zbyszko], from *Night and the City*.) Vince Edwards is punk pretty boy Val Cannon. And most memorably, there's demented sharpshooter Nikki Arano (Timothy Carey, once again clenched and inexplicable), and George and Sherry Peatty (Elisha Cook, Jr. and luminously wicked Marie Windsor) — voted by a jury of their peers Dark City's most perfectly married couple.

George: Been kinda sick today. Keep gettin' pains in my stomach.
Sherry: Maybe you got a hole in it. Suppose you have?
George: How would I get a hole in it?
Sherry: How'd you get the one in your head? Fix me a drink, George, I think I'm developing some pains myself.

The Killing: Johnny Clay (Sterling Hayden, top) stashes a gift-wrapped rifle in a bus station locker; George Peatty (Elisha Cook, Jr.) tries to impress his two-timing wife, Sherry (Marie Windsor).

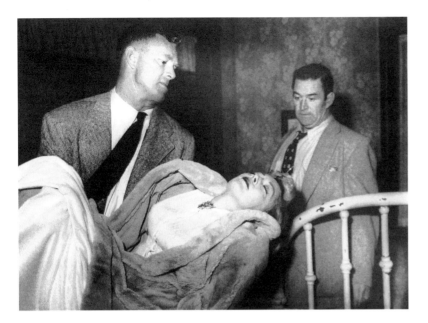

Johnny cold-cocks Sherry Peatty (Marie Windsor) while Randy Kennan (Ted de Corsia) watches; after leaving the track's counting room, Johnny deftly KO's a guard.

Unfortunately for Johnny, there's a crucial trait he doesn't share with Dix Handley: he goes soft at the wrong times. When he realizes that George, the weak link in his crew, has leaked details of the plan to Sherry, Johnny passes up the chance to ice her. Instead of "slapping that pretty face into hamburger meat," Johnny brushes her off and sends her home to resume systematic torture of her pitiful husband. Big mistake. Sherry is Johnny's only rival as a primal predator. She's feeding info she's coaxed out of George to her lover Val, who plans to highjack the loot.

Johnny floats through the incendiary core of the heist like a firewalker, immune to distraction. Stick to the plan. Play it out, no matter what. Million-to-one shots come in once in a while, you just have to be Johnny-on-the-spot. Mustering all his grace and guile, Johnny Clay is — at least for a few moments — the King of Thieves.

Not everyone is as cool. Nikki, the sniper Johnny hired to shoot thoroughbred Red Lightning as a distraction, doesn't make it. Nikki's been toting his death certificate around for years. A track security cop simply stamps the date on it.

Traffic around the track keeps Johnny from showing up on time to dole out the take — so he misses the fireworks when Val, dancing on Sherry's strings, bursts in to steal everything. George, realizing that his beloved Sherry has set him up, lets his pistol finally pop. Johnny's master plan flares into a massacre, bodies falling on bodies like useless puzzle pieces tossed in a pile. Johnny drives up and sees George stagger out of the hotel, bloodsplattered. He lams with the whole take, stuffed inside a cheap pawnshop suitcase.

Sherry, of course, has her own valise packed, ready to vamoose with Val. But it's cuckolded George who shows up. His flaccid firearm has one shot left, a parting gift for his wife. Plugged in the gut, Sherry sputters their epitaph: "It's a bad joke with no punchline."

Johnny, moving like Red Lightning, sprints to the airport with Fay in tow. But they make him check the suitcase. *Goddamn puny functionaries.* What glorious delusion, hidden under that stolid facade, made Johnny think he could beat the system? He's so close to the big dream of himself. So close — except for the yapping toy poodle that skitters across the tarmac, and the luggage cart swerving, and the cheap latch on the suitcase busting open. Johnny watches silently as his fortune gets scattered like so much confetti. He's too numb to run. Fay guides him through the airport. He's embalmed, can't even hail a cab. "What's the difference?" he mutters, giving up as the net closes. The weary philosophy of every two-time loser with ripe schemes but no real juice.

Kubrick received some notoriety for the film's unusual overlapping narrative, which backtracks to show the heist build-up from various characters' perspectives. But here he was merely being faithful to the structure of White's novel. A bolder stroke was hiring Jim Thompson to contribute to the screenplay. Celebrated years after his death as the toughest of noir novelists, Thompson at that time was sliding toward Skid Row, struggling under a hefty bar bill. He related to these hardcases, and popped some wonderful dialogue into the mouths of this flea-bitten menagerie.

"You know, I often thought that the artist and the gangster are the same in the eyes of the masses," Maurice muses for Johnny's benefit. "They are admired and hero-worshipped, but there is always present the underlying wish to see them destroyed at the peak of their glory."

"Like the man said: Life is like a glass of tea, huh?" is Johnny's riposte. "Oh, Johnny, my friend. You were never very bright. But I love you anyway."

When UA execs saw the first cut they were aghast, claiming it made no sense and that no audience would sit through it. Despondent, Kubrick recut the film conventionally, only to discover what Lionel White knew all along — the structure was essential to the story's originality. Kubrick defiantly returned the film to its original state; UA buried it on the bottom of double bills.

But Kubrick's style still drew notice, even if his unorthodox camera moves, lens flares, and wide focal lengths had irritated the hell out of veteran cameraman Lucien Ballard, who was at odds with the young director throughout the production. Kubrick, showing early indication of his obsessive perfectionism, usurped Ballard's camera to photograph the massacre aftermath himself, in a hand-held shot that lingers like gunsmoke. The film's lean, aggressive style signaled that a new approach to storytelling was in the air, several years before mainstream critics credited it to France's New Wave directors.

With *The Killing*, Stanley Kubrick offered a monument to the classic caper film, and a fresh gust of filmmaking in one clever package. Who knew when he wrapped it, that it would be the last amusing movie he'd ever make? His coronation as the Grand Omphaloskeptic of the cinema was still more than a decade away.

JOHNNY CLAY'S DEMISE WAS FORESHADOWED by the fate of Dave Purvis (William Talman), who pulls off an *Armored Car Robbery* (RKO, 1950), only to miss his flight at the airport, when an incoming plane casts his booty to the wind. This 67-minute "B," directed by the redoubtable Richard Fleischer, was one of the last noirs to present a "caper" as straight cops and robbers stuff. Its central scam was free of any complex moral shadings. There's no sympathy for this gang, because Purvis is as cold and unlikeable as his fellow masterminds, Doc Reidenschneider and Johnny Clay, were engagingly sympathetic.

A pair of noir aces: Charles McGraw puts the heat on William Talman in a publicity shot from *Armored Car Robbery*.

The supporting cast (Douglas Fowley, Steve Brodie, Gene Evans) is colorless compared to the two leads. Talman played some of the most reptilian villains in noir *(The Hitch-Hiker, Crashout, City That Never Sleeps)*. With his high forehead and protruding lizard eyes, it seemed like a forked tongue was likely to dart from between his cruel lips at any moment. Talman's baleful gaze could put any cliché'd scene on ice instantly. One of the few actors who could withstand the Talman treatment was the implacable Charles McGraw, who played Sgt. Cordell, a pitbull cop determined to avenge his partner, who was killed trying to thwart the robbery. McGraw actually looked like an armored car, draped in a pin-striped suit. The most distinctively gruff voice in the movies was strangled out of McGraw; it sounded like a fist was gripping his larynx whenever he deigned to utter dialogue.

McGraw took taciturn to tight-lipped extremes. Visiting his dead partner's widow in the hospital, he reaches deep for the appropriate words of sorrow and condolence. He fingers his fedora and finally clips off: "Tough break, Marsha" — and turns and exits before the emotion overwhelms him.

In a series of exciting film noirs — *The Killers, T-Men, Border Incident, The Story of Molly X, The Threat, Side Street, Road Block, His Kind of Woman, The Narrow Margin, Loophole,* and *Slaughter on Tenth Avenue* — McGraw's broad, blocky presence lent any scene additional heft. As villains, not many players were as physically threatening. As heroes, few conveyed juggernaut determination so off-handedly, or believably. McGraw was simply a natural on-screen. By the early '60s his bluntness had acquired a nicely weathered quality, used to good advantage by Stanley Kubrick *(Spartacus)*, Anthony Mann *(Cimarron)*, and Alfred Hitchcock *(The Birds)*. McGraw's career was tragically cut short by a horrendous fatal accident. He slipped in his shower and crashed through the doors, impaling himself on a huge glass shard. An awful end for one of the great faces and voices of noir.

KNOCKOVER SQUARE, OF ALL THE NEIGHBORHOODS IN DARK CITY, had the most generous ration of unique faces and voices. It's the characters in the crew, much more than the plots, that make caper films memorable.

In *Kansas City Confidential* (UA, 1952), an embittered ex-cop (Preston Foster) engineers a more ingenious armored car robbery than Dave Purvis ever considered. His motivation is deeply cynical, and emblematic of noir: he's steamed about his paltry pension after twenty years of futile crime fighting. He blackmails a trio of petty hoods into executing the robbery. The usual simmering paranoia within a high-strung crew is compounded by the fact that only Foster knows the identity of each man; masks prevent them from identifying each other.

Anonymity is key, as the robbers reunite months later in a Mexican fishing resort to divvy up the loot. Unmasked, no one is quite sure who's who, or who can be trusted, as the flunkies await instructions from the boss – who could be any of the vacationing marlin fishers. The gang is more than motley enough to earn a place in the Knockover Square pantheon:

Lee van Cleef (left) and Neville Brand put the screws to John Payne in *Kansas City Confidential*. Coleen Gray shouldn't be so shocked.

There's skittish Pete Harris, played by Jack Elam, who stepped into the movie business from a job as manager of the Bel-Air Hotel in Beverly Hills. Elam lost sight in his left eye after a youthful fight, and the resultant wall-eyed stare lent his silly-putty face an off-putting oddness that kept him employed for decades.

Chunky, thuggish Kane was a typical role for Neville Brand, whose mug made Charles Bronson look like Cary Grant. He'd reach the height of his popularity playing Al Capone on the hit television series *The Untouchables*. In reality, Brand was as far from a cowardly chiseler as you could get: he was the fourth most decorated soldier of World War II.

Playing Mutt (actually Tony) to Brand's Jeff was Lee van Cleef. The reedy, beak-nosed former accountant would knock around as a Hollywood henchman and saddle tramp for almost fifteen years before Sergio Leone made him an international star, casting him alongside fellow squint-meister Clint Eastwood in spaghetti westerns *A Fistful of Dollars* and *The Good, the Bad, and the Ugly*.

Odd man out in this band of plug-uglies is pretty boy Joe Rolfe (John Payne), an innocent truck driver cleverly set-up as fall guy for the robbery. The gang made its getaway in a duplicate of his florist delivery van, ensuring a diversion. As a result of the suspicion he draws, Rolfe — a paroled jailbird doing straight time — loses his job. He summons his own criminal savvy to hunt down the real robbers, and ends up replacing Pete Harris at the south-of-the-border square-up. The other goons are none the wiser, since they never saw Harris's face. The clever script, by George Bruce and Harry Essex, makes amusing use of this identity crisis. And the question of whether Rolfe will send up the robbers — or try to cut himself in on the spoils — generates terrific suspense.

Director Phil Karlson was in stride with *Kansas City Confidential*, having just released the sensational crime drama *Scandal Sheet* (Columbia, 1952), based on Samuel Fuller's novel *The Dark Page*. Karlson, like his two-fisted compatriot Anthony Mann, worked his way through the Forties grinding out Poverty Row programmers before finding his niche with violent, even brutal, crime pictures. He had a profitable association with leading man John Payne, making two other punchy noirs, *99 River Street* (UA, 1953) and *Hell's Island* (Paramount, 1955), in which he transformed the popular songbird into a lonesome nighthawk.

He'd go on to direct *The Phenix City Story* (Allied Artists, 1955), which signaled the end of stylish, artful noir. Replacing it was a slew of crimebusting "exposés" — *New York Confidential, New Orleans After Dark, Portland Exposé, Las Vegas Shakedown* — films in which noir's shadowy moral ambiguity was given the third degree by the Feds, and bureaucrats and G-Men once again held heroic sway over psychotic crooks.

Odds Against Tomorrow: Earl Slater's (Robert Ryan) quest for a big score scares his girlfriend Lorry (Shelley Winters).

Embittered ex-cop Dave Burke (Ed Begley, center) referees the racial hatred between cohorts Johnny Ingram (Harry Belafonte) and Earl.

Earl cheats on Lorry with his strange neighbor Helen (Gloria Grahame), who's excited by Earl's mean streak.

A RANCOROUS EX-COP would again provide the impetus for one of the last great capers from the "classic" noir period. Dave Burke (Ed Begley) was a typically ruddy-faced Irish cop, bounced from the force for refusing to rat out his colleagues before a crime commission. In *Odds Against Tomorrow* (UA/Harbel, 1959) he plots payback with a bank robbery he hopes will free him from the lonely confines of his dingy Dark City apartment.

His plan is a knockover of a bank in the small upstate town of Melton, easy pickings for a trio of big city slicks. He enlists the aid of Johnny Ingram (Harry Belafonte), a Harlem jazz musician who desperately needs a big score to pay off his gambling debts, and Earl Slater (Robert Ryan), a callous bigot who comes from the same poisoned family tree that spawned *Crossfire's* Monty Montgomery.

In the same way *Crossfire* used the murder mystery to explore anti-Semitism, *Odds Against Tomorrow* employs the heist formula to limn a hard-edged take on racism. The film was financed by Harry Belafonte's production company,

Harbel, and the first draft, adapted from William *(The Big Heat)* McGivern's novel, was done by John O. Killens, a young black novelist with no screenwriting experience. Belafonte brought in blacklisted Abraham Polonsky for the rewrite. During his excommunication from Hollywood, Polonsky wrote several politically-charged scripts based on African-American issues, a logical extension of his concern for the struggles of America's underclass. He thought that the popularity of stars such as Belafonte and Sidney Poitier might open the door for these challenging stories, but, as it turned out, neither man was willing to jeopardize his cross-over success by jabbing too hard at white America's conscience. For Poitier, films like *The Defiant Ones* and *Lilies of the Field* were a safer bet, sugarcoating anger with sentimentality.

For Belafonte, the structure of the crime drama proved more than adequate to support the added weight of social significance. The dynamics of men performing under pressure — shelving their resentments for the success of the job — was an acute metaphor for the American

workplace. Because it was a crime film, the race hatred that flares between Johnny and Earl was at a safe remove from the average film-goer. But its painfully irritating sting was deeply felt.

Johnny Ingram is the classic noir character: a good man struggling to hang onto his family and career, with a character flaw — gambling — he hopes won't be fatal. He bristles at the notion of a bank job: "Man, you're drifting. That's not your line, Dave. That's the firing squad. That's for junkies and joy-boys. We're people." Belafonte smartly underplays the racial angle — until Slater pushes him too far.

In one of the film's best scenes, the three conspirators meet to plan the robbery. Slater snidely dismisses any input from Ingram. A war veteran and ex-con, he pops off about the various firearms they'll need to take the bank by force. Earl reads Johnny's silence as a tip-off that the "boy" is yellow. Then Johnny proposes a simple but ingenious scheme for getting into the bank using nothing more than an oversized cardboard box. Burke lights up like a Christmas tree. Earl is humiliated. His anger will infect everyone he

The robbery should be a piece of cake. But Earl goes off plan by giving Dave, not Johnny, the car keys. He's afraid that the "boy" will run.

Johnny finally loses his cool and attacks Earl once the heist goes haywire.

Dave, shot by the cops trying to escape, sees his big scheme crumble. The car keys lie useless on the sidewalk.

encounters — and eventually doom them all.

Belafonte and his colleagues had their fingers on the pulse of a racial tension few films dared address without the requisite Hollywood sanctimony. He subtly, and presciently, suggested that Johnny's innate hipness — his black badge of cool — was a threat to lower class whites afraid of losing their waning hold on cultural dominance. In his Ray-Bans and turtleneck, and with his gravelly jive patter, Belafonte exuded a soulful, cavalier attitude even as his life fell apart. Peckerwood Earl was plenty jealous.

Ryan's virulent performance is almost unbearable. Earl Slater's racism is like gasoline in his veins; it keeps him going when he knows, deep down, that he doesn't fit in, and he has nowhere to go. Scenes of Earl wandering in the wintery city, seething with alienation, are both scary and sad. So are those of his girl Lorry (Shelley Winters) clinging to him in the cramped rooms they call home; she's like a wounded animal huddling with a predatory beast, helplessly hoping for the best. "It's never easy for you, is it, Earl?" she asks. "Only when I'm

angry," he responds sadly, pole-axed by his own character. "Then things get too easy." With that simple line, Ryan conveyed the confounding tragedy of men like Earl; but pity doesn't make them any less terrifying or any more tolerable. Ryan cheats on Lorry with neighbor Gloria Grahame in a scene that is played and shot with a hungry edge, both sexy and repellent.

Director Robert Wise created a bone-chilling tone in *Odds Against Tomorrow*, from the winter cityscapes to the desolation of defoliated upstate New York. His stripped-down, elliptical direction captured the cheerless, stunted lives of his desperate protagonists.

The scenes of the trio tensely biding their time in Melton, waiting for the cover of darkness, have a pungent bleakness: Wise shot them on infra-red film, conjuring an ominous starkness. He also abandoned the string-heavy scores of previous noirs (typically their weakest creative element) for a brassy, percussive soundtrack by the Modern Jazz Quartet. Ingram's life as a jazz man makes the nervy score logical, not a jive affectation.

After *West Side Story* (1961) and *The Sound of Music* (1965), a generation of film buffs weaned on the auteur theory would stamp Robert Wise as an "A" list Hollywood hack. It was a bum rap. Wise apprenticed with two geniuses, Orson Welles and Val Lewton, editing *Citizen Kane* and directing Lewton's creepy, touching *The Curse of the Cat People* (1944). In films as diverse as *The Body Snatcher* (1945), *Born to Kill* (1947) *Blood on the Moon* (1948), *The Set-Up* (1949), *The Day the Earth Stood Still* (1951), and *The Captive City* (1952) — he honed the ability to tell compelling stories concisely, whatever the genre. Like another sure-handed craftsman of this era, Richard Fleischer, Wise would soon be entrusted with bigger and bigger budgets — resulting in bloated movies that couldn't help but sag under the ponderous weight of the studios' expectations. Anyone who dismisses Robert Wise as a stodgy director-for-hire is only proving that they've never seen *Odds Against Tomorrow*, which demonstrated that messy social issues could be deftly addressed within the tidy framework of a small-scale crime picture.

Richard Widmark as Harry Fabian, Dark City's patron saint
of last chances and lost causes, in *Night and the City*.

This lousy town thinks I'm gonna knuckle under. Well, this town has another think coming. All those people up there will be readin' about me soon enough. They'll see my picture right there — staring at 'em over their coffee — and then they'll say: 'I shoulda done right by him. I shoulda known that he was gonna be a big man.' In their fancy digs, laughing and thinking they got it made. Like they got a leg up or something. Like they're better'n me. They'll just hafta learn. Somebody's gonna hafta teach 'em.

Losers' Lane

A guard makes his rounds outside a holding cell. One of the two guys in the tank cranes his neck to watch the bull patrol. "Lookit that cheap squirt, passing up and down," he grouses in an oddly high voice. "For a nickel I'd grab him... stick both thumbs right in his eyes...hang on till he drops dead." Then he chortles, and it's like staccato bleats of a raspy alto sax. The film is *Kiss of Death* (20th, 1947), the loser in stir is Tommy Udo, and the actor injecting Tommy with a new strain of dementia is Richard Widmark, making his Dark City debut. "Imagine me in here," he says to sloe-eyed cellmate Victor Mature. "Big man like me gettin' picked up. Just for shoving a guy's ears off his head. Traffic ticket stuff."

Once he's sprung, and hunting down a potential informer, Widmark makes movie history. He uses a torn-out electrical cord to lash Mildred Dunnock, the squealer's mother, to her wheelchair, then pitches her down the stairs of her tenement, cackling happily all the while. Audiences were brought up short by such berserk mayhem — but also guiltily beguiled.

Kiss of Death was an unusual hybrid, in limbo between the flamboyantly stylized cinematography of Norbert Brodine and the semidocumentary approach that director Henry Hathaway previously used in *The House on 92nd Street*. Mature played Nick Bianco, a hump trying to shake the crooked life who gets enlisted by the cops as a stoolie. Bianco fingers Udo for a job that's been nagging the law, but the prosecution bungles the case and the wacko walks. Nick sends his family away, knowing that he'll have to confront the vengeful Udo if he ever wants to be free of him.

Poor Victor Mature. He gave probably his best performance in *Kiss of Death*, but nobody noticed. They were breathlessly waiting for Widmark to reappear, eager for whatever fresh, twisted tricks he had up his sleeve. Ostensibly a story about Bianco's struggle to go straight, *Kiss of Death* is actually one of the earliest psychostalker movies. All its suspense is generated by wondering when and where Widmark will pop into the frame.

Tommy Udo wasn't the type of provocative, persuasive gangster Jimmy Cagney played to perfection in the 1930s; audiences weren't responding to Udo's anger and ambition, or relating to the simmering social motivations that made him turn bad. With Widmark inhabiting the baggy suits, white tie on black shirt, and fedora big as a lampshade, spectators were jazzed by his dizzy, dangerous charisma; he played it big and broad, with a spring in his step that might launch him over the top at any moment. All told, he had about 15 minutes of screen time, and he devoured it. He funnelled bad intentions, annoying habits, grating obnoxiousness, and total amorality into Tommy Udo, and let it rip. The result was a vicarious thrill, and it proved *very* influential. *Double Indemnity* had broached the unthinkable by making murder acceptable screen fare. Widmark took the next step — pathology as squirmy entertainment. And he raised the bar for all subsequent noir nutcases.

It was Darryl Zanuck who recognized the lunacy lurking in Widmark. Henry Hathaway didn't want to hire him, even after seeing the maniacal leer and hearing the freakish titter in a screen test. He thought Widmark was too clean-cut. But Zanuck prevailed, even outfitting Widmark with a hairpiece that lowered his forehead and made him look a little denser, and a lot scarier. *Kiss of Death* had only been in release for a month or two when college fraternities — ten in all — formed Tommy Udo fan clubs, celebrating the new craziness, particularly Udo's *I-oughta-smack-you* chauvinism.

Widmark scored an Oscar nomination for his *Kiss of Death* performance, and Zanuck promptly cast his suddenly hot contract player in *The Street With No Name* (1948), an old-fashioned racket-buster melodrama out of the 1930s. Director William Keighley sent a battalion of straight arrow Feds, holdovers from his earlier *G-Men*, after crooked fight promoter Alec Stiles (Widmark) — but it was no contest. Audiences instinctively sided with Widmark, whose nervy malevolence made

everyone else on-screen seem safe and tired.

Dark City was quickly becoming home to the man born in Sunrise, Minnesota, who'd spent his youth, oddly enough, as a wholesome honor student growing up in Sioux Falls, South Dakota. Unlike Depression-era roustabouts Mitchum and Hayden, Widmark enjoyed a secure, stable, all-American upbringing. He was president of the senior class at Illinois's Lake Forest College, a lettered receiver on the gridiron, captain of the debating team, and a movie-crazy member of the drama department. In 1942 he went to New York and broke into radio, before landing Broadway roles as a romantic leading man in *Kiss and Tell* and *Kiss Them for Me*. It seemed a sensible, if sinister, progression that *Kiss of Death* be his movie debut.

After wrapping *The Street With No Name*, Widmark was ushered directly into *Road House* (20th, 1948). It was another variation on Tommy Udo, with the flashier psychosis toned down, and the hairline allowed to revert to its natural level. It was Ida Lupino's vehicle all the way, and she requested Widmark specifically after being infected with Udomania herself. He went toe-to-toe with her, both delivering sensational drop-dead dialogue.

Road House was a simple story of the eternal triangle. Lili Stevens (Lupino) gets hired by the infatuated Jefty Robbins (Widmark) to work as a chanteuse in his roadhouse. But after some initial friction, she falls for Jefty's right-hand man, Pete (Cornel Wilde). When Jefty finds out, he retaliates by framing Pete for a trumped-up theft of the club's receipts. In a queasy twist, Jefty urges the judge to release Pete into his custody. From then on, he cruelly tortures the captive lovers while seeming to be a magnanimous benefactor. Widmark brought his special type of homicidal petulance to the part.

In *No Way Out* (20th, 1950), Widmark bunked in Robert Ryan's barracks. He played a fugitive killer who gets wounded and holds Sidney Poitier and Linda Darnell hostage. Poitier, a doctor, saves his captor's life. But that doesn't stop the bigoted

Widmark from race-baiting him at every opportunity. In a famous scene, Widmark and Poitier grapple and the wound in Widmark's leg reopens. Darnell, who's silently suffered the villain's virulence, snarls: "Tear it some more!" This bit was so loathsome it was clipped from many prints.

What separated Widmark from Ryan was the former's guileless demeanor. Ryan's rancor ran deep; it seemed to flow through generations. Widmark projected a callow immaturity. He came off like a spoiled kid who, if he didn't get the last cookie, would grab Dad's gun and open fire on the whole family. Ryan was all about ancient hatred, Widmark about newly-minted craziness.

By 1950 Widmark, like Ryan, risked being typecast. His defense was to kiss-off the Tommy Udo stigma with one last blowout. In *Night and the City* (20th, 1950), Widmark manufactured the quintessential noir loser. Man-child Harry Fabian was the culmination of all Widmark's previous ranting and raving. Jules Dassin pulled out all the stops, directing the film in a baroque style that verged perilously close to parody. Widmark matches him every step of the way. Whenever his dervish-like performance threatened to spin out of control, Widmark pulled Fabian back to earth with simple, poignant, sympathetic details. Playing a scheming hustler rather than a psycho killer, Widmark for the first time found tragedy at the core of a character.

Enough was enough. After Fabian, there were no darker avenues for Widmark to wander. He happily found himself cast as the health inspector hero of Elia Kazan's *Panic in the Streets* (20th, 1950), while Jack Palance essayed the infectious heavy that had been Widmark's stock-in-trade. This go-round Widmark didn't snicker whenever he smiled. The audience suddenly saw that the crooked smirk could also be disarmingly sweet. Probably because it represented a salvation of sorts, Widmark always cited *Panic* as his personal favorite among his many films. Once he'd established leading man credentials, he swung back and forth between the light and dark, bringing a shifty, ambiguous charm to films such as *Don't Bother to Knock* (which featured Marilyn Monroe's best performance) and the previously-lauded *Pickup on South Street*.

For the next fifteen years Hollywood detoured around Dark City. Widmark worked steadily in westerns, war dramas, and adventure sagas. In 1968, Don Siegel brought him back to the city, as *Madigan* (Universal), a veteran cop who seemed to embody the transition between the old and new Hollywood. The script, co-authored by Abraham Polonsky, was an Americanized version of Akira Kurosawa's *Stray Dog*, in which a cop has

his gun stolen and embarks on a 72-hour odyssey to capture the murderer who stole it. Widmark was perfect as the tired flatfoot trying to dodge the myriad treacheries of both the underworld and the politicized police department. The film was both an elegy for old-fashioned policers, and a preview of the rougher, more dyspeptic cop dramas that would later become a television staple.

During his career, Widmark himself proved to be anything but the crackpot character he perfected onscreen. He tied the knot with his college sweetheart, Jean Hazelwood, in 1942, and remained happily married to her. (Daughter Anne married baseball great Sandy Koufax.) He shunned publicity, preferring to live as a gentleman farmer on ranches in California and Connecticut. Though he premiered as a high-strung psychopath, Widmark's staying power made him one of the most stand-up guys in the business. As time takes its toll on Dark City's legendary citizens, Widmark could yet be the last man standing.

From *Road House*: Celeste Holm can plead all she wants, but she's not going to stop the inevitable. Audiences eagerly anticipated the scene where Widmark reached the end of his short tether, and flew into a keening, maniacal rage.

Widmark may have catapulted to stardom as Tommy Udo, but in truth he was not the original model for the fair-haired, lanky, laughing loon. That honor belongs to Dan Duryea, who during the 1940s occupied an exclusive enclave in Losers' Lane. He was Dark City's most enchanting villain, the man audiences loved to hate. For a number of years, Duryea's act was even more popular than Widmark's, although he never quite climbed into the upper echelon of leading men the way Widmark did.

The two men were remarkably similar, coming to Hollywood from Broadway, where they'd each mainly been cast in romantic blue-blooded parts. Both were slender, with lank, slicked-back blond hair. Both had a come-on smile that exuded an oddly cheerful menace. Both had unusual, high-pitched voices.

And most significantly, considering the Dark City milieu they inhabited, both men were riveting when they dropped the pretense of civilization and erupted into violence.

During the 1940s, Dan Duryea developed an odd, almost fetishistic on-screen forte — beating women. His deviate sexuality was first exploited by Fritz Lang in *The Woman in the Window* (1944). He padded the stick-thin actor with a double-breasted suit, bowtie and straw boater, a get-up that was, for awhile, his signature ensemble. Suitably decked out, Duryea struck the pose that would become his trademark: lounging in a doorframe, worrying a toothpick, a sly smile creeping across his face. "I'm just naturally what they call a cynic, honey," he drawls to co-star Joan Bennett. When Duryea paws his way around Joan's apartment, looking for the hidden murder weapon so he can blackmail her, Lang stages it like a gross sexual imposition. Bennett stands immobilized, panting slightly, while the insouciant Duryea rummages through her drawers, fondles her clothes, daubs himself with her perfume, and relishes her helplessness. Later, when Joan tries to feed him a poisoned scotch, Duryea wises up and turns malevolent. "You drink it," he seethes. When she demurs, he pops her with a curt backhand and throws her to the bed. "How could you lie like that to Pappy," he sneers. He takes her money and dismisses her with a flick of fingers off his chin. Duryea had the patent on all these rude bits of business.

In Lang's *Scarlet Street*, the actor upped the ante, having his way with sexy Joan, then blithely slapping her around. His caddish behavior struck a chord — especially in women. Duryea started getting fan mail by the truckload, most of it from infatuated females. Producers developed more inventive ways for Duryea to backhand distaff co-stars. These outbursts always caused Duryea's Brilliantined hair to come unglued, spilling long blond strands down his billboard-sized forehead. He was one of the first stars to act with his hair. This stylish affectation provided tonsorial precedent for, among others, rock and roller Jerry Lee Lewis.

Beatings administered by Duryea were so telegraphed that Universal's publicists felt it necessary to offer a disclaimer when promoting *Black Angel* (1946): "Something great has happened in Hollywood, land of great things. Beautiful June Vincent met dangerous Dan Duryea and escaped unscathed. Prolific Dan, beater of such gorgeous femmes as Joan Bennett, touches nary a strand of June's blonde hair in Universal's *Black Angel*, a story of guys and gals — some good, some bad. Maybe it was mother love that moved Duryea to confine his poundings to honky-tonk pianos — for this is June's first role since the birth of her baby. Quien sabe?"

Another memorable bit of Duryea business: in Fritz Lang's *Ministry of Fear* (Paramount, 1945) Duryea had a crucial cameo as the Nazi spy Cost, who dies during a séance, only to reappear as a tailor named Travers. Hair slicked and bowtie in place, Duryea contemplated either murder or suicide while artfully manipulating a huge pair of shears. Duryea was always the glowing center of attention in any scene, and Lang used his rail-thin radiance brilliantly in three films: *Ministry, The Woman in the Window,* and *Scarlet Street.*

In *Too Late For Tears* (UA, 1949), a clever and unjustly neglected Hate Street melodrama with a terrific Roy Huggins script, Duryea takes a whack at Lizabeth Scott. He plays a private detective who knows Liz is stashing a valise full of cash that someone tossed into her open convertible. She wants to keep the dough, while her husband, Arthur Kennedy, wants to turn it over to the cops. She and Dan hatch a plot to share the loot, and Liz bumps off her husband. Dan thinks that a few stiff smacks in the kisser will be enough to keep Liz in line, but she proves him wrong. By this time Duryea's facial treatments were so hugely popular that the studio used the ubiquitous slapping scene as its one-sheet art.

When Paramount later that year cast Dangerous Dan opposite Dorothy Lamour in *Manhandled*, audiences knew just what they were getting. Although Duryea had to dye his blond locks black — ostensibly to avoid confusion with the sixty-pounds thicker Sterling Hayden — the bowtie was firmly in place, and this time his oral fixation was chewing gum, which he'd masticate languorously, then deposit in inappropriate places. And, of course, the right hand got a workout. First he slaps Lamour, then hits her with a right cross — twice — and finally tries to throw her off a rooftop. His most dastardly act came in a remarkable scene where he chases Harold Vermilyea down in a huge Packard and pins him to a brick wall, grinding his foot down on the accelerator.

The same year Robert Siodmak cast him as Slim Dundee in *Criss Cross*, providing perhaps the finest visual record of Duryea's dandy duds. And, of course, he tagged Yvonne De Carlo once or twice before giving her a couple of lead ducats to Dreamland.

Somehow he managed to squeeze in another noir that amazing year, *Johnny Stool Pigeon* (Universal), in which he roughed up co-star Shelley Winters.

When Duryea made the same crossover as Widmark, playing only slightly crooked heroes in films like *The Underworld Story* and *World for Ransom*, he sacrificed some of his allure. He was a serviceable good guy, but a delectable bastard. When Duryea played things straight the strange music in his voice tended to go flat. When his riff was sharp and cunning, he exuded what one admirer described as "animal magnetism."

Duryea's off-screen life paralleled that of Richard Widmark, as well. Slapping women around made him a millionaire, but Duryea lived an uncomplicated, if opulent, life. He was one of Hollywood's more honorable citizens, considered a model husband and father. Married in 1931 to Helen Bryan, he remained with her until her death in 1967. Duryea followed her the next year.

BEFORE YOU START TO THINK Dark City's most infamous villains were all just clever put-ons brought to life by charming thespians, let's stop by the station house. Well, wouldn't you know? Look who they got jugged — Lawrence Tierney. Don't bother asking the desk cop if this is real life or a movie. It doesn't make any difference in this guy's case. If street credibility had been a requirement when it came to playing rat bastards, then Lawrence Tierney would be the undisputed heavyweight champion of Losers' Lane.

During the heyday of the noir crime drama, Tierney, a Brooklyn boy and son of an Irish cop, reeled off a string of rough-hewn "B" features made memorable by the actor's authentic mean streak. His breakthrough came at Poverty Row studio Monogram,

Claire Trevor gets sized up by Lawrence Tierney in Robert Wise's daringly depraved *Born to Kill*.

playing legendary bank robber *Dillinger* (1945). Although he did have formal acting training, Tierney never completely lost what he called the "doity poiple boids" in his Brooklyn accent, and it made him seem all the more believable, and unique, as an on-screen heavy. Pumping even more vitriol into his tough-guy persona was the rap sheet he built up along with his résumé.

After filming *Step by Step* in 1946, Tierney did a five-day stint in the drunk tank. It was only the first of many disagreements he'd have with John Law over the course of his checkered career, most stemming from a penchant for barroom brawling. Writers and directors were soon making hay off Tierney's public image. Young screenwriter Robert Altman fed Tierney the tongue-in-cheek line "Now you know me better than that — I never get into fights," in *Bodyguard* (1948), yet another of Richard Fleischer's short, sturdy programmers.

Tierney — like his brother, actor Scott Brady — was a big lug, broad-shouldered, and handsome. But his eyes narrowed into slits when he started thinking. And his thin-lipped grin was one of the most purely rapacious sights on film. He was the all-grown-up roughneck from high school who inexplicably had cute girls cozying up to him. Couldn't they see the callousness in his eyes? Didn't they know he had a nasty nickname for each of them?

In *The Devil Thumbs a Ride* (RKO, 1947), Tierney takes the conniving bully routine around the bend. Only seconds in, he shoots an old man in the back as he's making a night deposit at a bank. He fast-talks a soused newlywed into giving him a lift up the coast. At a filling station he picks up two gals fresh off the bus. He wastes no time trying to schmooze the dishier of the pair into a backseat clinch. When he commandeers the wheel he promptly runs over a motorcycle cop. The group ends up AWOL at a beach house, where Tierney coolly shuts off every avenue of escape, and resumes his lupine pursuit of the gullibly innocent gal. When she realizes he's a fugitive, he drowns her. Soon all hell is breaking loose.

Written and directed by Felix Feist, *The Devil Thumbs a Ride* is one of those dirt-cheap "B's" that are mesmerizing by virtue of the fact that they steamroll any logic that threatens to creep into the plot. With Tierney in the driver's seat, it's a fast ride, full of jittery laughs. He indulges in plenty of cruel put-downs, which had become his forte. When a gas jockey proudly displays a picture of his baby daughter, Tierney cracks: "From the looks of those ears, she's gonna fly before she walks." After he pitches some dreadfully purple woo at beautiful Carol, her shopworn friend Agnes turns on the car radio: "Anything not to have to listen to that." Snaps Tierney: "Quit yer gripin', grandma – you'll never have to listen to it."

Chock full of goony character actors, *The Devil Thumbs a Ride* is like a surreal, live-action cartoon. Darker and meaner is Robert Wise's *Born to Kill* (RKO, 1947), featuring Tierney as Sam Wild, perhaps the most unrepentently amoral character ever. After he kills two people in Reno, his weaselly buddy Marty (Elisha Cook, Jr.) scolds him: "Honest, Sam – you go nuts about nothin', nothin' at all. You can't go around killin' people whenever the notion strikes you. It's not feasible." But Sam finds it justifiable: "When I see what I want, I take it. Nobody cuts in on me." The cold-blooded killer insinuates himself into a clique of affluent San Franciscans. "Marrying into this crowd'll make it so I can spit in anybody's eye," he tells Marty. Sam meets his match in Helen Trent (Claire Trevor), a lustful society deviate, engaged to a local scion. Sam marries her half-sister Georgia (Audrey Long), but carries on a torrid affair with Helen. Their heavy-breathing scene in the kitchen pantry was hot stuff for the time:

"All my life I've lived on other people's money," Helen pants. "Now I want some of my own. There's another kind of security Fred can give me — without him I'm afraid of the things I'll do, afraid of what I might become. Fred is goodness and safety."

"And what am I?" Sam sneers. "You're strength and excitement — and depravity," she gasps. "There's a kind of corruptness inside you, Sam." Tierney reacts like he's being pinned with merit badges. They grapple in a wanton embrace. This pair would mug Walter Neff and Phyllis Dietrichsen and leave them hog-tied by the side of the road.

Tierney gained more notoriety as he started rehearsing his pugnacious patter in saloons. In '48 he did three months for busting a guy's jaw in a bar. Same year he was charged with kicking a cop while drunk and disorderly – a seemingly perpetual state. In '52 he sparred with a professional welterweight on the corner of Broadway and 53rd. He was the only actor in Hollywood who posed for more mug shots than publicity photos: belted a cop in '56; simple assault in '57; kicked in a dame's door the same year; another jawbreaker in '58, as well as a dust-up with cops outside a 6th Avenue tavern. The day his mother killed herself in 1960, Tierney was arrested for breaking down a woman's door and assaulting her boyfriend.

Amazingly, Tierney is still around, still working. Another scrapper of note, Norman Mailer, cast him in the author's foray into neo-noir, *Tough Guys Don't Dance* (1987), and Quentin Tarantino resurrected Tierney as the belligerent ringleader of his gang of *Reservoir Dogs* (1991). Now a hulking, chrome-domed, and still menacing, version of his once virile self, Tierney often shows up in cameos — none more appropriate then his uncredited stint as a drunken victim of a bloody beating on the television hospital show, *ER*.

EVERY YEAR WHEN THE CARNIVAL ROLLS ONTO A VACANT LOT at the outskirts of Dark City, you've got a chance to meet Stanton Carlisle, one of the wildest characters this town has ever seen. Once, as Stanton the Great, he had it all in the palm of his hand. But his fall was even steeper than his rise. The twisting tale of his life is told in *Nightmare Alley* (20th, 1947).

Stan (Tyrone Power) is a strikingly handsome young man learning the ropes of the carny dodge. He's fascinated by the flat joints the rubes fall for, night after night. A student of human nature, Stan is particularly entranced by the pitiful, chicken-gnawing geek, wondering what could make a once-proud human sink so low. The carny hustle also fuels his ambitious imagination. "It gives you kind of a superior feeling — as if you were on the inside and everybody else is on the outside, looking in," he tells Zeena (Joan Blondell) the veteran "mentalist" with whom he's having an affair. Zeena doesn't need her tarot cards to see the dangerous avarice in Stan. It's right there in his eyes.

Stan's after more than a fleshy fling with Zeena. He wants The Code, an intricate "mind reading" system she and her husband Pete (Ian Keith) long ago devised. It took them to the heights of the business, before booze brought Pete to his knees. One night Stan "accidentally" switches Pete's beloved moonshine with a bottle of pure wood alcohol. Once Pete's dead, Zeena needs a new partner. But after Stan's mastered the code himself, he dumps Zeena for Molly (Coleen Gray), a sexy young shill who's the main squeeze of the show's strongman, Bruno (Mike Mazurki). The lovely couple zoom to the top, leaving the road-show life for ritzy clubs where Stanton the Great entertains Dark City's elite with his amazing mental feats.

Stan finds a kindred spirit in Dr. Lilith Ritter (Helen Walker), an eminent psychologist drawn to Carlisle's shameless hucksterism. She's even more beguiled by Stan's devious plan to bilk her wealthy clients. Using

Stan Carlisle (Tyrone Power) has a way with women (both Coleen Gray and Joan Blondell), much to the chagrin of Bruno (Mike Mazurki) in *Nightmare Alley,* one of the bleakest films of the 1940s. Author William Lindsay Gresham wasn't just dabbling with fashionable nihilism: he committed suicide with this lone novel to his credit.

confidential information that Lilith feeds him from her sessions, Stan is able to convince several socialites of his miraculous powers. He tries to enlist Molly to portray one patron's dead lover; the old coot will give all his earthly riches just to see his dead sweetheart once more. Molly balks, fearful that Stan has become a Skygrifter:

"Everything you say and do is so true and wonderful," she blurts, "and you make it sound so sacred and holy – when all the time it's just a gag with you. You're laughing your head off at those chumps! You think God's gonna stand for that? He'll strike you dead!"

"I've met a lot of these spook workers," Stan counters. "And they're just like me — hustlers. I didn't see any of them wearing lightning rods." Molly snaps: "They don't act like you! They don't talk like a minister!"

But Stan gives her his God-fearing spiel, and coaxes Molly into participating in his ultimate hoax — convincing the delirious mark that there's life after death, by having the appropriately-attired Molly float ethereally around the perimeter of the man's estate. As the chump slumps to his knees in ecstasy, Stan has his own epiphany, imagining the riches he's going to bilk from this sorry sucker. But Molly, her conscience racked by the old guy's rapturous tears, blows the gaff. In the confusion, Stan knocks the old guy down, accidentally killing him.

He flees to Lilith to get his share of the dough they've scammed, then takes it on the arches. But he frantically returns to Ritter's office when he realizes she's pulled the old gypsy switch, substituting a single buck for each C-note. Stan, it seems, has been fleeced by an expert. Lilith turns out to be a real Larry: she has a wax recording of Stan during his own therapy session, admitting his involvement in Pete's death. She gives him the bum's rush. Flat broke and a fugitive from the law, Stan rides the rails. Like Pete before him, he starts hitting the bottle. Soon he's running routines on his new associates – hobos. When he tries to catch on again with the carnival, there's only one job left for a broke-down, boozed-up bum.

"You know what a geek is?" asks the carny manager. "Think you can handle it?" Stan downs another proferred shot of rotgut. "Mister," he says, "I was made for it."

Even a potentially fatuous coda that reunites Stan and Molly can't force a ray of light into *Nightmare Alley*. It is one of the most caustic, cynical movies that Billy Wilder never made. This exceptional film was the work of director Edmund Goulding, an industry stalwart whose facility with 1930s soap operas gave no indication of the black depths he'd explore in this venture. The film was a startling departure for everyone involved, especially Tyrone Power. He'd just come off the popular and critical success of *The Razor's Edge* (20th, 1946), playing a character far deeper than was his norm. Perhaps Hollywood's most popular and handsome leading man at the time, Power felt unappreciated as an actor and wanted to unleash an even bigger surprise on the public. When he read William Lindsay Gresham's novel *Nightmare Alley*, he immediately bought the film rights, realizing that Stan Carlisle was infinitely more intriguing than the swaggering swashbucklers the studio wanted him to play forever.

His performance is mesmerizing, making Carlisle one of the most compelling characters in all film noir. He's supported by terrific turns from Joan Blondell, Coleen Gray, and, especially, Helen Walker. When she reveals the cold, intellectual psychologist to be a calculating, demonic bitch, it's enough to make anyone swear off therapists. Dr. Ritter is the frostiest — and most believable — villain offered in any Forties film.

Nightmare Alley is unique among noirs. There's no gunplay, no gangsters, and the lone "crime" — the death of Pete — is handled with great ambiguity (unlike in the novel, where Stan clearly intends to poison him). In spirit it most closely resembles *Force of Evil*, another film that darkly delineates the predatory elements of the modern "success story." And just as Polonsky's film presciently envisioned a future filled with mob-infested lotteries and a criminal pox on Wall Street, so *Nightmare Alley* presages a world of televangelists, home shopping hucksterism, New Age charlatans, and the Psychic Friends Network.

Stan, you were born too soon.

Zeena (Joan Blondell) wonders what devious musings run through the mind of Stan Carlisle (Tyrone Power) in *Nightmare Alley*.

A COUPLE OF YEARS AFTER STAN CARLISLE RETURNED TO THE CARNIVAL, the geek was no longer the star attraction on the midway. Acing him out as the hottest act was a comely sharpshooter from the British Isles named Laurie Starr (Peggy Cummins). In her Annie Oakley outfit, twirling her six-guns, her eyes sparkling under the tent's spotlights, she was everything young Bart Tare (John Dall) wanted in a woman. She was *Gun Crazy* (UA, 1950).

Laurie recognizes the gunpowder glaze in Bart's eyes the first time she sees him, gazing up at her from the front row. When he accepts the house's challenge of a shooting contest, movies reach the zenith of outrageous sexual symbolism: flirtation by firearm. The two are so aroused by firing pistols at each other it's a miracle they don't go at it right on the stage — but then, they already have. For these two, sidearms have greater sensual allure than sex itself.

The film is ostensibly about Bart's fixation with guns. It quickly sketches his youthful yearning for weapons, but stresses that he doesn't want to kill anything. "It's just that when I shoot, I feel like I'm good at something," he explains to the local judge after he's caught red-handed trying to steal a majestic Colt revolver from a hardware store window. He's sent away to a reform school, and later joins the military, where he finds his niche as a shooting range instructor. But

he returns to his hometown utterly aimless — until he outshoots the sexy Miss Starr. From then on, he's got one direction: after her.

Bart and Laurie aren't together ten minutes before its clear who's running this show. "I want action," she declares. Literally in the blink of an eye, film noir's answer to Bonnie and Clyde are careering across the countryside, pulling stickups with a frenzy that borders on the nymphomaniacal. Laurie pretends that the robberies are about money, but they're really about the thrill she gets from them. In the heat of the heists, Laurie's face turns blissfully feral, like a cat tearing at raw meat. Bart is tortured by their outlaw lifestyle, but Laurie is unapologetic: "I told you I was no good, and I didn't kid you," she snaps at him.

Bart and Laurie marry, live like nomads robbing hand-to-mouth, then decide to pull one big job — knocking over the payroll office of a meat-packing plant. As they're fleeing, Laurie pumps a pair of slugs into an office manager who dares sound the alarm. Although he's disgusted at being a murderer now, Bart can't shake his deadly attraction to Laurie. For his benefit, she whimpers that she only kills when she gets scared, but it's another lie. She kills because she can't get enough.

With the murder rap hounding them, they flee like wild dogs, eventually ending up back in Bart's hometown, where he's shunned by his family and hunted down by his childhood buddies, now a reporter and a sheriff.

The fugitives hide out in a foggy marsh. As his old friends close in, warning Bart to give up, Laurie shrieks: "Come any closer and I'll kill you! I'll kill you all!" Distraught, Bart finally uses his gun to kill another living thing — his beloved Laurie. Hearing gunshots, his pursuers opens fire, killing Bart.

The script, written by blacklisted Dalton Trumbo, under the front Millard Kaufman (adapted from a *Saturday Evening Post* story by MacKinlay Kantor), couldn't have been honed more closely to the bone. As Bart, John Dall is saddled with chunks of blatant speechifying that are a Trumbo trademark, but for the most part the movie is paced at a breakneck speed not too conducive to idle philosophizing.

Joseph H. Lewis's direction is propulsive, possessed of a confident, vigorous simplicity that all the frantic editing and visual pyrotechnics of his filmmaking progeny never quite surpassed. *Bonnie and Clyde* may have been a better movie than *Gun Crazy*, but nothing in it matched the breathtaking four-minute single take in which Cummins and Dall rob a small-town bank. This uninterrupted shot, in which the audience is a virtual accomplice in the crime, is moviemaking at its exhilarating best.

Another jolt is the delirious scene in which the lovers are supposed to flee in separate cars after the payroll heist. Unable to pull away from each other, they wheel their land yachts into screeching U-turns and fall back into each others' arms. It should be laughable. Instead, it's the most ecstatic

"Two people dead! Just so we can
live without working! *Why?* Why
did you do it? Why do you have to
murder people? Why *can't* you let
them live?"

—Bart (John Dall) to Laurie
(Peggy Cummins) in *Gun Crazy*

moment in film noir. Lewis fires off one sharp scene after another, just like Bart fanning the hammer of his favorite Colt. Even today, there's a breathless freshness to *Gun Crazy*. The storytelling is so visually adept it could have been a silent movie, complemented solely by Victor Young's inventive score.

With all due apologies to Dalton Trumbo, it might have worked just as well.

The original Travis Bickle: Arthur Franz is God's lonely and deranged man, stalking the streets of San Francisco in *The Sniper*.

EDDIE MILLER (ARTHUR FRANZ) is another habitue of Losers' Lane whose obsession with firearms is inspired by uncontrollable libidinous urges. His fear of, and desire for, women — instilled in him by a loveless mother — drives him to murder. His only intimacy comes through a telescopic sight, his only release from pulling the trigger. *The Sniper* (Columbia, 1952) was the first film to explore what would eventually become something of a national pastime — assassination by high-powered rifle. It also took an unflinching look at the disorders behind sex crimes perpetrated against women.

Harry Brown's screenplay is based on research by associate producers Edna and Edward Anhalt, who disdained the grim fairy-tale romanticism of films like *Gun Crazy* in favor of a more straightforward accounting of violent sex offenses. The story is your basic manhunt thriller, familiar to film viewers of the past three decades. But in '52, the murder scenes were so shocking that the movie was jerked from release prematurely. There was no precedent for images such as Marie Windsor's head shattering a glassed-in billboard after being struck with a rifle shot. For the first time, a film directly addressed the homicidal rage of a lonely, disturbed man lashing out at women. There are provocative innuendos throughout, suggesting that women may be predestined victims of male predatory instincts, and that Miller's killing spree is just the twisted culmination of a chromosomal predilection.

The Sniper is seldom-seen, but it is central to a major shift that took place in film noir in the early 1950s. It was emblematic of what Paul Schrader, in his 1972 *Notes on Film Noir*, called the genre's "third and final phase" — the descent into psychopathology:

"After ten years of steadily shedding romantic conventions, the later noir films finally got down to the root causes of the period: the loss of public honor, heroic conventions, personal integrity and, finally, psychic stability." The disturbing themes of alienation, sexual confusion, and violent revenge rooted in *The Sniper* extend all the way through the 1960s, to Don Siegel's *Dirty Harry* (1972), in which modern marshal Clint Eastwood hunts through the same San Francisco streets that Arthur Franz terrorized in *The Sniper*, and reaching its apex in Schrader's own screenplay for the Über-noir *Taxi Driver* (1976).

The Sniper is notable for how it depicts Miller's derangement with a fresh sense of dispassion. It neither sympathizes with him nor treats him like a rabid animal. It's also one of the first films to take seriously the threat of brain-damaged individuals loose in the city. Miller wants to be put away — he knows he's dangerous — but the system is too overloaded to deal with him. The overcrowding of the VA Psych Ward has, by 1952, spilled over to the general hospital (the police even focus the manhunt on "section eights" — military mental cases). The film is loaded with scenes that capture the transition between an era when sexual deviance was considered a marginal problem — fodder for cavalier humor — and a new generation of armed and dangerous sexual predators.

After the guilt-wracked sniper intentionally burns his firing hand on a hot plate, he gets some old-school counseling from the male nurse bandaging him: "A man's got no business fooling around with a stove. They're strictly women's business. You're not married, huh? You're missing a big deal, friend. So you get married, your wife does all the cooking — so she's the one that gets burned. So what happens? She comes crying on your shoulder. You pat her head, give her a kiss or two — yeah, that's living."

A few years earlier, that would have passed

for homespun wisdom in a Hollywood movie. Here, the camera moves in on Miller's angry eyes as the nurse spouts off — his words serving only to stoke the killer's fury.

The idea that society is caught in the crosshairs of a new, deadly strain of urban menace — and unprepared to defend itself — is reflected in a police show-up in which a slew of sexual deviants are paraded before a roomful of cops. The inquisitor can't help himself: he treats the line-up like vaudeville shtick, making condescending jokes out of each man's perversion. The filmmakers clearly suggest that the joke is on the cops, who can't distinguish between garden variety peeping toms and a murderous psycho.

In an extraordinary scene, Miller attends a carnival and enjoys pitching baseballs at a bullseye, which dunks a pretty swimsuit-clad woman in a tank of water. His faultless aim attracts a crowd as she is soaked, over and over. Miller's misogynist rage finally erupts; he hurls balls directly at the woman, leaving her screaming in terror. Despite the considerable anxiety the film builds as the manhunt closes in on Miller, the filmmakers climax the proceedings with a scene of brilliant restraint: with the street cordoned off, and residents warned of an impending gun battle, the cops break into Miller's apartment to find him huddled on the bed, clutching his rifle. The camera dollies in on his relieved face, a tear dripping from his eye.

With *Murder, My Sweet, Cornered,* and *Crossfire* already on his résumé, director Edward Dmytryk's reputation should have been secure as a creator of excellent film noirs. But his personal life had a tendency to overshadow consideration of his artistic achievements. After serving a one-year prison sentence as one of the Hollywood Ten, the blacklisted Dmytryk lived in exile in England, until he recanted his defiant stance and turned informer against his former Communist comrades. The rancor his decision inspired in many of his contemporaries would always affect his reputation.

Once back in Hollywood, Dmytryk picked up the pieces of his career by returning to the fast and inexpensive trenches of "B" filmmaking. After the undistinguished *Mutiny* (1952), Stanley Kramer hired him to direct *The Sniper.* Dmytryk had insisted to his nine brethren that he was not

Marie Windsor was usually a little more savvy about men. But in *The Sniper* she plays a tavern crooner who enflames the tortured mind of Eddie Miller (Arthur Franz), a delivery man by day, and a psychotic sniper by night. Eddie comes to believe that his hand has a life of its own, and early in the film he burns it in an attempt to prevent himself from killing again. Note the bandage.

selling out, that he would never truly knuckle under to "the enemy." What must they have thought when for the role of Lt. Kafka (!), head of the manhunt, Dmytryk cast Adolphe Menjou — who, before the original HUAC committee in 1947, smugly presented himself as an expert on the Red Menace, and proceeded to indict half of Hollywood?

Despite the pressure he must have felt during this awkward period, Dmytryk turned in a highly effective job. He had cameraman Burnett Guffey, expert at chiaroscuro, eschew the dense shadows of his earlier noirs for the natural look of location photography. The more expressive moments are realized through bold compositions, camera moves, and editing. By 1952, the classic noir "look" was dissipating, as directors made the shift from studio sets to actual streets.

Although it's too obscure to be considered influential, *The Sniper* did predate the later development of stalker movies as a subgenre of crime dramas. Like those odd entertainments, its structure anticipates the predatory "catch and release" progression of pornographic movies. Instead of sexual capture and conquest, you get rejection and retaliation — the basic structure of all the "slasher" films to come — which reflect a social problem that, as *The Sniper* warned, has become an epidemic.

OF ALL THE GUN-TOTING CRAZIES THAT PASSED THROUGH LOSERS' LANE, none achieved greater infamy than Cody Jarrett (James Cagney) — a mama's boy who got homicidal whenever the *White Heat* (WB, 1949) cut through his brain like a buzzsaw. Jarrett was the poster boy for the criminal derangement made popular by Richard Widmark, Dan Duryea, and Lawrence Tierney. But *White Heat*'s reputation as a "classic gangster picture," which has steadily increased over the years, is a misnomer.

Cody Jarrett is an outlaw, not a gangster. The distinction is critical. In the 1930s, Cagney juked his way to fame in a series of "classic" gangster pictures: *The Public Enemy* (1931), *The Lady Killer* (1933), *Jimmy the Gent* (1934), *Angels with Dirty Faces* (1938), and *The Roaring Twenties*

(1939), the bedrock of Warner Bros.'s golden era. Those films were also notable for their "progressive" take on crime: it was the result of rugged conditions endemic to the modern city; the gangster was creating an organization alternative to the legit enterprises that a poor boy couldn't crack. Jarrett's lawlessness, on the other hand, stems from a mental disorder. Don't delve any deeper than his mother to find the root of his problems. Ma Jarrett (Margaret Wycherly) is a doting, smothering hardcase who'll alibi her boy for anything, including murder.

White Heat typifies the conservative subversion of the crime thriller. In the wake of the studios' Communist purge, blatant societal criticism was out. Films could no longer suggest that people did bad things because of economic pressures. Criminal instincts weren't the by-product of a social system, they were inherited from your mother. Eric Johnston, the head of the Motion Picture Association of America, who once defied HUAC's attempt to influence film content — only to later spearhead the studios' surrender to it — told the Screen Writers Guild in 1948: "We'll have no more *Grapes of Wrath*. We'll have no more *Tobacco Roads*. We'll have no more films that show the seamy side of American life. We'll have no more pictures that deal with labor strikes. We'll have no more pictures that show a banker as a villain." *Grapes of Wrath* author John Steinbeck certainly saw this day coming. "A Communist is anybody who wants thirty-five cents an hour when we're paying twenty-five," he sarcastically explained in that novel.

Ben Roberts' and Ivan Goff's script for *White Heat* came along just as Jimmy Cagney reached a personal and professional crossroads. After achieving huge stardom as George M. Cohan in *Yankee Doodle Dandy*, Cagney protected his fame by officially rejecting the associ-ation he'd had with left-wingers during his "progressive" days at Warner. But by '48 his misjudgments as an independent producer had dimmed his luster, and he was looking for a sure-fire comeback. *White Heat* was just the ticket — a new take on the old crook.

An Oedipus complex, not the hardship of poverty, is what drives Cody Jarrett to pull dangerous heists. The script charts Cody's renegade career: daring robberies to prove his worth to Ma; his capture and imprisonment; the betrayal by his wife Verna (Virginia Mayo) with Cody's underling, Big Ed (Steve Cochran); Ma's death, and the transference of Cody's affections to Hank Fallon (Edmond O'Brien), an undercover agent planted in stir with Cody. After he escapes from prison, Cody plots revenge against Verna and Big Ed, but doesn't realize it's Hank who's the more dangerous "traitor."

Cagney's flamboyant "toppers" — bits of show business that kick a scene over the top — are in ample evidence: falling into his Ma's lap when he's struck by a headache, gnawing a chicken leg as he shoots a cohort, kicking a chair out from beneath Virginia Mayo — all hundred-proof Cagney, with a psychotic twist. Most famous of all are the mess-hall breakdown, when he goes wild on learning of Ma's death, and the climax, in which he's trapped atop an oil refinery tank. Realizing it's curtains, Cody kisses tomorrow goodbye by pumping bullets into the tank and bellowing the most famous exit line in movie history. Credit Roberts and Goff for concocting the first cataclysmic climax in a crime thriller, but credit Cagney for the crazy smile, wounded dance steps, and giddy laughter — the ultimate Cagney "topper."

Despite the growing hue and cry against crime pictures in 1949, *White Heat* was a smash. Maybe people wanted nothing more than a riotously entertaining melodrama; thanks to Raoul Walsh's rambunctious direction, *White Heat* delivered the goods in spades. But critics were largely unkind. The film was deemed brutal and mean-spirited. One week after he'd written a laudatory review in *The New York Times*, critic Bosley Crowther recanted his view under pressure from social guardians, and branded the film a potentially harmful form of entertainment. In the intervening years, more viewers — and critics — have come to see the film as a savage black comedy, a send-up of Cagney's former screen persona. (Cagney came to loathe the film, angry that this snarling loser was the role with which he'd be most identified.)

An intriguing take on the film came from John Howard Lawson, of the Hollywood Ten, who viewed it with other inmates while serving his prison sentence. In a 1953 essay entitled *Film in the Battle of Ideas*, Lawson said that *White Heat* made a deep impression on the incarcerated audience, many of whom he described as "decent, well-intentioned people...who recognize the forces which drove them to vice or crime are inherent in our present social system. Related to this partial understanding is a deep bitterness, a feeling that the individual has no chance in a jungle society unless he adopts the way of the jungle.... *White Heat* idealizes this code of the jungle and advertises it as a way of life. The prison audience — and this is probably true of any audience — associated the fictitious character with Cagney's reputation. The spectators saw him as an attractive symbol of toughness, defending himself against a cruel and irrational society; at least, [inmates] said, 'he has the guts to stand up and fight back!'

"This emphasis on the individual's total depravity in a depraved society rejects the possibility of rational social cooperation," Lawson concluded. "Man is doomed to prowl alone, a beast in the jungle."

*"Made it, Ma!
Top o' the world!"*

— Cody Jarrett (Jimmy Cagney)
goes out in a blaze of glory
in *White Heat*.

Frank Lovejoy, William Talman, and Edmond O'Brien in *The Hitch-Hiker*.

E scape became the only option. Follow the blacktop out of Dark City and into a fresh start. Two hours ago the city lights dropped from the rearview, like stars blinking out a million miles away. Out here there'll be room to live, to make a move without knocking up against somebody. Listen – a train whistle. Not car horns, or an ambulance. I'll find a town where people still look you in the eye and call you by your first name, and know you're good for an IOU. Ah, look at this poor guy – his car must have conked out, right here in the middle of nowhere. "Hey Bud, you need a lift?"

Thieves' Highway

In the 1950s America reached its greatest prosperity since the mid-Twenties. The Cold War was terrific for business; consuming became a patriotic duty. And there was no greater badge of affluence than the automobile. President Eisenhower had a vision that hooked up the Cold War to the nation's burgeoning car culture: the Interstate Highway Act, a massive federal program that would link rural and urban America in what proponents called "farm to market" unity. The sinister aspect of the plan was that the new four-lanes were also designed as escape routes, should Soviet missiles rain on major U. S. cities.

The Highway Act had another unexpected dark side. It ensured that troubles once limited to the big city were now free to travel, in a big wide roadster, wherever they wanted to go. In terms of crime — and film noir — "Check the bus and train terminals and put a roadblock at the bridge!" would rarely be heard again.

A highly-publicized example of a new type of criminal in the nation's bloodstream was William Edward Cook, Jr., a 22-year-old ex-con who, in 1950, went on a murder rampage in the Southwest, cadging rides from his future victims. Among the unfortunate samaritans were a vacationing family from Illinois and a traveling salesman from Seattle. America thought it had buried the terrors of the old West under a veneer of grey flannel civility, but here was a clear indication that murder was just as likely to happen in the sticks as on city streets.

When Cook was finally apprehended, all the major magazines ran profiles. Journalists dutifully recounted the story of his brutal childhood — absent father, taunting from other kids because of a facial deformity, Dickensian boarding schools — searching for clues to his motives. Cook himself offered the most succinct explanation for his homicidal behavior: "I hate everybody's guts and everybody hates mine."

Cook represented an unrepentent viciousness that all but obliterated any notion in the media — especially the movies — of the criminal as a social rebel. Rebelliousness was kid's stuff, left to the slew of juvenile delinquent movies spawned by rock 'n' roll, and the rise of leather-clad motorcycle cults. Hardened criminals got more murderous than ever, in reality and in the movies. Their motives were still dutifully trotted out, but in Ike's America mitigating circumstances didn't count for much. A Red was a Red, and a crook was a crook. Both were threats to peace and prosperity. In films such as *The Night Holds Terror* (Columbia, 1955), *The Killer Is Loose* (UA, 1956), *Cry in the Night* (WB, 1956), *Cry Terror* (MGM, 1957), and even the "A" list *The Desperate Hours* (Paramount, 1955), the focus is on murderous outcasts invading lives of perfect middle-class tranquility.

In 1953, *The Hitch-Hiker* (RKO) would recount the harrowing eight-day ordeal two vacationing men suffered at the hands of Billy Cook. The story follows the basic outline of Cook's spree, changing the character's name to Emmett Myers (William Talman). When Ray Collins (Edmond O'Brien) and Gil Bowen (Frank Lovejoy) give Myers a lift, he commandeers their '52 Plymouth, and their lives. He revels in his animal instincts, which make him superior to the soft, bourgeois vacationers. Because Myers's deformed right eye cannot close, his captives are never sure if he's asleep, as they're held at gunpoint every night.

Myers represents the worst part of each man's ego, turned loose. When he asks what they do for a living, he learns that Gil is an architect, Roy a mechanic. "That makes *you* smarter," he sneers, jabbing the pistol at Gil. Even Myers's idle sniping wounds.

In a beautiful touch, Gil covertly slips off his inscribed wedding band and leaves it on the gas pump of a desolate Mexican filling station. It will either be the clue that rescues them, or the last trace he'll leave behind when his life is taken. Roy, meanwhile, is mired in a masculinity crisis: because he won't confront Myers — or run away from him — he's afraid that Myers's assessment of him as "soft" is all too true. His humiliation is a form of emas-

Talman terrorizes Lovejoy and O'Brien in Ida Lupino's *The Hitch-Hiker*.

culation. Roy's been suckered into seeing life through Myers's eyes — the eyes of a predator. In that narrow view, his failure to best his antagonist brands him as prey. The breakdown of his psyche follows. Gil doesn't get baited as easily. He's able to plot escapes more feasible than the mano-a-mano brawl Roy fantasizes. After riding the pair endlessly about how differences in class and education mean nothing now, Myers relishes one last joke – forcing Roy to trade clothes and walk into the trap that the

police have set. Symbolically, Roy keeps yelling into the darkness: "I'm not Myers! I'm not Myers!" Gil, who'd seemed resigned to his fate, strikes quickly: he overpowers the distracted Myers and wrestles the gun away. The killer is apprehended.

The Hitch-Hiker has the distinction of being the only film noir directed by a woman, Ida Lupino. If anything proved that Lupino was one of the boys, this did: there isn't a woman in the film, and the dynamics of machismo swirl at every turn. Although some of her earlier films have traces of noir, *The Hitch-Hiker* was her only directorial drive into (or out of) Dark City. Not that she didn't have several further excursions in mind. An investor's prospectus for The Filmakers, the production company she operated with husband Collier Young, mapped several Dark City projects: *I Bought a Gun*, about how a handgun in the house affects a family; *Something for Nothing*, a trilogy of gambling stories; and *The Story of a Murder*, described as "The first serious scientific approach...to tell audiences why people kill and why murder can be prevented." Finally, there was *Fire Bug*, featuring an arsonist who attempts to burn down the whole damn city.

Lupino turned to crime dramas only after attempts at socially-conscious films foundered. Inspired by the neo-realists, her first productions were heartfelt tales of ordinary people. She and Collier Young were both sick of the studios' "front office domination." *Not Wanted* (1949), Lupino's first independent film, was a look at unwed mothers. Elmer Clifton is credited as director, but the old veteran took ill before shooting, and Lupino helmed it, uncredited. She didn't yet have a Guild card, so she had to keep a low profile.

Never Fear (1950) was a romance about polio victims, featuring a wheelchair dance. Collier Young proudly declared to Hedda Hopper: "We're working on the theory that the ticket-buying public is more interested in *what's* in a picture than *who's* in it."

The Filmakers was broke in no time.

To salvage their investment, Lupino and Young signed a deal with the new head of RKO, Howard Hughes. Lupino didn't trust Hughes, and once the pact was inked she didn't trust her husband, either. Young handled final details, and the deal gave Hughes control of their creative lives. Rejected by Hughes was *The Atom Project*, on development of the A-bomb. Approved was *Outrage* (1950), concerning a rape victim. "Hughes liked things dealing with sex," said Malvin Wald, *Outrage*'s writer.

In addition to *Outrage* and *The Hitch-Hiker*, Lupino directed *Hard, Fast and Beautiful* for RKO, a sappy melodrama. More intriguing was *The Bigamist* (1953), in which Edmond O'Brien kept two families, and became equally bored with each. Lupino played against film noir conventions, making both women regular sorts instead of the typical virgin/whore dichotomy. Unfortunately, she also shed the noir convention of exciting storytelling. The film couldn't top Lupino's own story, anyway. After the Hughes debacle, she'd split from Collier Young, falling into the arms of rugged Howard Duff, who'd become her third husband. Young consoled himself with Joan Fontaine, whom he'd marry. Young and Lupino would, however, remain business partners. In *The Bigamist*, Lupino plays one of O'Brien's wives — Joan Fontaine plays the other. The following year, in *Private Hell 36* (written and produced by Young and Lupino), Ida would make love on-camera to Steve Cochran, under the eye of co-star (and current husband) Howard Duff, while her ex-husband observed from out of frame. Director Don Siegel recalled the principals as being intense, and intoxicated, throughout production.

Ida Lupino went on to a long career acting and directing in television. In the 1980s her films were "rediscovered," but proved to be a huge disappointment to revisionists seeking to proclaim her a maverick feminist who'd strained at her Hollywood bonds. No matter how many times critics watched her films, they couldn't realistically uncover a particularly gender-specific perspective. That's probably because Lupino saw herself as the equal of everybody else in the industry, and because her taste in material encompassed all of society, not just the distaff side. Although her ambition exceeded her achievements, she left a body of work that showed her to be a competent director, good writer, excellent producer, and a superior actress. Most important, she was a total pro, who never stooped to define herself in terms in gender.

ROY AND GIL CAME OFF THE ROAD IN FAR BETTER SHAPE THAN AL ROBERTS did in *Detour* (PRC, 1945). In this tawdry title, a masterwork of bargain-basement filmmaking, an innocent man picks up a psychopath only slightly less lethal than Billy Cook.

Roberts (Tom Neal) is a New York piano player whose girl, Sue (Claudia Drake), leaves him to seek a showbiz career in Hollywood. Lonely and distraught, Al pines for Sue, and finally decides to follow her, hitching west. In the southwest, he gets a lift from Charlie Haskell (Edmund MacDonald), a seemingly flush highroller in a halftrack-sized convertible. Al scopes the fresh scratches on Haskell's face and hands: "Whatever it was, it must have been big and vicious."

Tom Neal learns his own hard lessons about picking up hitch-hikers when he gives a lift to the meanest woman on earth, Ann Savage, in *Detour*. For some, Edgar G. Ulmer's six-day wonder — cheap, tawdry, rumpled and unshaven — is the ultimate expression of fatalistic film noir.

It was a woman, Haskell admits — an ingrate hitcher who went wild when he made a pass. Nice guy Charlie flashes a suspicious roll, and treats Al to a hash house dinner, which the hitcher inhales like a starving animal.

Belly-full and drowsy, Haskell lets Al takes the wheel. As Al contentedly ponders this good fortune, anticipating his reunion with Sue, Haskell mysteriously drops into the big sleep. It begins to rain, and when Al tries to roust his benefactor to put up the ragtop, Haskell pitches out and cracks his skull on a rock. Convinced that he'll be accused of murder, Roberts hides the body, switches wallets, and continues toward L.A. in Haskell's car. Bum call. At a filling station he makes an even worse one: he picks up a woman hitching a ride. After several miles of small talk, she blurts: "Okay, whad'ya do with his body?"

The woman, Vera (Ann Savage), turns out to be the feisty gal who raked Haskell miles back. Let's hope there's not another one like her back home. Vera is, hands down, the shrillest, meanest, bitchiest shrew to ever escape from Dark City. She's got Al knuckling under in no time. If he doesn't follow her orders, she'll finger him as Haskell's killer. At first her plan is no more devious than selling off the dead guy's glitzy wheels once they hit L.A. But in a fluke not uncommon on the impoverished outskirts of Dark City, she learns that Haskell was the heir of a dying millionaire. She demands that Al pose as Haskell so they can collect the inheritance. Screwed every which way, Al actually starts to go along with Vera's insane scheme. In a cheap hotel room, two lives at the end of their strings, Al and Vera battle it out like tethered cat and dog. Al calls her bluff, daring her to dial up the cops. She does, and he backs down before she can drop the rest of the dime, becoming, in essence, her slave. Vera celebrates by getting tight and gleefully locking herself in the bedroom, taking the telephone with her. Afraid she'll call the cops, Al tries to snap the phone cord, tugging with all his might. Something is wrong. Breaking down the bedroom door he finds Vera dead, the cord wrapped around her throat.

Fearing he'll be blamed for two murders, Al takes to the road like a fugitive. He waits for the day when the heat will finally swoop down. Hitching yet another ride, delusionally imagining his arrest, he utters one of the most famous lines in noir: "Fate, or some mysterious force, can put the finger on you or me for no good reason at all."

Detour was based on a 1939 novel by Martin Goldsmith, a young writer who, to finance his avocation, ran a coast-to-coast car service, hauling half a dozen passengers at a time in a Buick station wagon for $25 a head. The novel grew out of this experience. Its hard-luck flavor smacks more of the Depression than the immediate post-war period in which it was filmed. Goldsmith no doubt rued that he'd sold the film rights to producer Leon Fromkess in 1944 — before learning that John Garfield had read the book and wanted Warners to buy it. Garfield envisioned Ann Sheridan or Ida Lupino as his co-star. Fromkess relished telling a major studio to pound salt. He turned down a $25,000 offer for the property.

Fromkess's outfit, Producers Releasing Corporation (PRC), was the epitome of a Poverty Row studio. The entire production budget for *Detour*, including money paid for the rights and Goldsmith's own screenplay adaptation, was $30,000. The shooting schedule was six days. Only 15,000 feet of film was allotted to make a 63-minute movie. With that kind of money and time at stake, the production could only be entrusted to one man — Edgar G. Ulmer. Born in Vienna, Ulmer had studied philosophy at the University of Vienna, and was a contemporary of such future cine-

ma giants as F.W. Murnau (Ulmer worked on Murnau's silent masterpiece, *Sunrise*), Ernst Lubitsch, Robert Siodmak, and Billy Wilder. Once he came to the states, Ulmer developed a reputation as a virtually hubris-free director who could deliver competent films despite almost inconceivable limitations. Any hopes he had for an "A" list career were dashed when he and Shirley Castle, the continuity girl on his first major film, Universal's *The Black Cat* (1934), fell in love. She divorced husband Max Alexander, cousin of Universal chief Carl Laemmle, and married Ulmer. Laemmle got even by blackballing Ulmer at all the major studios. Poverty Row became home, but Castle remained his devoted wife for the rest of his life.

In *Detour*, Ulmer used every trick in his quiver to make an engrossing film out of virtually nothing. His first bit of magic was making more than half of Goldsmith's 144-page script disappear — and improving the story in the process. The "Arizona" desert in which much of the action takes place was all filmed within 15 miles of the PRC lot. Ulmer's vision was to transform the rambling roadside saga into a head-trip: The action is literally confined to what's roiling around in Al Roberts's mind. The bulk of the screen time is consumed with tortured close-ups of Tom Neal, pondering his miserable luck in the ultimate "why me?" voice-over.

Using this approach, Ulmer crafted a haunting blend of claustrophobia and paranoia. Roberts may believe there's some cruel invisible force working against him, but in truth he's his own worst enemy. His destiny would be different if he didn't work so hard at convincing himself that disaster will result from every twist of fate. *Detour* plays just like a nightmare — in which the unconscious locks rational thought in the closet and takes off on mesmerizing and implausible leaps of logic. That's why it works best at about 2:30 A.M., through half-closed eyes, when Neal's self-pitying soliloquies start snaking around your defenseless mind.

When watching movies that late, there's usually a chance of nodding off. Ann Savage obliterates any notion of that. The 24-year-old former bowling instructor turned actress was like Susan Hayward on a coke jag — a keening harpy from hell, with a singularly irritating nails-on-slate voice. Her spewed taunts — "I'm not through with you by a long shot," and "Not only don't you have any scruples, you don't have any brains," and "Shut up! You're making noises like a husband" — are scarier than anything Widmark slung in *Kiss of Death*. Savage played another vicious femme fatale in Monogram's *Apology for Murder*, a shameless knockoff of *Double Indemnity*, but her career was fairly short.

Her *Detour* performance, however, ensured her a top-floor suite in the low-rent Pantheon Hotel, home of characters you'll never forget.

Try as you might.

PARALLELS BETWEEN THE LIVES OF AL ROBERTS AND TOM NEAL have become the stuff of "B"-movie legend. Some fans of *Detour* suggest that its strange power haunted Neal, causing the film's fatalism to infect the actor's real life. In truth, Tom Neal was a sight more aggressive than Al Roberts. He'd probably have smacked a woman senseless if she popped off at him like Vera did in the film. Neal was a "poor man's Clark Gable," who worked steadily in "B's" during the Forties. He developed a reputation as a solid pro — and quite the Hollywood ladies' man. It was his passionate affair with blonde starlet Barbara Payton that threw a detour into his career. The pair were torrid lovers, as Payton recounted in her autobiography *I Am Not Ashamed.* "He had a chemical buzz for me that sent red peppers down my thighs." But when she decided to marry Franchot Tone in 1951, Neal saw red: The former boxer laid a savage beating on Tone. He didn't, however, lose Payton. She divorced Tone after 53 days, naming Neal as correspondent in the suit. Their tempestuous on-off affair had ugly overtones that cold-cocked both their careers. Neal quit the business, moved to Palm Springs, and married Patricia Fenton. He started a landscaping business, and had a son, Tom, Jr. But Patricia died of cancer when the boy was only a year old. Neal sent him to live with his sister in Illinois. He met Gail Kloke at the Palm Springs Tennis Club, and married her in 1961. Four years later, Kloke was shot to death, and Neal was arrested for the murder. Payton sat in the courtroom, in dark glasses, watching the noose tighten. Despite some damning evidence indicating first-degree murder — Neal claimed it was an accident, but the gun was never found — he was sentenced to prison for involuntary manslaughter. He was freed after six years, but died of heart failure in a Hollywood apartment several months later. His son, who'd come to California to live with him, found the body. In 1990, Tom Neal, Jr., starred in a remake of *Detour,* in the role of Al Roberts.

HITCH-HIKING IS CLEARLY NOT THE IDEAL TRANSIT OPTION. Safer to ride the rails — unless you happened to be a passenger on a particular UP train from Chicago to L.A. in 1952, when all variety of intrigue and murder squeezed through the corridors and into the cloistered sleepers. In *The Narrow Margin* (RKO, 1952) a full ration of cops, dames, and hitmen were onboard for the ultimate "can" movie (slang for a story set in the confines of a moving vehicle).

Writer Martin Goldsmith has the honor of inspiring what may be Hollywood's two best "B" movies, *Detour* and *The Narrow Margin*. The latter is based on an unpublished Goldsmith story, adapted by Earl Felton. As in *Detour*, logic gets locked in the baggage car, while momentum travels up front.

Walter Brown (Charles McGraw) and Gus Forbes (Don Beddoe) are assigned to escort a gangster's widow from Chicago to L.A. "I hear she's a dish," says Forbes as they alight in the Windy City. "She's the sixty-cent special," growls Brown. "Cheap, flashy, strictly poison under the gravy." We've got McGraw at his surliest, and it doesn't get any better than that. At least not until we meet their baggage, Mrs. Neil (Marie Windsor). From the first shot of her, sucking on a tar-bar, flipping back her jet-black wave, and giving the cops the once-over with her impossibly huge, sexy eyes, we know McGraw has finally met his match.

Marie Windsor tests Charles McGraw's loyalty to police work on a cross-country train trip in *The Narrow Margin. Opposite:* Marvelous Marie is menaced by hoods.

Before they even get Mrs. Neil to the waiting taxi, Forbes takes a fatal bullet. The syndicate is out to ensure that she won't talk to the grand jury about a payoff list linking them to the LAPD. The death of his partner ignites Brown's contempt for Mrs. Neil; the match-up of McGraw and Windsor is tough-talk nirvana. "You make me sick to my stomach," snaps McGraw. "Well, use your own sink," Windsor fires back. Nobody could throw brass-knuckled palaver like these two.

When a mob soldier offers Brown a hefty bribe to hand over Mrs. Neil, it results in a knock-down-drag-out brawl. After risking his neck for her, Brown is further revolted when Mrs. Neil says they should take the deal, and split the bribe.

Casing out the train, Brown meets a lovely woman, Ann Sinclair (Jacqueline White), traveling with her wiseacre kid, Tommy (Gordon Gebert). He pulls a clever ruse, redirecting the heat by letting the hoods think that Sinclair is Mrs. Neil.

In the meantime, Windsor and McGraw shovel verbal coal. "The food stinks and so does your company, but I'll hand you one thing, Brown — you're beginning to show real genius," Mrs. Neil cracks. "Making this other dame the target shows you're using your head."

"For your information, I didn't rig it that way," Brown counters. "Well, if you didn't, the DA's entitled to a refund," she tells him.

"I've seen some real hardcases in my time, but you make 'em all look like putty. We're not talking about a sack of gumdrops that's gonna be smashed, we're talking about a dame's life." The banter gets as overheated as the engine's boiler.

The tables turn on Brown. While he's cozying up to Miss Sinclair, the mob manages to get a hitman, Densel (Peter Virgo), onboard. The villains locate Mrs. Neil, break in, and murder her. Realizing he's failed to protect both his partner and the witness, McGraw bawls himself out in front of Ann. She comes clean — *she's* the real Mrs. Neil. The other woman was an undercover cop, used as both a decoy and as a test of Brown's incorruptibility. More guilty than ever now that *two* cops have died on his watch, Brown finally becomes the proper McGraw juggernaut, and he completes the mission, dispatching the crooks and delivering the witness safely to Los Angeles.

The Narrow Margin was the zenith of director Richard Fleischer's "B" movie career. The genetic roots of his flair for manic action were in his dad, Max, and his uncle, Dave — the legendary cartoonists and animators who ranked as the only rivals to Walt Disney in the 1930s. The Fleischers produced such classic animated fare as *Out of the Inkwell*, *Betty Boop*, and *Popeye the Sailor*. Richard studied medicine at Brown and drama at Yale, but by 1942 he was a newsreel editor at RKO. A feature

director by the time he was 30, Fleischer carved a niche as a specialist at crisp programmers: the previously cited *Bodyguard* and *The Clay Pigeon*, as well as *Follow Me Quietly* (RKO, 1949), and Eagle-Lion's excellent *Trapped* (1950). He didn't dwell on noir atmospherics, but displayed a genuine talent for the all-important left-right combination: vigorous

Is any caption necessary when Marie Windsor has it working like this? These lovely folk are all citizens of *Hell's Half Acre* (Republic, 1954), Honolulu's notorious red light district. Marie is the reprobate wife of lowlife Jesse White, who nurses a split lip while her gangster lover, Philip Ahn, jukes up weaselly stool pigeon Leonard Strong, doing his best Peter Lorre imitation. Wendell Corey stars as a WWII vet, believed dead, who is mixed up in the island's underworld. His wife, Evelyn Keyes, searches for him by posing as a taxi dancer. The film is one of a series of down and dirty "B" noirs written by Steve Fisher for Republic.

action and sustained suspense. The dexterity he showed in 63-minute melodramas earned him the helm of such top-of-the-line 1950s spectacles as *20,000 Leagues Under the Sea* and *The Vikings*. By the Sixties he was shepherding such bloated efforts as *Barabbas*, *Dr. Doolittle*, and *Fantastic Voyage*. Still active in the Eighties, he hacked out *Conan the Destroyer* and *Red Sonja*, tapping little of the vigor of his early efforts. Other marginal noirs on his résumé include *Violent Saturday* (1955), a colorful Cinemascope caper long on soap, short on grit. *Mr. Majestyk* (1974), was closer to Fleischer's early form, and remains one of the best adaptations of crime fiction impresario Elmore Leonard. Along with *Thieves' Highway* and *Border Incident*, it's a terrific example of the little-known subgenre, agri-noir.

In *The Narrow Margin*, Fleischer's inventive direction reached its peak. Some scenes couldn't have been any better: the killing of Forbes and McGraw's backalley pursuit of the shooter, the brutal fistfight between McGraw and David Clarke in a cramped train compartment, the multiple planes of action layered on the train windows, the inspired visual transitions (dissolving from Windsor scraping her nails with an emery board to the wheels chugging inside the train's journal box to the chattering crawl of a Western Union ticker, all in about four seconds). But despite all that, it's the omission of one single image that keeps *The Narrow Margin* from being easily heralded as a minor "masterwork": where is the shot of McGraw watching Marie

Windsor's body being taken off the train? It's unpardonable neglect of a character who is, frankly, the most memorable part of the movie.

Sadly, this rude dismissal is typical of a career that included *Cat Women on the Moon*. Although indelible in most every part she played, Windsor never broke into the top rank of female stars. She was just too physically intimidating – statuesque, 5' 9," with a balcony that could support a double run of pinochle. Sexy, evil femme fatales were her lot. She handled the role effortlessly in such noirs as *Force of Evil*, *City That Never Sleeps*, *The Sniper*, and, most effectively, *The Killing*.

Windsor was a one-time Miss Utah whose youthful ambition was to follow in the high-heeled footsteps of her screen idol, Clara Bow. Legendary pin-up artist Alberto Vargas certainly saw that Windsor had "It" when he hired her as a model. She put herself through Maria Ouspenskaya's famous acting school by working as a cigarette girl at the Mocambo nightclub, where she caught the eye of producer Arthur Hornblow, Jr. She started her career in "B's" in the early 1940s, and was once Gloria Grahame's understudy on stage. Windsor married realtor Jack Hupp in 1943 (he was a devoted fan, seeing one of her early plays, *The Bar Off Melrose*, twenty-nine times). They remained happily married.

Windsor stayed active in television right up into the Nineties. She was also a dedicated official of the Screen Actors Guild, and spearheaded charities aimed at helping orphans and mentally disturbed children. Though never given the meaty roles she deserved, she was the undisputed Queen of "B" noirs.

Who wouldn't have forgiven Charles McGraw for making the obvious play: locking himself in Marie's compartment and enjoying the rhythm of that long ride to the coast?

Wendell Corey interrupts a tender moment between John Hodiak and his rival for Hodiak's affection, Liz Scott, in *Desert Fury*.

OUT IN THE PAINTED DESERT is the town of Chuckawalla, setting for a very strange crime "drama." Hal Wallis's *Desert Fury* (Paramount, 1947), scripted by Robert Rossen, is the gayest movie ever produced in Hollywood's golden era. Recitation of the "plot" is hopeless: the action swirls around a band of sexually ambiguous miscreants hiding out in the middle of nowhere. Fritzie Haller (Mary Astor) runs the Purple Sage casino, while dominating her gorgeous and spoiled daughter Paula (Lizabeth Scott). The two women play it like sapphic temptresses. When Scott appears, Astor says, "You look good, baby — gimme a kiss." Liz, in her full Technicolor glory, looks like fifty million bucks. Determined to break away from "mother," she romances on-the-lam gangster Eddie Bendix (John Hodiak), another character of indeterminate sexuality. Their dalliance doesn't sit too well with Bendix's longtime companion, Johnny Ryan (Wendell Corey, in a memorable debut role), nor Paula's other suitor, the town's stud sheriff, Tom Hanson (Burt Lancaster). In this air-conditioned desert, everyone saunters around in fabulous Edith Head fashions, pondering all kinds of offbeat sexual desires. The film, directed by Lewis Allen, is saturated — with incredibly lush color, fast and furious dialogue dripping with innuendo, double entendres, dark secrets, outraged face-slappings, overwrought Miklos Rozsa violins. How has this film escaped revival, or cult status? It's Hollywood at its most gloriously berserk.

COMBINE THE FERTILE SOIL OF CALIFORNIA'S central valley with year-round sunshine and a steady supply of water from the majestic Sierra Nevada mountains, and you've got food for practically all of America. Mix in the treachery of how that bounty gets to market and you've got a "subversive" produce-noir.

Thieves' Highway (RKO, 1949) is unjustly overlooked, bookended in limbo between direc-

Thieves' Highway: **Produce broker Mike Figlia (Lee J. Cobb, right) tries everything to avoid paying gypsy trucker Nick Garcos (Richard Conte) a fair price for his load of Golden Delicious apples. Figlia's henchmen slash Nick's tires while his truck's illegally parked, trying to force him to sell before the cops arrive. But Nick's after more than a fair price. He wants revenge for his father, who was crippled in a Figlia-staged "accident" after arguing over money. "Figlia, you're used to pushing around old men," Nick advises. "Touch my truck and I'll climb into your head."**

tor Jules Dassin's more famous *Naked City* (1948) and *Night and the City* (1950). It didn't have a high-powered producer like *Naked City*'s Mark Hellinger, nor a high-powered visual style like *Night and the City*. What it did have was a perfectly-honed screenplay by A. I. Bezzerides, a fantastic cast, and Dassin's most graceful, light-fingered direction (something he'd rarely be accused of again).

When it came to prose, Bezzerides was a real prole. He grew up in Fresno — raisin capital of the world — during the Depression, and learned first-hand about making a living off the land and surviving the betrayals that crop up later in the food chain. His novel *Thieves' Market*, upon which the film is based, offered a hard-edged look at how greed and chicanery infect the agri-business system. Call it Steinbeck noir. If you're going to cook up a melodramatic potboiler from serious literature, this is the recipe.

Nick Garcos (Richard Conte) returns home from the war to find his old man crippled by a trucking accident. The culprit is Bay Area produce broker Mike Figlia (Lee J. Cobb), who has a rep for cheating small operators and "fixing" them if they protest. Nick, an immigrant child, has picked up a new American brand of piss and vinegar in combat. He reclaims the truck that his father had to sell, and looks for a load that will get him near Figlia. Another driver, crafty old Ed (Millard Mitchell) knows of a hidden orchard of early apples, and the two men strike a deal. Tailing them to the Bay Area are two other truckers, Pete (Joe Pevney) and Slob (Jack Oakie), who don't think Ed's old truck will make the run. They're poised to scavenge the load.

Dassin handles the trucking montages with great panache, including a suspenseful scene in which Conte is pinned by his rig when he tries to fix a flat on a soft, sandy shoulder. Ed, who'd been a conniver up until then, shows his true colors by saving Nick. Bezzerides's flair for off-the-cuff dialogue quickly sketches a masculine bond between the duo, now pals for life.

When Nick shows up at the bustling Produce Market, he and Figlia engage in some nasty negotiating. Knowing he can make a killing on the first apples of the season, Figlia tries all his grifts to cheat Nick. He cuts his tires in an attempt to force him to unload; he complains about the fruit's "pulpy" quality; he lies about the going price. When all else fails, Figlia pays sexy Italian refugee Rica (Valentina Cortesa) to lure Nick to her room.

In her garret, we're treated to scenes that combine Rica's lonesome stranger-in-a-strange-land pathos with a tense erotic charge. The constraints of the Production Code forced Bezzerides and Dassin to be creative, and they conjure the type of exquisite sexual by-play that would disappear from the screen once the Code was obsolete: Both shower in the cramped room with only a curtain separating them; in an embrace, Cortesa rubs her dark curls on Conte's face; she uses her sharp fingernails to play tic-tac-toe on his bare chest. In her American film debut, Cortesa uses her heavy accent, sharp features, and flashing, cunning eyes to create one of the most full-blooded supporting characters in Dark City.

While Rica toys with Nick, Figlia sells his load right off the truck. Bezzerides depicts the marketplace as an arena, and cutthroat business as the all-American sport. When Nick confronts Figlia, demanding full price for his fruit, the two men square off like heavyweights. Early-morning buyers watch from ringside. "Figlia's gonna eat that kid alive," chimes one. "I'll take odds on the kid," says a savvy broad who's gone toe-to-toe with Figlia herself.

Meanwhile, Ed struggles to bring in his load, vexed by a weak universal joint on his drive shaft. On the winding roads of the steep Altamont pass, it finally blows. Ed cracks up. Apples avalanche down the hillside. Ed burns to death in the truck's cab. Pete and Slob, stunned, head on to S. F. to tell Nick the news.

Nick has forced top dollar — six bucks a box — out of Figlia, and celebrates by calling his Waspy girlfriend Polly (Barbara Lawrence), telling her to come to the city so they can be married. Rica's sweet on Nick, though, and on a stroll through the railyards, she tries to convince him to forget Polly. They're jumped by Figlia's boys, and Nick's money is stolen. When he wakes up in Rica's room, Nick's convinced she set him up. Rica leaves him to recuperate, then picks Polly up at the depot and escorts her back to the crib. When Polly sees her fiancé in another woman's bed — and learns that he's lost all his money — she dumps him flat. Exactly as Rica expected. "Polly and I have one thing in common," she tells Nick, smiling slyly. "She loves money, too."

Figlia learns that Ed's haul of Golden Delicious was spilled, but undamaged. He offers Pete fifty cents a box to bring in the dead man's load. Pete takes the money, but Slob spurns him. When Nick emerges in the cold morning light, he learns from Slob what's happened. Nick goes wild. "Four bits a box!" he screams, kicking over crates. "Four bits a box!"

He has Slob drive him to the spot where Ed augered in. He finds Figlia celebrating in a roadside tavern. Smashing his hand with an ax-handle, Nick forces Figlia to confess that he shorted Pete on the apples. As Pete and Slob keep Figlia's thugs at bay, Nick drops the pretense

and finally gets down to it: He beats Figlia senseless — "For Dad." In one of the few satisfying romantic fade-outs in noir, Nick returns for Rica and takes her away from Dark City in his rumbling rig.

Your tour guide confesses a soft spot for *Thieves' Highway*. It was the first noir he'd ever seen, although at that time there wasn't the handy label for this kind of dark, crime-tinged melodrama. All he knew was that its treacherous mix of crime, business, sex, loyalty, and submerged politics was intoxicating. From then on he was always looking for the 90 proof kick that only a 90-minute thriller, laden with meaning but light on its feet, can provide.

The corruption of America's agri-business was seen from a more Republican perspective in *Border Incident* (MGM, 1949), released two months after the left-leaning *Thieves' Highway*. The film aimed to coattail on the success of Anthony Mann's *T-Men*, made the previous year. Again, a pair of undercover agents infiltrate a crime ring — not counterfeiters, but farm labor racketeers. Cameraman John Alton transposed his noir vision to the Southwest, painting mesas and fertile fields with the same ominous shadows found in his cities.

Mann, who'd already displayed an unsettling flair for brutality in *T-Men*, offered greater shocks in the wide open spaces. When agent Jack Bearnes (George Murphy) has his cover blown, he's set up for a grim farming "accident": he's shredded by the swirling blades of a reaper as his colleague, Pablo Rodriguez (Ricardo Montalban), looks on helplessly.

Border Incident, like *T-Men*, is undermined by its association with the Federal gov-

ernment. In exchange for the imprimatur of the Justice Department and the Immigration and Naturalization Service, the film was obligated to show criminal labor practices as the work of a few small renegades. In 1949, unlike today, the trail of crime could never lead to corporate America. *Border Incident* ends with the voice of authority assuring us that the crisis of illegal farm workers has been alleviated through the dedicated work of agents like George Murphy and Ricardo Montalban.

It looks like the end of the line for Mexican undercover agent Ricardo Montalban in *Border Incident*. Evil rancher Owen Parkson (Howard Da Silva, *center*) operates an illegal labor ring, with right-hand man Jeff Amboy (Charles McGraw) and Jeff's wife, Bella (Lynn Whitney). Scripted by crime specialist John C. Higgins, the film was another of the racket-busting noirs director Anthony Mann began at Eagle-Lion studios. MGM's bigger budget didn't dull Mann's cutting edge.

They Live by Night: (clockwise from top left) Jay C. Flippen, Cathy O'Donnell, Howard Da Silva, Farley Granger.

"SOMEDAY I'D LIKE TO SEE SOME OF THIS COUNTRY we've been travelin' through," the young man tells his sweetheart. "By daylight, you mean? That'd be nice." Some hope. It's not going to happen for Bowie (Farley Granger) and Keechie (Cathy O'Donnell), because *They Live by Night* (RKO, 1949). These starry-eyed kids — "Never properly introduced to the world we live in..." — are fugitives, skulking through the backroads and motor courts of an angry every-man-for-himself country.

Based on the Depression-era novel *Thieves Like Us*, by Edward Anderson, *They Live by Night* was the directorial debut of Nicholas Ray, a young man of considerable heart and talent. Producer John Houseman, who prospected many of the most creative minds in 1940s Hollywood, had known Ray since their days at New York's Federal Theater. He sensed a brilliant future for Ray as a movie man. Houseman gave him a copy of Anderson's novel, and Ray produced a thoroughly-detailed treatment that displayed a firm grasp of the filmmaker's art.

The storyline is simple: Bowie, a youngster sent up on a specious murder rap, escapes with a pair of seasoned criminals, T-Dub (Jay C. Flippen) and Chickamaw (Howard Da Silva). In hiding, he finds his soulmate, Chickamaw's niece, Keechie. Together, they gradually drop their defiant defenses and imagine that they can live normal, happy lives. But the veteran crooks won't let Bowie loose. He assists in another bank job, deluding himself that his share will help hire a lawyer to clear him of the murder charge. Fleeing, Chickamaw shoots a cop – and Bowie's gun, covered with fingerprints, is left at the scene. His innocence is gone forever. Bowie and Keechie are married, but it's honeymoon interruptus when the gang puts the touch on him for another knockover. T-Dub is killed this go-round, and Bowie and Chickamaw angrily split.

With Keechie pregnant, the lovers take to the road. Each time they begin to feel like "real people," reality kicks them in the teeth. They return to Hawkins (Ian Wolfe), the crooked judge who married them, hoping he can rig passage to Mexico. But they don't have juice, even with the lowest of the low: "I believe in helping people get what they want as long as they can pay for it," Hawkins informs them. "I marry people 'cause there's a little hope they'll be happy. But I can't take this money of yours. No, sir. In a way I'm a thief just the same as you are — but I won't sell you hope when there ain't any." It's T-Dub's bitter sister-in-law, Mattie (Helen Craig) who sells out Bowie, in a deal to win release of her own convict husband. Realizing Keechie can never get straight while attached to him, Bowie returns to their motel to bid her farewell. He never makes it. The law is laying for him, and he's shot to death. Keechie finds the goodbye note on his body, professing love for her and their unborn child.

During the Thirties, Nicholas Ray had journeyed throughout rural America with the legendary Alan Lomax, helping record indigenous folk music for the Library of Congress. The experience was clearly influential. At his best, Ray worked like a jazz man (in fact, a treatment called "Jazz Man" was one of his earliest proposed projects): his eyes and ears open to nuance, colorations, unexpected ways of riffing within a familiar refrain. Where some directors saved their wind for the flashy solos, biding time in the bridges, Ray committed to the whole piece. He constructed a brilliant soundtrack, showing as much attention to aural aspects as did Welles. George Diskant (who deserves a reputation as lofty as John Alton's and Nick Musuraca's) offered camerawork that perfectly captured the swings between fitful repose and frantic flight. The cast was letter perfect, with the hardened mugs of the veterans looming over the wet-behind-the-ears newcomers. There's hardly a note in *They Live by Night* that doesn't resound — gracefully — with freshness and conviction.

Like a genuine folk, blues, or jazz artist, Ray was respectful of the tradition in which he worked. Although brighter than most, he never came off like a wiseguy, looking to cut those who'd played before. His goal was always to deepen the material, not subvert it with egotistical showboating.

Made in 1947, *They Live by Night* wasn't released in the U.S. until late '49, due to confusion wrought by Howard Hughes's takeover of RKO. More film noirs were issued that year than any other, and Ray's was lost in the shuffle. Had it been distributed earlier, perhaps Ray would have garnered more enthusiastic reviews, leading Hughes to offer him better material than tired soapers like *A Woman's Secret* (1949) and *Born to Be Bad* (1950). On loan to Columbia, Ray directed the Humphrey Bogart-sponsored *Knock on Any Door* (1949), in which the script's percussive message-mongering overwhelmed Ray's finesse. The association would, however, lead to creation of *In a Lonely Place*, a genuine masterpiece.

Ray was a great artist, but a mediocre craftsman. When inspired — as in *They Live by Night*, *In a Lonely Place*, *On Dangerous Ground*, *The Lusty Men*, *Johnny Guitar*, and *Rebel Without a Cause* — his work was emotional, evocative, and inventive. When less than fully engaged, a disdainful torpor could creep in. After *Rebel*, Ray's identification with lonely outsiders became too strong, and too self-destructive, for him to survive in Hollywood. He battled chronic illness and depression with drink and drugs. Eventually, that long struggle did him in. He'd finished his cinematic career as a teacher, which was appropriate considering his thematic obsession with the (often doomed) promise of youth. He attained a mythic stature among his charges, but he probably would have traded it for the relentless health and stamina of Samuel Fuller.

As Nicholas Ray was making his debut, aging veteran director Frank Borzage was spiraling downward. A two-time Oscar winner, Borzage left his home in Utah and started in films with Thomas Ince way back in 1913. Although he'd helmed several popular Thirties titles such as *A Farewell to Arms* (1932) and *Desire* (1936), Borzage's 98-film legacy is fat with forgettable fodder. By 1946 Borzage, who once stalked the plush carpets of Paramount's executive offices, was reduced to a three-picture deal with Republic — the magenta-colored lots on Hollywood's Monopoly board.

If ever there were proof that in the late Forties noir "infected" Hollywood — like a virus of resurgent creativity — it was Borzage's 1948 *Moonrise* (Republic). The film, based on Theodore Strauss's novel, was originally proposed as an "A" picture, to be directed by William Wellman, and starring either James Stewart or John Garfield. When talks with the majors didn't pan out, independent producer Marshall Grant took the project to Republic, where Borzage was handed the reins of the relatively low-budget picture. If Grant's initial plan had been borne out, *Moonrise* would certainly be more well-known — but it's doubtful that it would have been much better.

The story resembles *They Live by Night*, in that both focus on young men branded as outcasts, living on the fringes of the rural South. They're also the most romanticized, poetic works in noir.

Danny Hawkins (Dane Clark) is haunted by the legacy of his father, who was hanged for murder. Taunted throughout his life in the small southern town of Woodville, Danny fears that his "bad blood" will doom him to a violent, unhappy life. When boyhood rival Jerry Sykes (Lloyd Bridges) competes with Danny for the attention of beautiful schoolteacher Gilly (Gail Russell), Jerry sneers that she'll never go for a guy with killer's blood in his veins. The two brawl out back of the summer dance. In a blind rage, Danny crushes Jerry's skull with a rock. He hides the body in the swamps.

The disappearance of Sykes throws the tiny town into an uproar. As the manhunt inexorably closes in, Danny comes to believe his fate is predestined. He takes to the swamps, convinced he's no better than a wild animal, unfit to live among humans. When Sykes's body turns up, the philosophical sheriff (Allyn Joslyn) muses: "If you went into all the reasons why that rock struck Jerry Sykes's head, you'd end up writin' the history of the world."

This tale is directed with a simplicity that is spare, earnest, and deep. Borzage's most vital work was done in the silent era, and *Moonrise* is an example of an artist returning to his roots for a last-call shot of adrenalin. The opening montage is stunning: in several heartbeats, we see the senior

Hawkins's execution, Danny's birth, his torment at the hands of other children, and his emergence as a sullen adult. The dark images flow like the "tainted" blood in Danny's veins. Borzage applies his very stagy studio style to this crime drama, and the result is a kind of magic unrealism. John L. Russell's camera prowls through swamps with reeds of the deepest, inky black and highlights shimmering like floating jewels. The bayous presaged Charles Laughton's similar visions in *Night of the Hunter* (UA, 1955). The young lovers secretly meeting in a deserted antebellum mansion were ancestors of James Dean and Natalie Wood in Nick Ray's *Rebel Without a Cause* (WB, 1955).

As in *They Live by Night*, analogies are drawn between animals and the hunted human. Borzage's symbolism is brazen — dissolving from a close-up of Dane Clark to the face of a scared raccoon. But in the finest tradition of silent film storytelling, Borzage transcends the obvious. Accompanying a band of hunters dangerously close to the spot where he buried Sykes, Danny climbs a tree to shake out the trapped 'coon. Man and animal stare at each other. We feel the shiver as Danny suddenly recognizes his kinship with the helpless critter. But Danny must sacrifice it, to divert the group's attention from the burial spot. The 'coon is finally shaken loose, falling into a circle of predators. We hear the hounds and hunters pounce on it as Danny breaks down in tears.

Danny's disintegration comes on a Ferris wheel at the county fair. He explains to Gilly that his father murdered a doctor in a blind rage after malpractice resulted in the death of Danny's mother. His soul-searching is interrupted by the appearance of the sheriff, who also boards the ride. Borzage has found the perfect visual corollary for Danny's feelings of entrapment and guilt. Disoriented and panic-stricken, Danny leaps from the top of the Ferris wheel. In a vertiginous shot, we assume Danny's point-of-view for a terrifying fall into the carnival crowd.

These scenes exemplify a type of blunt but beautiful visual poetry that craftsmen like Borzage created in the silent days, but which evaporated from movies about the time that the last of these pioneers faded away. Because "crime dramas" relied on hyper-charged emotions, an old warhorse like Borzage was able to indulge his flair for pictorial storytelling, rather than restrain it. Like the best of the silents, *Moonrise* drew emotion — and complex themes — directly from its juxtaposition of vivid images. There isn't a trace of the irony that would permeate later, "smarter" films. The movie's only faults are aural: an overwrought score by William Lava, and Borzage's disdain for the veracity of regional dialect in a story ostensibly set in the Deep South. With title cards replacing its dialogue, it could have been the greatest silent picture Borzage ever made.

Dane Clark and Gail Russell
in Frank Borzage's *Moonrise*.

Dane Clark, the "B"-budget John Garfield, is affecting as the tortured Danny. Gail Russell comes off as one of the true Dark Angels of film noir. John Russell photographs her with the same rapture Borzage lavished on Janet Gaynor in a series of sentimental silents in the late Twenties. When she tracks Danny down, hiding amid the cobwebs of the vacant plantation house, she offers him a lovely benediction: "You should have sent me away when I might have gone. It's too late now." True to his reputation as a hopeless romantic, Borzage would never allow Gilly to betray Danny. She's a savior, not a femme fatale.

Unfortunately, Gail Russell had no savior herself. She chased her stage fright with booze, and spent the Fifties shuttling between sound

stages and sanitariums. In '57 she drove her convertible through the front of Jan's Coffee Shop in L.A., nearly killing the janitor who was pinned under the chassis. In August of '61 she was found dead in her Hollywood apartment, surrounded by empty vodka bottles.

There's no such grim demise for Borzage's characters. *Moonrise* is unique in that it's one of the few noirs in which the redemptive power of love holds nihilism at bay. The ending — in which Danny reclaims his place in society by turning himself in for Jerry's murder — at first plays false. If Danny were extradited to Dark City, his spiritual awakening would be rudely acknowleged by a spell in the Tombs. But here, in the thin air of Borzage's ethereal realm, it actually works. The ending may have been written as your typically pat wind-up, but Borzage's unabashed commitment to the theme of redemption convinces you that peace of mind counts all the more in a world where injustice and hatred rule.

The End of the Road

For many years the authorities have tried to nail down the facts surrounding the death of "classic film noir." Some reports indicated that it died in 1957, on the edge of a polluted creek in the California border town of Los Robles. Others claimed that in 1959 it was blown to kingdom come in a refinery explosion outside the upstate New York town of Melton. Our sources indicate that Noir — the original, the one bred from the craft and politics of the Hollywood studio system — actually perished in a lonely motel room in California's central valley.

Noir had registered under an assumed name — Marie Samuels — after stealing twenty-five grand from the real estate office in Phoenix where she worked. Typical of Noir — an impetuous crime, committed in the throes of passion. We'd been down this road before: the volatile sexuality leading to criminal behavior, the moral ambivalence, the desperate flight. All the icons and imagery were firmly in place.

Then Noir had a nice long talk with lonely young Norman, the proprietor of the motel, and she decided that crime didn't pay after all. She realized it was a hopeless blind alley. Like Danny Hawkins in *Moonrise*, she decided to turn herself in and face the music. A nice hot shower would cleanse her of her sins.

That was the night Noir died.

When he stepped into that bathroom, brandishing a butcher knife and clad in his dead mother's housecoat and wig, it was one small step for Norman Bates, but one giant leap for the movies. When Norman — reverting to his normal schizophrenic self — cleaned up the gory mess, he washed the last vestiges of "classic noir" down the drain with the blood.

But Alfred Hitchcock was the real culprit. If he tried to profess his innocence, he'd be lying. He knew exactly what he was doing. Can't you see that schoolboy smirk right now? This was a case of murder, open-and-shut: Hitchcock slaughtered our expectations.

Psycho (Universal, 1960) was an astonishing landmark in the history of cinema. A generation of movie-watchers who came of age in the Seventies and Eighties, when the bloodletting of slasher movies became standard adolescent fare, and MTV provided a daily visual and aural assault, can't comprehend the impact *Psycho* had when it was first released. Before audiences had recovered from the unsettling image of a toilet, actually shown functioning on-screen (a Hollywood first) — Hitchcock murdered his star actress a third of the way into the film, in a scene that has never been surpassed for both filmmaking artistry and pure shock value.

It's not a stretch to contend that *Psycho* did for movies what the assassination of JFK would soon do for politics. It loosened all the bearings, shattered all the preconceived notions of how things worked, and it ushered us into a strange new American fear-scape where suspicion replaced complacency as the pervasive national backdrop.

Psycho didn't manage this all by itself. But its incredible influence over the next generation of filmmakers had a lot to do with it. For all the cinematic brilliance — it's by far the most accomplished "B" movie ever — *Psycho* is also a sensational tent show, a freak carny attraction. "No one seated after the show has begun!" screamed the ads. "Don't Dare Reveal the Shocking Ending!" Hitchcock liked to say that he perceived *Psycho* — and the surrounding hoopla — as a "black comedy." No doubt it was, for him.

When it was first released, no one was laughing, rest assured. It was only later, when the cultural elite had adopted its post-everything attitude, effectively disregarding the main thrust of any popular art in favor of the deconstructive irony beneath, that critics detected humor — and began to appreciate how Hitchcock had hustled audiences with mesmerizing technique.

Hitchcock had a lot of Stanton the Great in him. He set up his audience with cold disdain, confident he could easily fleece them with his dazzling sleight-of-hand tricks, and his audacious powers of misdirection. Like Stan Carlisle, Hitchcock knew we were suckers for a good story, and like the ill-fated huckster, he knew the heady euphoria that came with "getting over" on a crowd. "It gives you a kind of superior feeling," Stan had said. "As if you were on the inside and everybody else was on the outside, looking in."

It was a sensation sought by many of America's next wave of filmmakers, for whom Hitchcock would reign as the ultimate master, with *Psycho* the medium's touchstone. They were responding not just to the film, but to its facility for manipulating viewers.

That shiver of cruel power would become a goal to which many new filmmakers would aspire. There was scant reward offered to those who embraced subtlety, or restrained artistry, or even seamless, coherent storytelling. Sensation would compensate for any shortcomings. *Psycho*'s sensational power spawned a legion of imitators — copycat killers, if you will. They've taken many of the dark themes once emblematic of classic film noir and steadily pushed them toward vulgar excess, all in the hope of garnering attention in a market saturated with noise and violence.

If the film noirs of the late Forties were warning flares, as suggested at the start of this excursion, their radiance would be barely noticed in the bomb blasts of today's cinematic offerings. As far as "classic film noir" is concerned, *Psycho* was the film that brought down the curtain on that now-lost world.

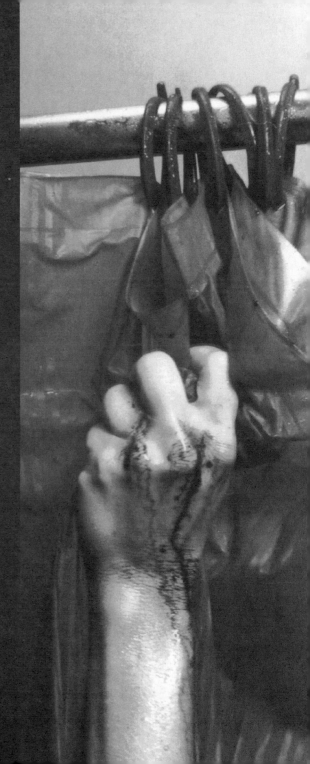

Poster Gallery

On the following pages are examples of poster art from the classic noir period. Like the films themselves, the advertising art was the product of studio factories. They kept hundreds of illustrators busy churning out breathtaking artwork for even the lowliest "B" thriller.

Filmmakers today often attempt to recapture the spirit and feel of classic film noir movies. But like the mosaics in Dark City's subway stations, there's no chance that artwork like this will ever be commissioned again. Photography-based posters have entirely supplanted their painted predecessors, and, believe it or not, images such as these are considered too graphically complex for the average contemporary filmgoer to scan and comprehend. Increasingly sophisticated tastes and advanced technology have raised movie marketing to a science. The result: an endless series of unimaginative designs that display little more than close-up photographs of stars' faces, either scowling in a stark key light (drama) or smiling in full light (comedy).

Film poster art is a lost world unto itself. Enjoy these few examples, because you'll never again see anything like the promo pieces for *Sorry, Wrong Number*, *Blonde Ice*, or *Manhandled*.

Thieves' Highway (20th Century-Fox, 1949)

Desperate (RKO, 1947)

Side Street (MGM, 1949)

Raw Deal (Eagle-Lion, 1948)

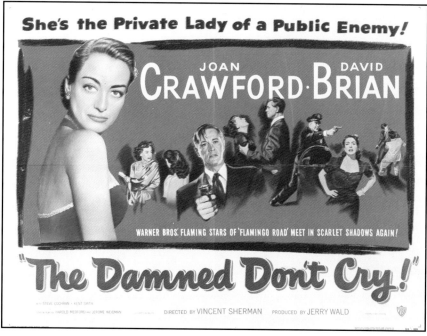

Sorry, Wrong Number (Paramount, 1948)

Out of the Past (RKO, 1947)

The Damned Don't Cry (Warner Bros., 1950)

Woman in Hiding (Universal-International, 1950)

Two of a Kind (Columbia, 1951)

The Big Heat (Columbia, 1953)

The Prowler (United Artists, 1951)

Shield for Murder (United Artists, 1954)

Touch of Evil (Universal-International, 1957)

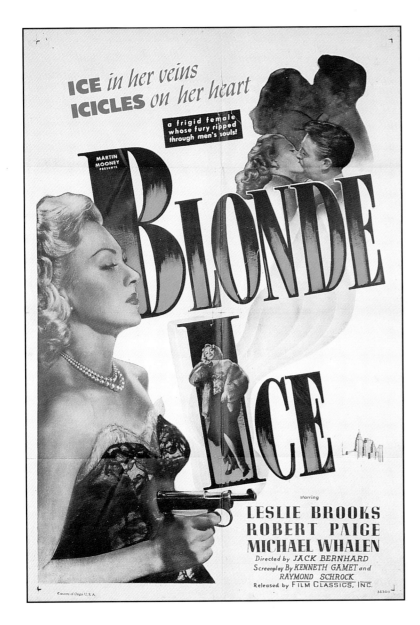

The Crooked Web (Columbia, 1955)

Blonde Ice (Film Classics, 1948)

Pushover (Columbia, 1954)

Scarlet Street (Universal-International, 1945)

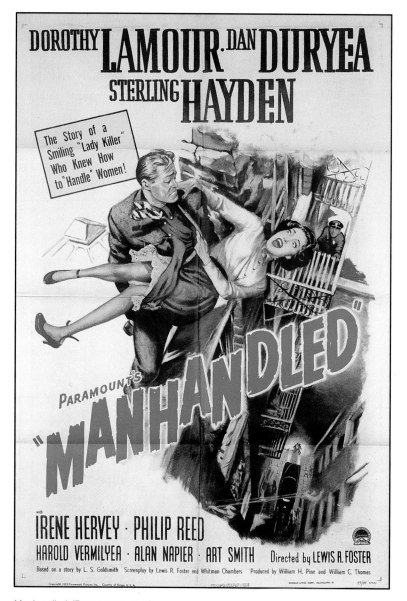

Manhandled (Paramount, 1949)

Black Angel (Universal-International, 1946)

Armored Car Robbery (RKO, 1950)

The Crooked Way (United Artists, 1949)

Somewhere in the Night (20th Century-Fox, 1946)

The Devil Thumbs a Ride (RKO, 1947)

Roadblock (RKO, 1951)

The Big Combo (Allied Artists, 1955)

Naked Alibi (Universal-International, 1954)

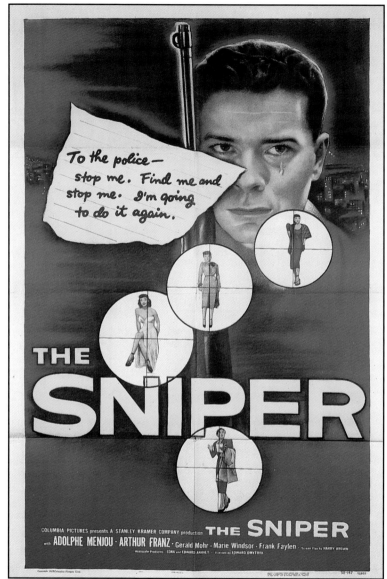

The Sniper (Columbia, 1952)

Pickup on South Street (20th Century-Fox, 1953)

Afterword

Dark City, it should be evident by now, was Hollywood. New York, Chicago, San Francisco, and many other cities, large and small, provided the necessary backgrounds for our stories. But the sense of desire and despair, the greed and alienation and the unflinching take on the venal depths of human nature are the product of a specific place, the Dream Factory, and a specific time — the final days of the once-powerful studio system, a volatile period when politics and paranoia, economics and ego, and avarice and alcohol conspired to bust up one of the great rackets of the Twentieth century.

Nobody saw the whole grand scheme quite so clearly, or mordantly, as Billy Wilder. He didn't invent film noir, but with *Double Indemnity* in '44, he came as close as anyone to defining it, and perfecting it, in 106 minutes. Several years later, his film having spawned countless imitations, Wilder laid the noir template over his own industry, and produced a trenchant blend of darkness and wit, *Sunset Boulevard*. It left no doubt that he was the most talented combination of writer and director ever to work in Hollywood.

Sunset Boulevard takes off from the traditional noir detective story. A cynical young writer, down on his luck, is "retained" by a strange client:

Gloria Swanson as Norma Desmond in *Sunset Boulevard*.

he must warily tread his way through sepulchral secrets and the flames of narcissism, dealing with an array of grotesque, and possibly dangerous, eccentrics. Wilder parodied the weary first-person narration that was, by 1950, all too common in crime dramas: his "hero," Joe Gillis (William Holden) recaps the story while floating, dead as dead gets, in the swimming pool he'd always wanted. Gillis tells how he conned faded silent screen queen Norma Desmond into supporting him while he wrote the script for her triumphant return to the big time. But he'd fatally underestimated the combustible, neurotic mix of fear, neediness, desperation, loneliness and vanity he faced. Norma was Hollywood incarnate, the ulti-

mate femme fatale, and she was far too much for Joe to handle. Like so many chumps before him, and many more to follow, he thought he could take what he wanted, toss it aside when he was done, and walk away unmarked. Norma nudges him along with a few parting shots. He was a hack anyway, with only a couple of lousy "B's" to his credit. Dime a dozen in this town.

Wilder offers Hollywood as an American city under a distorted magnifying glass: bustling with activity, surging forward with fresh ideas, its residents yearning for success and relentless in their quest of it. So much so that as they barrel-ass through their pretense of a community, they zoom right past the side streets where isolation, misery, and rejection fester into madness. Wilder surveys all this with a baleful gaze, and a cold, cynical laugh. Perhaps it's the only appropriate attitude in this terrain.

AT THE SAME TIME Wilder was concocting *Sunset Boulevard*, an even darker assessment of Hollywood life was being created at Columbia. *In a Lonely Place* (1950) is a film that uses its crime-drama spine only as support for a jumble of raw nerve endings. The film transparently lays open the lives of its principal creators, and transcendantly charts sad corners of the human heart.

After making *Knock on Any Door* together in 1948, Humphrey Bogart and Nicholas Ray sought out another project, which Bogart would produce through his independent company, Santana Productions. They chose Dorothy Hughes' novel *In a Lonely Place*, though they would retain little other than the basic premise and the evocative title. Step by step, they brought the project closer to "home." The locale was shifted to Hollywood. The main character became a screenwriter. And rather than

The artist as suspect:
Frank Lovejoy, Carl Benton Reid,
and Gloria Grahame are suspicious
of what makes screenwriter Dixon
Steele (Humphrey Bogart) tick, in
In a Lonely Place.

have him be the cold-blooded killer of the novel, Ray and Bogart made him something altogether more unsettling and ambiguous — the artist as suspect. Not an uncommon notion in Hollywood, 1949, but in the case of Bogart, and Ray, the character had very personal dimensions. Here was a tale in which the paranoia went deeper than the politics of the period.

Dixon Steele (Bogart) is a once-major talent whose deft touch with a script has been undermined by his attachment to the bottle, and uncontrollable bursts of temper. His loyal, dedicated agent Mel Lippman (Art Smith) sets Dix up with one last shot, adapting a turgid novel for a major studio. Dix and Wilder's Joe Gillis are cut from the same cloth: intelligent, witty men filled with self-loathing because they can't wean themselves from Hollywood's glamorous, sugary tit. To achieve the kind of status Joe always craved, Dixon Steele had to encase himself in a carapace of snide cynicism. (He probably laughed like hell when he opened his morning paper to the headline: FADED MOVIE QUEEN MURDERS WRITER.)

Dix is so disdainful of his assignment that he brings home a coat-check girl familiar with the odious bestseller, so she can describe the plot to him. He nurses a drink, smiles at the sound of the wind between her ears, and eventually sends her home. But the next day she turns up murdered, and Dix becomes the prime suspect. The only witness to his actions is Laurel Gray (Gloria Grahame), an aspiring actress who's just moved in across the courtyard. She provides Dix with a fair alibi, and soon their mutual attraction sparks into romance. And as so often happens in Dark City, the attention of a beautiful woman inspires the dissolute artist. Fresh ideas and smart dialogue stream from Dix's typewriter.

But gradually Laurel begins to see that jealousy and violence are an essential part of Dix's character. Seething because the cops still consider him a suspect, Dix blows up and attacks another motorist on a beach road. Laurel begins to fear that Dix may be a killer after all. She holds out little hope for their life together. The more lasting relationship is between Dix and Mel. The battle-scarred agent understands that in exchange for the chance to tap into Dix's genius, he'll have to absorb the anger and contempt as well. Laurel, however, won't stand for it. When Dix realizes she intends to leave him, he tries to strangle her. The police call to say they've caught the actual killer, but the news comes too late. Looking at Laurel's horrified face, Dix understands that he may as well be a murderer. He walks away, any chance at love and happiness evaporated.

Bogart and Ray didn't need guns, gangsters, or byzantine schemes to get to the heart of Dark City. They'd both been there. Ray had fallen in love with Gloria Grahame when they made *A Woman's Secret* together in 1948. She'd inspired in him the same kind of excitement that Laurel gave

Dixon Steele. Then she got pregnant, and Ray, adhering to his stand-up Midwestern principles, saw marriage as the only appropriate course of action. By the time they tied the knot, though, the bloom was off the rose. Gloria spent their Vegas wedding night alone in her hotel room, while Nick — in a move Dix surely would have toasted — drunkenly gambled away forty grand in an all-night stint at the casino tables. The pair's attempt at a cordial professional life shattered when Gloria had an affair with Ray's 13-year-old son by a previous marriage.

Ray's commitment to his craft — characterized by some, Bogart included, as obsessive — made him an outcast at the studios. "He always felt people were out to get him," said Rodney Amateau, an RKO assistant who worked on several Ray films, including *In a Lonely Place*. "And nobody was out to get him, you know? But if you feel somebody's out to get you long enough...they play the part."

For Bogart, the part of Dix Steele could have been rote. In the end, it was revelatory. Bogart's nasty streak was legend in Hollywood. He was a notorious needler, who'd get several sheets to the wind at Romanoff's and sarcastically insult anybody he thought deserved it. That part of Dix Steele came naturally to him. The revelatory part was the ineffable sadness he exposed at the core of the character. This too was familiar to Bogart, although unlike Dix, he found a way past it. When *In a Lonely Place* was released, all of America was enthralled with the storybook romance between tough-guy Bogart and sultry young Lauren Bacall. It was a classic Hollywood match-up, milked for all it was worth by Warner Bros., and the ravenous, star-struck public.

Less known was the tricky feat Bogart had pulled off extricating himself from wife Mayo Methot. She too had come to Hollywood seeking stardom, a big beautiful blonde, ready to take the place by storm. But her marriage to Bogart, and their prodigious boozing and brawling, took their toll. Her looks went, and so did the film offers. As Bogart's popularity grew, so did Methot's jealousy and possessiveness. Mayo begged him not to leave her for Bacall, and promised she'd stop drinking. Bogart was loyal; he steered clear of Bacall, and gave it another go with his wife of six years. But when Warner Bros. reunited Bogart and Bacall for *The Big Sleep*, the Bogarts' booze and bouts were uncorked again.

Methot spiraled into depression. She humiliated herself by begging Bogart — in the press — to return to her. After Bogart divorced her and married Bacall, Methot left Dark City, crushed and alone. In an 80 proof haze, she drifted out Thieves' Highway, back to her home state of Oregon.

Not long after the release of *In a Lonely Place*, Mayo Methot was found dead in a roadside motel. No lights, no cameras, no retakes.

Bibliography

Barson, Michael. *The Illustrated Who's Who of Hollywood Directors, Volume 1: The Sound Era*. New York: The Noonday Press, 1995.

Bessie, Alvah. *Inquisition in Eden*. New York: McMillan Co., 1965.

Cameron, Ian and Elizabeth. *The Heavies*. New York: Praeger, 1969.

Ceplair, Larry & Englund, Steven. *The Inquisition in Hollywood: Politics in the Film Community, 1930–1960*. Garden City, NY: Anchor Press, 1980.

Christopher, Nicholas. *Somewhere in the Night: Film Noir and the American City*. New York: The Free Press, 1997.

Clarens, Carlos. *Crime Movies: An Illustrated History*. New York: W. W. Norton & Company, 1980.

Clark, Al. *Raymond Chandler in Hollywood*. New York: Proteus Publishing, 1982.

Crawford, Christina. *Mommie Dearest*. New York: William Morrow and Company, 1978.

Curcio, Vincent. *Suicide Blonde: The Life of Gloria Grahame*. New York: William Morrow and Company, 1989.

Davies, Nigel. *The Rampant God: Eros Throughout the World*. New York: William Morrow and Company, 1984.

Davis, Mike. *City of Quartz: Excavating the Future in Los Angeles*. London, New York: Verso, 1990.

Donati, William. *Ida Lupino: A Biography*. Lexington, Kentucky: The University Press of Kentucky, 1996.

Eisenschitz, Bernard (Translated by Tom Milne). *Nicholas Ray: An American Journey*. London: Faber and Faber Limited, 1993.

Eisner, Lotte. *Fritz Lang*. London: Martin Secker & Warburg Ltd., 1976. (Reprinted by Da Capo Press, New York, 1986.)

Friedman, Lester D. *The Jewish Image in American Film*. Secaucus, New Jersey: The Citadel Press, 1987.

Friedrich, Otto. *City of Nets: A Portrait of Hollywood in the 1940's*. Berkeley and Los Angeles: University of California Press, 1986.

Gabler, Neal. *An Empire of Their Own: How the Jews Invented Hollywood*. New York: Crown Publishers, 1988.

Garnham, Nicholas. *Samuel Fuller*. New York: The Viking Press (in association with the British Film Institute), 1971.

Gelman, Howard. *The Films of John Garfield*. Secaucus, New Jersey: The Citadel Press, 1975.

Gifford, Barry. *The Devil Thumbs a Ride & Other Unforgettable Films*. New York: Grove Press, 1988.

Grobel, Lawrence. *The Hustons*. New York: Charles Scribner's Sons, 1989.

Hayden, Sterling. *Wanderer*. New York: Alfred A. Knopf, 1963.

Higham, Charles. *The Films of Orson Welles*. Berkeley, California: University of California Press, 1970.

Hill, James. *Rita Hayworth, A Memoir*. New York: Simon & Schuster, 1983.

Hirsch, Foster. *Film Noir: The Dark Side of the Screen*. San Diego: A. S. Barnes and Company, 1981. (Reprinted by Da Capo Press, New York, 1983.)

Houston, David. "The Two Tom Neals: A Legacy." Evanston, Illinois: *Filmfax #11*. July, 1988.

Kahn, Gordon. *Hollywood on Trial: The Story of the Ten Who Were Indicted*. New York: Boni & Gaer, 1948.

Kaplan, E. Ann (editor). *Women in Film Noir*. London: The British Film Institute, 1978.

Klein, Robert. *Wounded Men, Broken Promises: How the Veterans Administration Betrays Yesterday's Heroes*. New York: Macmillan Publishing Co., 1981.

Kuhn, Annette (editor). *Queen of the B's: Ida Lupino Behind the Camera*. Westport, Connecticut: Praeger, 1995.

Lasky, Betty. *RKO, The Biggest Little Major of Them All*. Englewood Cliffs, New Jersey: Prentice-Hall, Inc., 1984.

MacShane, Frank. *The Life of Raymond Chandler*. New York: E. P. Dutton & Co., 1976.

McArthur, Colin. *Underworld USA*. New York: The Viking Press (in association with the British Film Institute), 1972.

McGilligan, Patrick. *Cagney: Actor as Auteur*. San Diego: A.S. Barnes & Co., 1975.

Madsen, Axel. *Stanwyck*. New York: Harper Collins, 1994.

Miller, Mark A. "Marie Windsor Interview." Evanston, Illinois: *Filmfax #30*. Dec./Jan., 1992.

Mumford, Lewis. *The Culture of Cities*. New York: Harcourt, Brace and Company, 1938.

Murphy, Michael and Cheryl. "The Devil Thumbs His Nose: To Hell and Back with Lawrence Tierney." New York: *Psychotronic #8*. Winter, 1990.

Navasky, Victor S. *Naming Names*. New York: The Viking Press, 1980.

Nevins Jr., Francis M. *Cornell Woolrich: First You Dream, Then You Die*. New York: The Mysterious Press, 1988.

Nielsen, Mike and Mailes, Gene. *Hollywood's Other Blacklist: Union Struggles in the Studio System*. London: British Film Institute, 1995.

O'Brien, Geoffrey. *Hardboiled America: The Lurid Years of Paperbacks*. New York: Van Nostrand Reinhold Company, 1981.

Ott, Frederick W. *The Films of Fritz Lang*. Secaucus, New Jersey: Citadel Press, 1979.

Parish, James Robert. *The Tough Guys*. New Rochelle, New York: Arlington House Publishers, 1976.

Polonsky, Abraham. (John Schultheiss and Mark Schaubert, editors) *Force of Evil: The Critical Edition*. Northridge, California: The Center for Telecommunications Studies, Film as Literature Series, 1996.

Pratley, Gerald. *The Cinema of Otto Preminger*. New York: Castle Books, 1971.

Ragan, David. *Movie Stars of the '40s: A Complete Reference Guide for the Film Historian or Trivia Buff*. Englewood Cliffs, New Jersey: Prentice-Hall, 1985.

Sarris, Andrew. *Interviews with Film Directors*. New York: Avon Books, 1969.

Selby, Spencer. *Dark City: The Film Noir*. Jefferson, North Carolina: McFarland & Company, 1984.

Server, Lee. *Sam Fuller: Film Is a Battleground: A Critical Study*. Jefferson, North Carolina: McFarland & Company, 1994.

Skenazy, Paul. *James M. Cain*. New York: The Continuum Publishing Company, 1989.

Silver, Alain and Ward, Elizabeth, editors (with Carl Macek and Robert Porfirio). *Film Noir: An Encyclopedic Reference to the American Style*. Woodstock, New York: The Overlook Press, 1979.

Silver, Alain and Ursini, James (editors). *The Film Noir Reader*. New York: Limelight Editions, 1996.

Spoto, Donald. *The Dark Side of Genius: The Life of Alfred Hitchcock*. Boston: Little, Brown and Company, 1983.

Taylor, John Russell. *Hollywood 1940s*. London: Multimedia Publications (UK) Ltd., 1985. (Published in the U.S. by Gallery Books, New York, 1985.)

Thomas, Bob. *Joan Crawford*. New York: Simon & Schuster, 1978.

Thomas, Tony. *Howard Hughes in Hollywood*. Secaucus, New Jersey: Citadel Press, 1985.

Thomson, David. *A Biographical Dictionary of Film*, Third Edition. New York: Alfred A. Knopf, 1994.

Thomson, David. *Rosebud: The Story of Orson Welles*. New York: Alfred A. Knopf, 1996.

Thomson, David. *America in the Dark: The Impact of Hollywood Films on American Culture*. New York: William Morrow and Company, Inc., 1977.

Tierney, Gene (with Herskowitz, Mickey). *Self-Portrait*. Wyden Books, 1979.

Turner, Peter. *Film Stars Don't Die in Liverpool*. New York: Grove Press, 1986.

Twomey, Alfred E. and McClure, Arthur F. *The Versatiles: A Study of Supporting Character Actors and Actresses in the American Motion Picture, 1930-1955*. Cranbury, New Jersey: A. S. Barnes and Co., Inc., 1969.

Index

Italic numerals indicate photos

A

About Mrs. Leslie, 142
Accused, The, 115
Act of Murder, An, 117
Act of Violence, 138–139
Adams, Dorothy, 88
Adler, Luther, *117*
Adrian, Gilbert, 60
Ahn, Philip, *182*
Alda, Robert, 29, 106, *107*
Aldrich, Robert, 66, 80–81
Alexander, Max, 178
All My Sons, 101
Alonzo, John, 82
Altman, Robert, 165
Alton, John, 31, 40-41, 131, 185, 187
Amateau, Rodney, 195
American Authors' Authority, 59
ACLU (American Civil Liberties Union), 142
American Mercury, The, 58
amnesia as plot device, 131–133, 136
Anderson, Edward, 187
Anderson, Judith, 88
Andrews, Dana, *43,* 87, *88–89*
*Angel Face, 103–*104
Angel Heart, 132
Angels with Dirty Faces, 171
Anhalt, Edward and Edna, 170
anti-communist campaign in Hollywood, 21, 33, 34, 37, 48, 66, 73, 80, 96, 134–135, 141, 149, 171, 172

anti-Semitism, 139–141, 156
Apology for Murder, 59, 178
Arlen, Harold, 107
Armored Car Robbery, 154
*Asphalt Jungle, The, 144–*148, 149, 152
Astor, Mary, 72, 138, *139,* 183
Atlantic City, 102
Attack!, 82

B

Bacall, Lauren, *74,* 75, 195
Backfire, 117
Backus, Georgia, *22*
Bad and the Beautiful, The, 53
Bad Day at Black Rock, 142
Baer, Max, 26
Balaban, John and Barney, 24
Ball, Lucille, 76
Ball of Fire, 64
Ballard, Lucien, 154
Bankhead, Tallulah, 95
Basehart, Richard, *17–18,* 41
Beddoe, Don, 180
Begley, Ed, *156–157*
Behind the Rising Sun, 130
Behrmann, Paul, 78
Belafonte, Harry, *156–157*
Bellaver, Harry, 112, *113*
Bendix, William, *135,* 136
Bennett, Bruce, 106
Bennett, Joan, *92–93,* 94, 162
Bernhardt, Curtis, 62, 133
Berry, John, 33
Berserk, 63
Best Years of Our Lives, The, 129
Between Midnight and Dawn, 117
Beware, My Lovely, 143
Bezzerides, A. I., *42–*43, 80–81, 184

Big Combo, The, 30–31, 122
Big Heat, The, 43–45, 156
Big Night, The, 48
Big Red One, The, 36
*Big Sleep, The, 74–*75, 116, 195
Big Sleep (the bad one), *The,* 104
Bigamist, The, 177
Billy Budd, 142
Bioff, Willie, 23–25, 41
Birds, The, 155
Black Angel, 29, 120, *121,* 162
Black Cat, The, 178
Black Mask magazine, 68, 70, 73
Blackton, Gloria, 118–119
Blackton, J. Stuart, 118
Blonde Fever, 52
Blondell, Joan, *166, 167*
Blood on the Moon, 102, 157
Bloom, Howard, 84
Blue Angel, The, 93
*Blue Dahlia, The, 135–*136
Body and Soul, 24, *25–*26, 27, 32
Body Snatcher, The, 157
Bodyguard, 165, 182
Boehm, Sydney, 45, 112, 134
Bogart, Humphrey, 26, 53, 70, *71, 72–*73, *74–*75, 83, *106, 132–*133, 138, 187, 193, *194,* 195
Bogeaus, Ben, 107
Bond, James, 82
Bond, Ward, *42*
Bonnie and Clyde, 168
Boomerang, 40
Border Incident, 154, 182, *185*
Born to Be Bad, 187
Born to Kill, 157, *164,* 165
Borzage, Frank, 188, 190
Bourde, Paul, 125
Bow, Clara, 182
boxing, film noirs about, 25–27
Boy with the Green Hair, The, 46

Boyle, Robert, 126
Brackett, Charles, 56
Bradley, Gen. Omar, 131
Brady, Scott, 165
Brand, Neville, 116, *155*
Breaking Point, The, 32–33
Brecht, Bertolt, 48
Breen, Joe, 41, 56
Brian, David, *62*
Bridges, Lloyd, 136, *137,* 138, 188
Brodie, Steve, 76, 87, 114, *140,* 154
Brodine, Norbert, 159
Bronson (Buchinsky), Charles, 150, *151,* 155
Brooks, Geraldine, 62
Brooks, Richard, 34, 142
Brown, Harry, 170
Browne, George, 23–24, 41
Bruce, George, 155
Brute Force, 34–35, 100
Bryan, Helen (Mrs. Dan Duryea), 163
Burnett, W. R., 145, 146, 147
Burr, Raymond, *67,* 94–95, 114
Butler, Hugo, 33, 48

C

Cadwalader, Jessica (Mrs. Robert Ryan), 141, 143
Caesar, Augustus and Livia, 84
Caged, 34
Cagney, Jeanne, 111
Cagney, Jimmy, 32, 40, 72, 160, 171–*173*
Cain, James M., 56–60
Caine Mutiny, The, 133
Calhern, Louis, 146, 147, 148
Call Northside 777, 40
Calleia, Joseph, 50
Canon City, 34, 41

Drew, Ellen, 131
Driscoll, Bobby, *122*
Duff, Howard, 34, *35*, *49*, 100, 138, 177
Dunaway, Faye, 82–83
Dunnock, Mildred, 159
Duryea, Dan, 29, 92, *93*, 94, 101–102, 120, *121*, *162–163*, 171
Dwan, Allan, 105

E

Eastwood, Clint, 43, 155
Edwards, Vince, 152
Eisenger, Jo, 67
Eisenhower, Dwight D., 175
Elam, Jack, 155
Elliot, Biff, 80
Elliott, Laura, *124*
Emhardt, Roger, *36*
Endfield, Cyril, 137–138
Endore, Guy, 33
English, Marla, 48
Englund, George, 52
Enterprise Studios, 25
Erskine, Chester, 103
Essex, Harry, 17, 155
Evans, Gene, 36, 154
Evans, Robert, 82, 83

F

Fairbanks, Jr., Douglas, 60
Falcon Takes Over, The, 74
Fall Guy, 120
Fallen Angel, 86–87
Fantastic Voyage, 182
Farewell, My Lovely, 104
Farewell to Arms, A, 188
fate in noir, the theme of, 111–127

Faulkner, William, 75
Fay, Frank, 63, 64
Faye, Alice, 87
Fear and Desire, 152
Fear in the Night, *120*
Federal Bureau of Investigation, 39–40, 46, 149
Federal Theater, the, 46, 48, 187
Feist, Felix, 165
Feldman, Charles, 107
Felton, Earl, 180
female animal, the, 84
Fenton, Patricia, 179
Ferguson, Helen, 66, 67
File on Thelma Jordon, The, 66-67
Filmakers, The, 176–177
Films and Filming magazine, 142
Films in Review magazine, 142
Fisher, Steve, 16, 133
Fistful of Dollars, A, 155
Fitzgerald, F. Scott, 118
Fixed Bayonets, 36
Fleischer, Max and Dave, 180
Fleischer, Richard, 154, 157, 165, 180–181
Fleming, Rhonda, 151
Fletcher, Lucille, 66
Flippen, Jay C., 152, *186*, 187
Florey, Robert, 131
Follow Me Quietly, 182
Fonda, Henry, *126–127*
Fontaine, Joan, 177
Forbes, Charles, 129, 131
Force of Evil, *20*, *22–23*, 25, 32, 167, 182
Ford, Glenn, *45*, *54*, 97–98
Ford, John, 114
Ford, Wallace, 41
Foreman, Carl, 135

Forty Guns, 64
Foster, Preston, 155
Fourteen Hours, 17, *18*
Fowler, Gene, 36
Fowley, Douglas, 154
Frankenheimer, John, 143
Franz, Arthur, *170*, *171*
Friedrich, Otto, 24
Friends of Eddie Coyle, The, 104
Frings, Ketti, 115
Fromkess, Leon, 178
Fuchs, Daniel, 101
Fuller, Samuel, 36–37, 64, 155, 187
Furthman, Jules, 75
Fury, 137

G

G-Men, 40, 160
Gabin, Jean, 106
Gable, Clark, 60, 100
Gabor, Zsa Zsa, 51
Gangster, The, 30, 154,
Garbo, Greta, 52
Gardner, Ava, *100*
Garfield, John, *22–26*, *32–33*, 106, 130, 139, 178, 188, 190
Gaynor, Janet, 190
Gebert, Gordon, 180
Gentleman's Agreement, 141
George, Gladys, *33*
Giancana, Sam, 23
Giesler, Jerry, 96
Gilda, 97–98
Glass.Key, The, 136
Glennon, Bert, 151
"God" in noir, the theme of, 126–127
Godfather, The, 82, 150
Goff, Ivan, 172

Goldsmith, Martin, 178, 180
Goldwater, Barry, 25, 80
Goldwyn, Samuel, 139
Gomez, Thomas, *22*
Good, the Bad, and the Ugly, The, 155
Gough, Lloyd, *25*
Goulding, Edmund, 167
Graham, Fred, *148*
Grahame, Gloria, *44–45*, *52–53*, *54*, 62, 78, *156*, 157, 182, *194*, 195, *207*
Granger, Farley, *112*, *113*, 124, *186*, 187
Grant, Cary, 142, 155
Grant, Marshall, 188
Grapes of Wrath, The, 172
Gray, Coleen, 152, *155*, *166*
Greer, Jane, 76, 78, 87
Gresham, William Lindsay, 166, 167
Griffith, D. W., 97
Griffith, Edward, 148
Gross, Nancy Roe, 75
Group Theater, The, 32, 120
Guare, John, 102
Guffey, Burnett, 171
Gun Crazy, *168–169*

H

Hadley, Reed, 40
Hagen, Jean, *xii*, 112, 146, *147*
Hale, Barbara, 132
Halton, Charles, 109
Hammett, Dashiell, 68, 70–73, 74, 80, 82
Hamill, Pete, 143
"hard-boiled" fiction, 68–81
Hard, Fast, and Beautiful, 177
Hard Way, The, 106

Photo Credits

All photographs used in this book are from the
Lester Glassner Collection, or the private collection
of the author, except for the following:

Courtesy of the Academy of
Motion Picture Arts and Sciences

Angel Face, page 103
Border Incident, page 185
Brute Force, pages 34 and 35
Crossfire, page 140
On Dangerous Ground, page 42
Quicksand, page 111
Touch of Evil, pages 50 and 51
Thieves' Highway, page 184

Courtesy of the Museum of
Modern Art Film Stills Archive

Kansas City Confidential, page 155
Murder, My Sweet, page 73
Pickup on South Street, page 37

Opposite: Gloria Grahame and Humphrey Bogart, *In a Lonely Place.*